UPDRAFT

THE AERODYNAMICS OF GREAT LEADERSHIP

JACQUELYN S. FREEDMAN

STATION
SQUARE
MEDIA

NEW YORK, NEW YORK

UPDRAFT: The Aerodynamics of Great Leadership

Editor: Diane O'Connell, Write to Sell Your Book, LLC
Cover Design: Kathi Dunn
Interior Design: Steven Plummer
Post-production Management: Janet Spencer King

Printed in the United States of America for Worldwide Distribution

ISBN: 978-0-9861560-3-8

Electronic editions:
Mobi ISBN: 978-0-9861560-4-5
EPUB ISBN: 978-0-9861560-5-2

First Edition

For Renee, my mom, who would have loved this.
I wish you were here to see it.

And for Dan, this never would have happened without you.

Acknowledgments

Sitting down to write a book feels like one of the loneliest activities on the planet—especially when you're staring at a blank screen or an empty piece of paper and are sure it is destined to stay that way. However, I have learned the right support, encouragement and expertise make all the difference in the world.

I have to start with Diane O'Connell of Write to Sell Your Book. Saying she is a brilliant editor doesn't come close to describing the impact she has. I admit it—I was disappointed that my original manuscript wasn't the best thing she ever read, but her insights and observations were right on target and she seemed to intuitively understand what I was trying to accomplish. Not only did Diane help me find my voice as an author but her feedback challenged me to develop and focus my message until it became worthy of publishing. And, she's a joy to work with.

Diane's team was superb. Copyeditor Linda Dolan smoothed out every rough spot, helping to polish the manuscript. Cover designer Kathi Dunn knew just what questions to ask and hit a home run the first time out. Interior designer Steven Plummer was so patient, letting me explore concepts until I realized that his initial direction was, in fact, the way to go. Indexer Jane Scott helped me to appreciate the complexity of something I had never even given a second thought to. And post-production guru Janet Spencer King responded with lightning speed and could answer any question I had.

A special thanks to my knights in shining armor at Farotech: Chris David, Greg Dietrich, Denis Kurganskiy, Chris Carr and Mark Oestreicher. Not only did their team do exceptional work but they came to my rescue, handling a last minute issue as if they had planned for it months ago. And illustrator Lea R. Segarra was so easy to work with and so responsive. I just love the simplicity and elegance of her illustrations.

There are so many friends and family members who have supported, cajoled, encouraged, guided and annoyed me—all in a wonderful effort to keep me motivated and moving forward. Thank you all so much. Here it is—now stop bugging me!

And of course, Dan, my husband and best friend, who was confident this would happen before I had even finished page one and whose love, support and willingness to live without access to the kitchen table made this possible.

client satisfaction and retention). Another questioned the competency of several managers who made excuses and wouldn't act without explicit instructions. And yet another faced pressure from an impatient Board of Directors who was pressing him for results. Each one was worried about his organization as well as himself. I could see their concerns, as well as their sleepless nights, written all over their faces.

Wing Vortex

While the symptoms vary, the bottom line is that far too many leaders are no longer enjoying their jobs. The word I hear most often from owners, executives and board members is "frustrated." I believe it doesn't have to be this way, and it is this belief that drove me to write this book. While it is true that leading an organization can be one of the most difficult and frustrating jobs on the planet, it can also be one of the most gratifying and rewarding professions ever imagined. So, what do you do? The same thing the lead goose does. Remember we mentioned that these birds often fly in a v-formation? They do this to take advantage of the updraft created by the swirling air coming off the wing tip of the bird in front of them. This updraft reduces air resistance and increases lift so each bird can flap its wings less often. Less work means that in a group, the birds can cover much more distance—as much as 70 percent more than if they were flying solo. As the leader, it is your job to create the conditions where each and every member of your organization is both creating and taking advantage of that updraft. Maybe an example with less altitude would help.

The very first car I owned was a Nissan 200SX. It was a silver hatchback with a manual transmission, and we took great care of each other, parting only once the amount of oil leaking out exceeded the amount poured in. Next, I bought an Acura Integra. It was a silver hatchback with a manual transmission (some say rut; I say pattern). Both cars were wonderfully fun to drive. The challenge was my driveway, which required a leap of faith to traverse. The house sat on a hill so the second floor was at street level. We had a ridiculously steep driveway with a lovely turn in it so you would come down the hill in one direction and then have to make a less than 90-degree turn in order to head into the garage. Needless to say, even the smallest amount of snow, slush or freezing rain made it almost impossible to get back up to the street. The Nissan had rear-wheel drive, so as winter approached I would put several sandbags in the trunk over the wheel wells to weigh down the back of the car. And we were first in line when the pallets of ice melt showed up at the hardware stores. Despite that, I can recall several harrowing attempts to get up the driveway where I ended up either stuck partway without sufficient traction to move forward or sliding backwards until the tires caught (experiences I definitely do not wish to duplicate).

The Acura, however, has front-wheel drive. I was absolutely amazed at the difference that made. Instead of the engine revving and the tires spinning, I was able, more often than not, to make my way right up the driveway. Most of the leaders I talk to are like my Nissan, trying to push 2,700 pounds up the driveway. They are using a tremendous amount of energy, their wheels are spinning, and they can't even see where they are going. The answer isn't to push harder; the answer is to get up front and lead the way, creating the momentum to move forward.

The good news is that you can banish your symptoms along with your frustration, and you can enjoy going to work again. *Your organization can soar under your leadership.* But you are not alone in being frustrated, and that leads me to the bad news. As the leader, you do not benefit from this updraft. In fact, the lead bird has to work the hardest, and that is why flying in the lead position requires experience, determination, resilience and a demanding combination of skills. However, once you understand updraft and its relationship to the job of leadership, you will be able to focus your efforts, harnessing the power of aerodynamics to take your organization to new heights.

In *Updraft*, we're going to delve into the areas that require your attention because they directly affect your organization's ability to soar. Some of you may not like Part I, as it shines the spotlight on you as an individual. After all, you need to be the kind of person who people want to follow—if you aren't aerodynamic, how can your organization be? In Part II, we'll look at the issues that enable your organization to get off the ground. Then, once you are aloft, Part III will set the stage for updrafts that will support the organization at altitudes you never thought possible.

PART I:
AERODYNAMICS

As the lead bird, it is imperative you have the ability to create updraft. In order to do that, you need to understand exactly what updraft is and how critical you are, both as an individual and a leader, in creating or destroying it.

CHAPTER 1

What is updraft and how does leadership create it?

Thrust. Drag. Gravity. Lift. These are the four forces exerting pressure on any object moving through the air—whether it be a bird, a ball, a feather, a Frisbee® or an airplane. If you were learning to fly a plane, you would be busy analyzing everything there is to know about how these forces affect the plane and its ability to fly—these are not things you want to learn about at an altitude of 7,000 feet. Similarly, if you want your organization to fly, you need to understand how leadership exerts pressure on the organization and how those pressures affect its ability to fly. Liftoff occurs only when the forces of lift and thrust are able to overcome gravity and drag. If you aren't getting off the ground, then your organization must be weighed down by an excess of drag and gravity that have jeopardized its ability to fly. The question is, why? Why are we experiencing an excess of drag and gravity, *or* why aren't we generating sufficient lift and thrust? Regardless of what you may think, the hard truth of the matter is that this inability to take flight comes back to leadership and its ability (or inability) to create updraft.

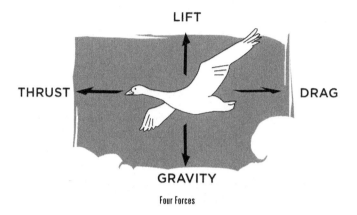

Four Forces

Before you can begin to create updraft, we need to discuss exactly what we mean by it, how it is created, and how it radiates throughout your organization. I mentioned earlier that many of the leaders I speak with are pushing—they are using too much energy and not getting enough in return. This happens because their attention is focused in the wrong places. We need to step back and examine this issue in the context of defining leadership and its specific roles and responsibilities. The very first thing you need in order to create updraft is a thorough understanding of what updraft is and how it relates to and is dependent on leadership.

UPDRAFT AND ENGAGEMENT

Earlier, I explained that by flapping its wings, each goose creates an updraft that helps the bird behind it—if the birds are in a v-formation. Each bird is contributing to the effort by lifting his own weight and also by helping those around him. That is, each bird is dedicated to his specific role and to the progress of the entire flock. What would your organization look and feel like if each person's efforts extended beyond his or her functional or operational area to the entire organization where people were helping each other and feeding off each other's successes?

4

What we're talking about is an organization full of *engaged* people—people who are talented, passionate, focused and committed to the goals, values and mission of the organization. These are people who have a positive emotional connection to their organization; in other words, they care. And when people care, they care about everything—not just their jobs or areas or departments. When meeting the staff of a new client or prospect, I often informally "test" for this by asking questions or pointing out an issue that lies outside their functional area. Do they essentially dismiss it, giving the issue (and me) some lip service or do they embrace it as something they can and will do something about?

On my way into a meeting with the finance director of a retail chain, I passed a public area that was littered with cigarette butts (probably where the staff took their breaks). I mentioned it during our meeting but left doubtful anything would happen—after all, this was outside the finance director's scope of authority. At our next meeting, much to my delight, I saw that the area had been cleaned up. Certainly an issue of this nature was not in the finance director's "job description," but her connection to the organization drove her to reach out and initiate action. Just imagine the possibilities when the vast majority of people in your organization are performing at this higher level! People who have this positive emotional connection demonstrate it every day by achieving and surpassing goals, taking a win-win approach with colleagues, voluntarily going the extra mile, being an advocate for their company, and continually finding opportunities to make improvements.

When your people care about their organization and what they are doing, the results are nothing less than astounding. I've seen this firsthand, and you've probably experienced it too. I remember a customer service person taking on a customer's problem as if it were her own, reaching out to product management, product development and production for answers. Then, she patiently explained the solution to the customer and offered to send out a few products, free of charge, which would be helpful in resolving the issue. On the other end of the spectrum, we've all encountered the customer service agent who compounded our anger and frustration by serving us an insincere "sorry" with a "nothing I can do" chaser. The problem is you can't make people care or pay them to care—that decision rests solely with them.

When I've asked business owners, "What percentage of your staff do you think is engaged?" Responses typically range from 50 percent up to 80 percent. Most people are shocked and saddened to hear that the employee engagement level in North America is estimated to be 29 percent.[1] Think about what that means. A 29 percent engagement rate means you are benefiting from less than one-third of the value of your most important and most expensive asset. While this explains why so many leaders feel their organizations aren't soaring, it also means there is a lot of opportunity for those who figure it out. As you'll see, updraft relies on many of the same factors that impact employee engagement, but it requires us to go even further. While a handful of talented, dedicated managers can do wonders for employee engagement within their scopes of influence, they are not powerful enough to lift the entire organization.

You may have heard about employee engagement. Please don't dismiss it as the most recent fad in leadership. Despite what you may or may not think, it is the key not only to creating updraft but also to creating the organization you've envisioned and dreamed about. Can you really afford to ignore a concept that has been proven to have a strong, positive relationship with things like sales growth, innovation, quality, earnings per share, customer satisfaction and retention, reduced turnover, lower cost of goods sold, and so on? Consider just a few examples:

- Bottom line: Hewitt Associates found that "organizations with high levels of engagement (where 65 percent or more of employees are engaged) outperformed the total stock market index even in volatile economic conditions." What they saw was a staggering 63-point difference in share-holder return between companies with high (65 percent or more) and low (less than 40 percent) engagement.[2]

- Productivity: Moving an employee from low to high levels of engagement can result in an improvement in employee performance of 20 percentile points—and decreases the probability of departure by 87 percent.[3]

- Customer loyalty: Highly engaged teams achieved a 37 percent net promoter score (a metric designed to measure customer loyalty) versus just 10 percent for teams with low engagement.[4]

- Quality: A Fortune 100 manufacturing firm found that the low-engagement group had 5,658 quality errors (parts per million) versus 52 (no, that's not a typo) quality errors for the high-engagement group.[5]

I could go on and on. Where there was once a trickle of research proving and validating the connection between engagement and stellar organizational performance, now there's a tsunami of case studies and research.

Why is engagement so important to creating updraft? Think back to the v-formation where each bird physically creates updraft for the birds that flank them. If your next in line is not engaged, then he's not creating updraft and all the birds behind him lack that support. Each and every bird needs to create updraft. Just one disengaged person, especially one in a leadership or management role, can easily com-promise the performance of an entire department or division, and before you know it, your organization is grounded. Shockingly, only 34 percent of managers and executives are estimated to be engaged.[6] This means an awful lot of birds are forced to flap harder, expending more energy because they are flying without the benefit of updraft. You

> **High levels of engagement lead to teamwork, cooperation and an esprit de corps that promotes progress and lifts the entire organization.**

cannot afford to keep even a single turkey on your payroll—the cost is so much higher than you realize. When the right person—i.e., one who is talented, passionate, enthusiastic and committed—is plugged into the right position, he or she creates updraft just by doing his or her job. Those high levels of engagement lead to teamwork, cooperation and an *esprit de corps* that promotes progress and lifts the entire organization, helping it to get off the ground.

ACCEPTING CHAOS

Avian v-formations have fascinated observers for years, and only very recently have researchers confirmed their suspicions that birds fly in a v-formation for its energy-saving effects (i.e., updraft). In doing so, they found that birds that fly in a v-formation maximize performance even more effectively than scientists ever thought possible; the birds actually adopt the exact position fixed-wing aerodynamics would predict.[7] In other words, the birds position themselves to take full advantage of the updraft coming off the preceding bird,[8] something previously considered impossible due to "the complex flight dynamics and sensory feedback that would be required."[9] Even more unexpected, researchers discovered not only do the birds get into the optimal position for updraft, but based on their spacing, they synchronize their wingbeats.[10] By either flapping in unison with the bird in front of them or timing their downbeat with the preceding bird's upbeat, they further their ability to utilize the upward-moving air. (Maybe "birdbrain" isn't quite the pejorative term we thought it was.)

What researchers didn't find, however, is a goose off to the side or the leader of the flock yelling, "Bob, your flapping is out of synch," or

"Downwind side, close ranks — you're too far apart." The geese move and fine-tune their positions, interacting, communicating and making in-flight adjustments designed to maximize their performance and that of the flock. Sometimes this results in a picture-perfect v-formation and sometimes in a seemingly incoherent mass of birds, shifting positions faster than you can say "corporate restructuring." This process works because the flock is a self-organizing system.[11] As such, it is complex, dynamic and chaotic, but also highly adaptable, creative and spontaneous.

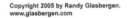

"I would like you to be more self-reliant, show more initiative, and take greater personal responsibility — but check with me first!"

So, what does all this have to do with our discussion of engagement and updraft? Well, without diving too deeply into the theories behind self-organizing systems, one of the characteristics of such a system is that the agents (or members of the system) initiate action on their own within certain global limits. They do this based on the information and feedback they receive and the interactions they have. The v-formation is not imposed by some authority (i.e., there's no goose yelling instructions) but is the result of the actions of each individual goose. Most of the business owners and executives I speak with want their people to act like agents of a self-organizing system. They want their people to do the work of the organization and deal with the problems and opportunities that arise without waiting for instructions, but at the same time, they can't help directing and managing and coordinating. Leaders want the responsiveness and creativity of the system, but have trouble accepting and trusting the chaos. As a result, they impose structure through an ongoing barrage of processes, procedures and policies.

Now go back to our flock and think about trying to dictate the v-formation. As soon as you get one or two geese into the proper position, even the slightest breeze means starting all over again. You can't orchestrate the v-formation.

- There are far too many variables.

- Conditions change too quickly.

- Complexity increases exponentially with the size of the flock.

- It reduces each individual's role to that of a cog, being told what to do.

- It takes you out of formation, so you are no longer creating updraft, and forces you to neglect the responsibilities of leadership.

- It is exhausting and leads to exactly the kind of frustration and burnout so many leaders experience.

In the same way the flock relies on each goose's ability to do its job, you need to get the right people into the right positions (more on this later) and let them do their jobs. Disengagement (or a lack of engagement) occurs when those top-down controls—which reflect the philosophies, attitudes and beliefs of leadership—come between your employees and their ability to do their jobs and feel good about where they work and what they do. Think of the customer service agent who can't satisfy an unhappy customer because his or her hands are tied by an inflexible, no exceptions refund policy. Or a manager who wants to individualize rewards and training efforts for his or her staff but is limited by the organization's one-size-fits-all programs. Or the manufacturing engineer who needs four levels of approvals before he can resolve a production problem. These kinds of situations quickly destroy initiative and creativity and result in confusion, frustration, anger and resentment. And by interfering with your people's ability to assess and adjust their positions, you impede their ability not only to harness updraft but to create it.

I've seen engagement survey after engagement survey asking, "What can we do to increase engagement?" Leadership's interest is commendable and indicates that they acknowledge, at least to some extent, engagement's importance, but the very question reveals an incomplete understanding of the subject. The question shouldn't be "What can we do to increase engagement?" it should be "What are we doing that is getting in the way of engagement?" In other words, "What do we need to stop doing?" The vast majority of your people walked through the door on their first day of work eager, excited and optimistic, but little by little, that enthusiasm was crushed out of them. The fact it was done unintentionally makes it no less destructive.

I hope you are starting to see how engagement leads to the creation of updraft and how the very presence of updraft begins to transform your organization. Now think about how this new model affects you. As the leader, how does it help you? Think back to your own frustration and concern over the lack of progress. Once your people are creating updraft, you are no longer spending your days mired in operational issues. Your highly competent and engaged staff comes to you when they need you, but they are eminently capable of doing their jobs, leaving you free to...dare I say it . . . lead. Suddenly, you have the bandwidth to meet with clients, investors, board members and your own staff to assess situations, consider opportunities and address strategic issues.

Instead of spending day after day trying to take off or feeling stuck in a holding pattern, you find the quality of your day changes dramatically as you spend time focusing on those areas affecting updraft. In many cases, these will be the very areas you've always wanted to work on but never had time for. Going to work can be exciting, inspiring and fun for your entire organization—including yourself. And it should be. Because your job is not just critical to the success of your organization but has implications far beyond your own parking lot. Leaders who can create updraft are scarce (remember that 29 percent engagement level?), and that is bad, not just for leaders and their organizations but for society as a whole.

CATBIRD INDUSTRIES

Maybe you feel I'm exaggerating the importance of leadership, but think about all the things great leadership and its subsequent updraft make possible in an organizational setting, say at Catbird Industries, a manufacturer of cat-related products. New toys, beds and litter boxes are developed. Research is conducted, giving new insights into cat behavior and health issues. Manufacturing and sourcing procedures are improved and new processes are implemented, resulting in better quality products at lower costs of manufacture. People are learning and developing and contributing; they are engaged and happy and spreading that attitude throughout the organization. Production is humming along as raw materials come in and products go out. Profits are healthy, enabling the company to grow. Employees are hired and on-boarded. Kitties are leading longer, healthier lives. And as a result, customers are happy and spreading the word about Catbird Industries' products. (If you are unsure or even skeptical as to how you impact all the areas I've just mentioned, stay tuned, that's what this book is all about.) Catbird Industries is soaring, and that's obviously great for anyone affiliated with them. But their achievements extend far beyond the edges of their organization. During the holiday season, you've probably seen that great Jimmy Stewart movie, *It's A Wonderful Life*. In it, a good, kind man (Jimmy Stewart), who is angry and frustrated over a serious business problem he didn't create, is shown by an angel what life would have been like had he never existed. He has no idea of the impact he's had on the lives around him, and he's surprised at the difference he's made for close family and friends as well as the people he's touched only tangentially. In the same way that a ripple in a pond continues to radiate out far from its point of origin, his influence has travelled considerably further than he realizes. Great leadership has the same far-reaching effects.

Let's ask Clarence (Jimmy Stewart's angel in the movie) to show us what Catbird Industries might look like without updraft. Without strong guidance and leadership, the organization simply fails to thrive. Just like a ship with no one at the helm, the organization has no control over its direction. Without that, there is no cohesiveness or focus, and performance at all levels is compromised. Like rust on the hull of our ship, the lack of progress and goal-achievement slowly eats away at the organization. Over time, sales decrease. Production is cut back. Revenues and profits fall. People are increasingly frustrated, insecure and disengaged. As these emotions and attitudes spread throughout the organization, they are reflected in the culture, and before long, top performers jump ship, accelerating the downward spiral. No new products, procedures or processes are developed—and on and on it goes.

But what are the bigger-picture, broader implications for this lack of leadership? Take the decrease in sales, for instance, which will eventually lead to a reduction in production. As the manufacture of toys, furniture and cat beds is cut back, people may be laid off, requiring them to tap into unemployment programs. Fewer jobs in the community may affect the area's ability to attract residents, which could impact housing prices. Lower revenues and fewer workers also mean reduced tax revenues for the area with implications for public services and schools. If Catbird Industries is a major player in the local community, then these effects will be even more dramatic and far-reaching.

In addition to layoffs, less output means fewer inputs, so vendors of lamb's wool, plastics, carpet and string will all see demand drop. Catbird Industries' issues negatively affect all of their suppliers and partners, potentially initiating a similar cycle for them, depending on their situations and the quality of their leadership. And what about those who have been laid off or are miserable at work? What is the effect on them, their spouses and their kids? Both the local and national economies are negatively impacted as residents, suppliers and governments feel the pinch created by the flailing Catbird Industries organization as it sinks.

Without strong leadership, there is no emphasis on development and growth—in fact, there's no emphasis on anything. This further reduces the number of great leaders available, not just to this company but also to other organizations, the government and the community. New product development and process improvement come to a standstill as creativity and innovation all but disappear. Who knows what life-changing products or industry-shifting processes will never be developed. People become frustrated and insecure, simultaneously unhappy with their jobs but terrified they may lose them. Such high levels of stress may impact their health, contributing to the rising costs of healthcare.

This is far from an exhaustive list, but you get the idea. While this state of affairs can persist for years, months or weeks, it will ultimately destroy the organization if left unchecked. The organization's potential is lost. Resources are wasted and value is destroyed—and not just at the organizational level. Think about how the larger economy has been impacted by bad leadership and dubious decision making at places like Lehman Brothers, WorldCom, Arthur Andersen and Enron—companies that no longer exist but have had a material impact on the world around them. And the larger the organization, the larger its impact will be—positive or negative—on the world around it.

No pressure, right?! You already have plenty on your shoulders without me making you responsible for the entire economy. I just want you to take a moment to recognize how important your job is. Leadership is a noble profession, and leaders need to be proud of what they do and inspired by the tremendous potential they see. My intent is simply to remind you of the impact and importance of great leadership and that it is leaders like yourself who create the future.

FIVE MYTHS ABOUT THE JOB OF LEADERSHIP

Being in a position of leadership doesn't make you a great leader any more than having a body makes you a great athlete or having wings makes you capable of flight—just ask a penguin. While most of us know people who are in positions of leadership, few of us have had the awesome opportunity of learning from or working with a truly great leader. The vast majority of people who I speak with possess or could possess the capabilities necessary for great leadership. The issue isn't one of supply; we have plenty of raw material. To a great extent, the problem lies with the fact that the job of leadership is dangerously misunderstood and as a result of these misperceptions, we often end up with the wrong people in leadership and/or with poorly structured positions. You need to be aware of these myths and confront them head-on as they will compromise your ability to create updraft.

Myth #1: Leadership means power.

Myth #1 concerns those people who *want* a leadership position but for the wrong reasons. These people are often committed to the old-style command-and-control philosophy. They are eager for the power and authority the position brings and are more interested in "what's in it for them" than the challenges and successes of true leadership. They lack passion for the mission, vision and values of the organization (if those even exist). Their true motives are obvious, and they do not engender loyalty or trust, never mind any level of engagement. Out of frustration, even good leaders sometimes pull rank, reminding others they rule the roost, but true leadership is not about power or ego. In fact, great leaders know that leadership is more about the ability to give up and grant others power and authority. This is not to say great leaders are intimidated by or uncomfortable with power. The fundamental difference is that power and control isn't the great leader's objective; it simply comes with the job.

Myth #2: Great technical skills translate to leadership talent.

Myth #2 is born out of the assumption that technical competence translates to leadership competence, and you can see this clearly demonstrated in the common practice of promoting from within. Don't misunderstand me, promoting from within is a great philosophy, but think about how it typically works. Let's say we have a top-performing salesperson who sells paint and decorating items to small and mid-sized retailers. His territory explodes as he increases sales to existing customers while also adding a few new retailers. He excels in his position, running past established goals and targets, and in doing so, he gains the attention of management. Eventually, a position opens up for a sales manager, and he becomes the obvious choice for promotion. Eagerly, he moves into his new position, but it doesn't take long before he is struggling and everyone is disappointed but mystified by his inability to perform.

Many people would simply say that our salesperson had been promoted to his level of incompetence, explaining away his downfall with the Peter Principle. You've no doubt heard of it. It was formulated by Laurence J. Peter, who studied how people move through an organization, and it states "in a hierarchy, every employee tends to rise to his level of incompetence."[12] I think what Peter observed was not so much that people are promoted into a position where they are incompetent but that they are promoted into a position that isn't a good fit for them or for which they haven't been properly prepared. Semantics? Maybe. But the distinction is an important one. It isn't so much that the person suddenly loses his or her abilities but that the organization has failed to understand the true nature of the new position.

© MARK ANDERSON, WWW.ANDERTOONS.COM

"It's a brand new position, and we're still figuring out your duties. So I won't be able to tell you how you're doing it wrong for a few weeks."

Go back to our salesperson. He met and exceeded his targets by excelling in all aspects of sales from lead generation to closing. His hard work and talent were rewarded with a promotion to sales manager. But look at what *that* job entails. The sales job exists to close sales and keep clients happy, while the sales manager position exists to advance the development and performance of the sales team.

ROLES AND RESPONSIBILITIES	
Sales Position	**Sales Manager**
• Find and qualify prospects	• Hire and direct a sales team
• Establish relationships with clients	• Establish plans and strategies for the department
• Possess a thorough knowledge of products/ services	• Interact extensively and participate with senior management
• Create proposals	• Establish and control budgets
• Close sales	• Conduct ongoing coaching and development for all team members
• Handle customer issues	• Assist team members with proposals, presentations and meetings, as needed
• Interact with internal departments	

While there is some overlap, these are two completely different jobs, requiring completely different skill sets, talents and competencies, and there is no reason to assume that someone who excels in one will necessarily excel in the other. This is not to say a great salesperson doesn't have what it takes to be or to become a great sales manager, just that expertise in one does not necessarily correlate to proficiency in the other and vice versa.

Years ago, early in my husband's IT career, he worked for a project manager who was highly regarded by both those for whom he worked and those who worked for him. While he was an excellent project manager, their boss used to joke (somewhat inappropriately) that "his technical knowledge about mainframes would fit in an ashtray." Although his technical skills were lacking, his ability to plan, coordinate and motivate were outstanding. Most hierarchical structures (i.e., organizations) eventually reward what we'll call "technical expertise" with a promotion to a position that requires less emphasis on the technical and instead requires "leadership/management expertise." I think this disconnect is what Laurence Peter observed and what led him to formulate the Peter Principle.

These situations develop thanks to two organizational realities that do not occur in organizations that have updraft. The first relates to the amount of training, support and guidance most employees receive with their promotions, which usually sits on a continuum somewhere between little and none. Many people fail simply because they are thrown off the ledge to either take wing or drop like a stone. There are people who possess the competencies necessary to move up from a technical position to a leadership position, but as we've just seen, organizations are ignorant of the magnitude of this transition. They don't do a good job communicating the expectations, priorities and responsibilities of the new position, and leadership fails to provide the attention and mentoring that would lead to success. The second organizational reality that contributes to this situation is the sad but true fact that organizations do not do a good job assessing the performance of the leaders and managers within their ranks, so those who secure a leadership position for the wrong reasons find it relatively easy to retain it.

Myth #3: It's okay to hire an executive for skills other than leadership.

Myth #3 is closely related to Myth #2 as it results in putting the wrong person into a leadership position and, once again, is the result of misunderstanding the job. Myth #2 was the result of a tactical misconception about the position, while Myth #3 is a strategic misconception regarding the position. In this case, the organization doesn't understand the true job of leadership or its role in creating updraft. This occurs most commonly with high-level executive positions. It can happen for many reasons, but oftentimes the owners or the board become so focused on a particular challenge they believe to be hampering the company's growth that they bring in someone to address that specific issue.

I've seen CEOs and presidents hired for a whole host of reasons—because they had access to capital, a background in process improvement, a reputation for cost-cutting, experience in sales, extensive industry knowledge...all kinds of things. I'm not saying these areas of expertise are not important. I am saying they are not disciplines that create updraft, and therefore, they do not automatically qualify someone to be the lead bird. In one organization I know, the president was hired because of his industry connections, in the hopes he could open doors at a few retailers the company had been unable to penetrate. Not only did these connections not pan out, but this gentleman was so uncomfortable dealing with people that he had a bathroom built in his office so he wouldn't have to bump into his own employees.

Needless to say, his leadership abilities were essentially nonexistent, and instead of growth and expansion, his tenure was characterized by layoffs, lost clients, massive disengagement and the departure of several top performers. The company would have been better off hiring a true leader and then creating a position, or hiring a consultant who could have addressed the sales issue. And taking it a step further, had they hired a leader who understood the job of leadership and was capable of creating updraft, they may well have found the organization wholly capable of solving the issue on its own. An understanding of updraft and the ability to create it is the most important qualification for leadership—anything else is icing on the cake.

Myth #4: Leadership can be a part-time job.

The misconceptions surrounding the job of leadership can also lead organizations to structure the role in such a way that the job itself interferes with the promise of great performance. Myth #4 is that leadership can be a part-time job, but the reality is there are far too many concerns, commitments and responsibilities that extend to every corner of the organization and outside the organization as well. This manifests itself most often in firms using the "managing partner" structure, common to accounting and law firms.

In this scenario, a partner who has successfully built his practice and contributed to the growth of the firm is appointed the senior partner.

Like a CEO or president, this partner's responsibilities encompass a huge array of issues, starting with leadership (i.e., setting direction, leading the executive team, identifying business opportunities, establishing organizational objectives, etc.) but extending out to human resources (i.e., hiring and promoting employees, dealing with disciplinary issues, handling partnership performance reviews and development, reviewing compensation plans, etc.), marketing (i.e., developing brand identity and messaging, representing the firm, etc.), sales (i.e., tracking progress, assisting others as needed, etc.), and any and all organizational issues that arise. At the same time, that partner is usually expected to maintain and continue growing his personal practice—something that was a full-time job before the promotion and remains a full-time job for all the other partners. So now, the managing partner is expected to do two full-time jobs. While CEO or president is a full-time position everywhere else, these responsibilities are expected to take only a percentage of the managing partner's day. Rarely does a firm have the talent, structure and processes in place that would enable a managing partner to be truly successful. In this case, it is the structure and expectations of the position that make great leadership all but impossible.

Myth #5: Leaders should have all the answers.

Myth #5 goes right to the heart of so many of the discussions I've had. In many cases, company growth (or a lack thereof), a merger or acquisition, new ownership or investors, competitive developments, a lack of progress, industry shifts, and so on have left the leader feeling unsure of himself and questioning his own ability. These leaders are beating themselves up for not having all the answers. Unlike athletes who are always working with coaches to improve performance, many leaders hesitate to reach out. Consider Phil Mickelson, a professional golfer, who relies on a team of people to keep him on his game—his caddy, a putting coach, a swing coach, a short-game coach and even a mental coach.[13]

©Amy Nathan/www.BigHairMetamorphosis.com

As a business owner or executive, you've spent years amassing a tremendous amount of expertise and experience in your field and industry, but if your company decided to automate its warehousing systems or needed a completely new branding and marketing program, you wouldn't hesitate to reach out to someone who had spent years amassing expertise and experience in that field. Moreover, you wouldn't see it as a short-coming or a reflection of your ability. So many of the leaders I speak with seem to feel that leadership is something they should instinctively know how to do. But leadership is another discipline to learn just like finance, production, marketing or sales. What leadership does require is the strength to reach out to advisors and experts who can support your growth and development, enabling you to rise above the never-ending stream of challenges that come with your job.

LEADERSHIP DEFINED

James MacGregor Burns said, "Leadership is one of the most observed and least understood phenomena on earth."[14] And yet, in order to transform your organization and create updraft, you need to thoroughly understand the role of leadership and its impact on an organization. The difference between average performance, exceptional performance and poor performance comes down to leadership. We need to explore the concept of leadership in order to understand the effect it has on people. For example, how is it that Wegmans, a chain of grocery stores, manages operating margins double the earnings of the big four grocers and sales per square foot estimated to be 50 percent higher than industry averages?[15] Wegmans has buildings, produce, stacked shelves, prepared foods and employees. So, what is it that makes their clients such fanatics that they drive out of their way and right past the competition?

Wegmans and its competitors all start with the same basic inputs. Money is money. Cash registers are cash registers. A gallon of bleach is a gallon of bleach. It isn't the quality of the bleach that makes for a great shopping experience, it is the smiling, friendly, helpful faces you encounter at every turn. Even a restaurant with a lovely ambience and excellent food can't thrive if the waitstaff is rude and discourteous. More than any other factor, the customer's experience will depend on the quality of your people. It is the introduction of leadership energy and its effect on people that creates something greater than the sum of its parts—but how much greater depends on the quality of that energy.

Think about an organization as a chemical reaction, like the kind that occurs when you bake a cake. While mixing together flour, baking powder, butter, sugar, eggs and vanilla may result in some tasty batter, until you put it in the oven and introduce energy in the form of heat, you do not have a cake. In the same way our cake requires the introduction of heat energy, our organization requires the introduction of leadership energy; without it, we just have a bunch of ingredients—and to a great extent, the same ingredients our competition has. But when we introduce positive leadership energy, something happens. Earlier we talked about the impact of engaged people on customer service, quality, productivity, costs, profits and innovation—and its importance to the creation of updraft. Wegmans' positive leadership energy generates a powerful updraft. That updraft, in turn, has engaged their people and led to performance that has made it a customer service legend, garnering awards, press coverage, profits and employee retention industry competitors would kill for. How many grocery stores do you know that receive requests from people to *please* put a store in their area? Wegmans received more than 5,200 requests[16] in 2012 alone.

> **When people are supercharged, the updraft they create provides one of the most difficult to reproduce strategic advantages out there.**

Leadership is the ability to supercharge an organization's most important asset—its people. And when those people are supercharged, the updraft they create provides one of the most difficult to reproduce strategic advantages out there. Leadership energy is rarely neutral. If it isn't positive, then it is introducing a negative energy where the effects are just as predictable—disengaged people, resulting in inconsistent quality, uninspired customer service, low productivity and a lack of innovation.

Remember our cake? Well, now it is dried out, burned on top or not fully baked. What you are getting from your organization starts with what you are giving—or, more specifically, with the kind of leadership energy you are infusing it with. This issue goes right to the heart of what leadership is and how it creates (or destroys) updraft.

THE JOB OF LEADERSHIP

If you want your organization to soar, we've established that you need to imbue it with positive leadership energy that supercharges each and every member of your flock. Inspiring and encouraging the creation of updraft is a huge job, and while we've talked about what you need to accomplish, we've said nothing about how you do this. Of course, this book is all about what it takes to get everybody into formation and flying in the same direction, but let's take a quick look at the three critical areas affecting updraft—resources, culture and direction—and, as such, require leadership's attention.

Resources

Before geese and other migratory birds take flight, they are a common sight in and around ponds, lakes and other bodies of water. They stop to feed, drink and rest, making certain each bird has what it needs to go the distance. As the leader, ensuring each member of your flock has what he or she needs is your responsibility. I'm not saying you should be involved with the purchase of paper for the copier but that you are responsible, at the highest levels, for making absolutely sure the organization and each individual has what they need—both physically, mentally and emotionally. Do people have everything they need to do their jobs to the best of their ability?

The knee-jerk reaction of most owners and executives is a quick, "Yes, of course, we have desks and computers and processes," or, "Sure, we have cash registers and shelves and a warehousing system." But the question goes much deeper than that. As consumers, we've all witnessed the customer service agent who is uncomfortable with the long silence and feels compelled to explain that the computer is very slow, or the repairman who is embarrassed that he has to come back because they don't stock the part, or the retail associate who is apologizing because their policy doesn't allow her to...(fill in the blank).

I remember performing reconnaissance on one retail establishment before meeting with the owner. The associate at the customer service area (no less) apologized over and over because a simple transaction was taking so much time. The cash register kept freezing up, and she had to go through a several step process to restart it. When I asked her about it, she said it happened all the time. "Have you told anybody about the issue?" I asked, and in response, I got the all-too-familiar eye roll that told me the company's executives didn't understand that they were responsible if she was unable to take care of clients the way she (and they) wanted to. The implications of not having the right resources are far more serious than it might seem at first blush, and they correlate very strongly with a lack of engagement.

Think about it this way. Imagine starting a home project: perhaps you and your significant other decide to paint the living room. The colors are all picked out, so you get an early start to the hardware store. You buy the paint, a couple of drop cloths, and then you head home. As you begin moving furniture out of the way, you notice several holes. You are a bit annoyed to find that the spackle you have on hand has hardened in the container, so back to the store. Once the spackle has dried, you need to sand those areas, but you can't find the sandpaper. As you rummage through your workshop, you become increasingly angry. Finally ready to dip a brush into paint, you discover that the brush isn't thoroughly clean.

By now, you are angry at your spouse, annoyed at yourself and hate your house for even having a living room. Now imagine what it is like for customer service people who have to apologize to clients because the computer system doesn't work correctly, or for factory workers who have to stop assembly in order to scrounge up the tools and parts necessary to repair a machine, or for salespeople who can't get the product information they need. It is no less frustrating for them.

As the leader, you need to guarantee that your organization has access to the best-quality resources it can get. While a bit more complex than the flock's needs, there are really just three resources that provide for the other inputs—time, people and money. Technically, we could say there are only two inputs—time and money—since money allows us to hire people. However, as we will discuss, people are *the* most significant resource, so we will consider them separately. While even the best leader cannot procure more time, it is leadership that ensures time is being used effectively and efficiently by focusing attention on the vision, mission and goals of the organization. And since the talent and commitment of your people determine the success of the company, acquiring, developing and retaining the best of the best is essential. Leaders who do not devote sufficient time and energy to this responsibility do not recognize the connection between stellar financial performance and talented, engaged employees.

Culture

Extremely social animals, Canada geese have their own set of routines and conduct that guide behavior both on the ground and in the air. While instinct drives goslings to peck soon after they hatch, it is their parents who teach them what to eat and what not to eat.[17] Migration and migratory routes are passed down from generation to generation, and in the same way we teach our children how to communicate, so do the geese.[18] Goslings, for instance, must learn to recognize the threat call and its accompanying body language (head pumping, an open bill with tongue extended, and possibly vibrating feathers)[19] so they don't accidentally provoke an attack from another goose. These habits and behaviors increase the likelihood of survival and also reduce conflict within the established family groups. For remarkably similar reasons, it is your responsibility to set the standards for behavior and to shape the environment inside your organization. You must ask, as well as answer, the important questions. What do we, as an organization, believe in? What do we stand for? What won't we tolerate?

The answers to these and similar questions establish the shared standards and values that help to guide actions and decisions. When used and understood correctly, these values serve as ethical guidelines and become part of the foundation for the organization's culture. The goal is to create and maintain a supportive culture—one that inspires passion and engagement rather than one that fuels indifference and resentment. It is the leader's job—your job—to monitor and tend the culture in order to ensure it remains an asset of the organization rather than a liability. While we've discussed this as one of the three areas requiring leadership's attention, a positive, nurturing culture could also be considered one of the resources leadership needs to provide.

Direction

You've finally gotten off the ground, and everybody is working together, flying in a beautiful v-formation—just like the geese. At this point, you might think you've made it. But those birds aren't flying around just because they can. They are following the lead bird in search of food, water, mating grounds or warmer weather, and every mile they cover brings them closer to their destination. Your people are expecting you to take them somewhere too. They are counting on you to have a destination in mind—i.e., a vision (more on this later)—and to have answers to those questions that revolve around the reasons for our existence as an organization. Why are we here? What is the purpose of this organization? Where are we going? What do we want to accomplish? Having a specific direction provides a shared focus that concentrates the efforts, resources and energy of the organization and is crucial to supercharging performance. Just flapping their wings isn't enough; people want to accomplish something.

Resources. Culture. Direction. Your attention to these three areas is absolutely vital to creating updraft. We will revisit these issues many times and in much greater detail as we dive into our discussion of updraft and how to use it to transform your organization.

STRETCHING YOUR WINGS...

We've just gotten started, and while I hope that you are finding our discussion interesting, I'm more concerned that you are finding it thought-provoking. It is never easy to stare into the mirror and take responsibility, but in order to explore new ideas and perspectives, you'll need to put aside your preconceived notions about leadership, your organization, your people and even yourself. At the end of each chapter, I've included questions designed to help you zero in on your particular situation. I encourage you to consider these questions carefully, as they will help you to understand why your organization isn't soaring...yet.

1. To help you experience the beauty and grace of the v-formation, take a moment to watch a short slideshow at www.DeltaVstrategies.com/Resources taken from the vast database of geese photographs I mentioned earlier.

2. Close your eyes, relax and picture the organization functioning the way you've always imagined. What is your role? What are you doing? Are you enjoying yourself? What is stopping you from attaining your vision?

3. What do you think is the engagement level at your organization? How does that make you feel? Is it contributing to the issues you see?

4. Go to www.DeltaVstrategies.com/Resources and take the Updraft Assessment. Review it carefully. Have your executive team complete the assessment as well.

5. Which of the Five Myths of Leadership applies to you? Are you sure? How can you address it?

6. Are you bringing leadership energy to your organization? What kind? Are you truly supercharging your people? All of them?

7. Of the three focus areas—resources, culture and direction—which one needs the most attention? Why has it been overlooked?

8. Bring your executive team together to discuss engagement. (For more case studies and research, go to www.DeltaVstrategies.com/Resources.) Some possible discussion points could include:

   - How do team members define engagement?

   - What do they know about it?

   - What do they think the engagement level is at your organization? Why?

   - How is this related to the issues and challenges you face?

   - What kind of leadership energy is this team providing? Is it helping or hurting the engagement level?

   - Using the Updraft Assessment from #4 above, have your executive team share their results from Part 2 and Part 3 of the assessment.

   - On a scale of 1 to 10, what is the status of each of the three areas of focus—resources, culture and direction? Start with the area with the lowest score. How could you, as a team, begin to address it?

CHAPTER 2

Are you worthy of being followed?

Your ability to create updraft starts not with your leadership skills, but with who you are as a human being. Before we can discuss getting your organization into the skies, we need to address those characteristics and factors contributing to your personal aerodynamics. We've just talked about the tremendous effect you have on your organization. If you are not aerodynamic enough to get off the ground, what hope does your organization have? As a leader striving to create updraft, you need to inflame passion, instill confidence and stimulate progress. Look at those again—inflame passion, instill confidence and stimulate progress. Notice these are not the kinds of things that can be done by issuing memos or giving orders. Your success in these endeavors starts with your ability to connect with your people, engendering feelings of respect, trust and loyalty—characteristics that are essential to getting you, as an individual, off the ground. But before we look at respect, trust and loyalty and how they contribute to your ability to create updraft, we need to lay the foundation with a discussion of integrity.

TOO MUCH SUGAR

There is a wonderful story involving Mahatma Gandhi.[20] Apparently, during the 1930s, a mother in India was at her wit's end in her efforts to get her son to stop his obsessive sugar eating. She decided to take him to see Gandhi, hoping he could convince her son to change his habits. They made the journey, and the mother explained the situation to Gandhi. He thought a moment and then instructed the mother to return in a week's time with her son, which they did. At their second visit, Gandhi smiled at the boy and told him that he must stop eating sugar. The boy agreed. As they turned to leave, the mother, somewhat perplexed, asked Gandhi why he couldn't have asked that of the boy a week ago. Gandhi replied, "Because last week, I too was eating too much sugar."

Integrity is an inner strength and confidence that comes from knowing who you are and what you stand for. As Gandhi demonstrated, however, just knowing who you are and what you stand for isn't enough. Integrity demands consistency between the internal (values, beliefs and principles) and the external (words, actions and behaviors). It is not so hard to have values and principles, but having the courage to live by them is another matter entirely. It is easy to decide you are going to eat healthier food, but it takes tremendous self-discipline and determination to do so when you have 15 minutes to grab lunch and you find yourself surrounded by fast food joints. Your values and beliefs are expressed and tested in the decisions you make, the words you choose and the behaviors you exhibit. Every day, challenges arise that require a choice between what is right and ethical over what is easy and convenient. For a person to have integrity, there must be consistency between what they believe, what they say and what they do.

© Mike Baldwin / Cornered

"Your integrity is on the line. Want me
to say you're in a meeting?"

Having such a powerful internal compass contributes to emotional stability as well as inner peace. In a sense, integrity is the decision you won't lie to yourself and you will hold yourself accountable to what you believe so you can always "look yourself in the mirror." People who know themselves and what they stand for have this sense of balance, of harmony, of integrity. Integrity is a foundational character trait because it comes from within. Only you truly know if you are living up to your own principles. A person alone on a desert island can have integrity if he or she conducts himself or herself according to his or her values and beliefs. Leaders, however, do not have this luxury.

Leaders need the courage not only to live by their values but to "go public" about them. By going public, you do two important things. First, you are actively communicating about what is important by talking openly about your values and referring to them on a daily basis, especially when making decisions. This establishes expectations and, as we will discuss, is closely tied to organizational values. Second, you are sending the message that you are willing to be "under surveillance," inviting those around you to judge whether you are upholding the ideals you claim to embrace. If you say you value honesty and openness but you withhold the truth from your people, you will be judged to be without integrity and there will be little you can do to change those perceptions. General Norman Schwarzkopf said, "Leadership is a potent combination of strategy and character. But if you must be without one, be without the strategy."[21] Great leaders don't just *walk* their talk, great leaders *are* their talk.

Integrity is a crucial, foundational character trait. It enables you to establish credibility, engender respect, and build trust and loyalty. Integrity means your word is sacred. It frees people to trust your judgment as well as your motives, encouraging them to act rather than hesitate out of the fear of being blindsided or conned. It establishes you as a positive role model to be imitated and reinforces your commitment to the standards and principles you promote. High levels of personal integrity contribute enormously in making you a person who others want to follow. Often confused with trust, honesty, sincerity and other similar traits, integrity is inextricably linked with these qualities. While integrity comes from within, these other traits are based on the perceptions and judgments of others and, as such, are also critical to your ability to create updraft.

Think about it. Your goal is to establish a tight v-formation; otherwise the birds will be too far apart to take advantage of the updraft each one is creating. Flying in such a close formation is exciting and exhilarating, but it's also risky and hazardous. If we are going to maneuver successfully with our wings just inches apart, like the Thunderbirds or Blue Angels (the Air Force and Navy's flight demonstration squadrons, respectively, who fly jet fighters in choreographed programs sometimes just 18 inches from each other),[22] then we must have the utmost respect and trust for our leader (as well as for each member of the team). As a result, we need to take a closer look at what it takes to build respect, trust and loyalty and at how they figure into your success as the squadron leader. Needless to say, respect, trust and loyalty are the proverbial two-way street.

> **High levels of personal integrity contribute enormously in making you a person who others want to follow.**

We will discuss the other half of the equation as it relates to your treatment of your people later on. Right now, the focus is on you.

RESPECT

The link between respect and integrity is simple. As human beings, we are surrounded by examples of deceit, corruption and hypocrisy. We live in a world where it is so much easier to choose what is convenient or popular over what is right. We are constantly bombarded by examples of people who have made decisions based on greed, ambition and short-term thinking, to the detriment of entire companies, communities, industries and themselves. (Think Bernie Madoff, Enron and a host of others.) As a result, when we cross paths with someone who exhibits integrity, he or she earns our respect. In a little while, I'm going to tell you about someone who gave up a coveted position and salary to pursue what was most important to him. You may or may not agree with his decision, but it's hard not to respect his passion, conviction and strength of character. People like him remind us that it is not necessary to abandon or compromise our principles in order to succeed, and their strength and determination are contagious. Being respected means you are esteemed, admired and looked up to for who you are, what you do and what you know.

Contrary to what many believe, respect cannot be demanded and is not automatically granted just because of a person's title. I finally left my last corporate position because I could no longer work for people who I did not respect. While my own professionalism, standards of behavior and upbringing dictated that I *treat them* with respect by responding to their requests and interacting with them in a courteous, attentive manner, their lack of leadership and interpersonal skills made it impossible for me to actually respect them. They provided no guidance, direction or feedback—the CEO couldn't even look people in the eyes when speaking with them.

© Randy Glasbergen / glasbergen.com

"Of course I respect my employees. I think they should be treated just like real people."

Respect must be earned, and it develops over time based on experience. As we build a relationship with someone, we are constantly judging him or her, from the moment we first set eyes (or ears) on them. We form a first impression, often in a matter of seconds, and then we use information from additional interactions to either confirm or to revise our initial conclusions. This includes nonverbal communications as well as things like the following:

- How do they carry themselves? Do they seem confident?
- What do their clothes say? Their jewelry?
- What do they exude? Friendliness? Boldness? Shyness?
- What is their body language saying?
- How do they make me feel?

As we continue getting to know each other, we start to look below the surface. What do we have in common? What opinions, experiences or interests do we share? Through discussions and interactions, we build on those initial connections and begin to establish the foundation for a relationship. In a professional environment, our observations focus on specific areas where we assess information about job-related abilities and experience as well as clues about work ethic, the potential for cooperation and teamwork, attitude, and a host of other work-related (and personal) attributes. Over time, I may come to admire the breadth and depth of your knowledge and expertise. I may come to appreciate the way you handle difficult situations. I may come to have a high opinion of the way you handle yourself and how you interact with others. In other words, I may come to develop respect for you, your opinions and your abilities. (We're talking here about respect from a holistic viewpoint. It is certainly possible for me to have respect for your expertise but abhor the way you treat others and have no respect for you.) Your people need to respect you, both as a person and as a leader. Without respect, you will lack the ability to inspire confidence in your abilities as a leader and you will be hard pressed to find people willing to fly anywhere near you.

TRUST

Once your organization is riding high on the updrafts, you won't be contending with speeds of up to 700 mph (just under Mach 1, the speed of sound) or 6 G's of force like the Blue Angels[23] I mentioned. Despite that, getting people to safely and confidently fly within close proximity of each other is going to mean garnering more than respect. It requires tremendous levels of trust in the leader and the leader's ability. Your people need to trust you unconditionally.

Like respect, trust is built over time. It is a confidence or belief in the character, strength and integrity of someone or something, and it too grows out of experience and observations. In a sense, trust is the ability to predict the future. It is the belief one has sufficient knowledge to anticipate how someone will act or react to a situation—an understanding of what they will or won't do. In this case, and with all apologies to the financial services industry, past performance *is* expected to be indicative of future results or, more accurately, of future behavior. This does not mean the foretelling of specific actions or decisions, but rather expectations around how someone will perform. Will they keep their word? Will they share the credit? Will they take responsibility?

Here's a wonderful thought. Let's say your organization has been soaring along. Expansion plans are on the horizon, and you are preparing to build your own 20-story office building. While you'd want the building to be aesthetically pleasing and to accommodate your business needs, your most pressing concern would be knowing the building was sound—that it would stand. Toward that end, you would most certainly want a structural engineer on board to guarantee the finished building had structural integrity. This would ensure that it would perform as expected and that it was designed to resist any loads or stresses put upon it. You certainly don't want your new building falling over the first time wind gusts exceed 40 mph. Trust is very similar. It is the belief someone will act or react in a manner consistent with who he or she is known to be, regardless of the situation (i.e., the stresses put upon him or her). Since trust must be established over a period of time, honesty, reliability and consistency are crucial. And all those things are natural by-products of integrity.

Why is trust such a big deal for human beings? Because even the smallest act of trust requires some degree of vulnerability. When your dog rolls over and lets you pet his belly, he is displaying a tremendous amount of trust that you are not going to hurt him. Animals instinctively protect their stomach area as it houses their vital organs. Exposing that area requires a high level of trust based on what your pet knows about your behavior or about people in general. Similarly, humans protect themselves from physical and emotional harm and won't allow themselves to be vulnerable unless they are reasonably sure they are safe. That decision stems from the information and experience they have gathered about how someone will act and whether he or she has been judged to be a risk. When someone breaks our trust and betrays us, we are doubly wounded. I'm sure you've heard the expression "Fool me once, shame on you. Fool me twice, shame on me." We are angry with that person, but we are also angry at ourselves for having been fooled.

> **Even the smallest act of trust requires some degree of vulnerability.**

Many of the leaders I work with have a difficult time with this. They are reticent to expose their bellies (figuratively, people, figuratively!), and I do understand their concern. I have worked with owners who were so "chummy" with their staff that their advice and guidance was often ignored. Then, there were those who were perceived as aloof, unfriendly and completely uninterested in their own people. When you are in a position of authority, you are always teetering on the line between personal and professional. You want to get to know your people and have them get to know you, but you don't want to go too far—becoming their "best" friend can make life very complicated. Having to evaluate or, even worse, lay off someone with whom you have a close personal relationship can be difficult and uncomfortable at best. As a result, leaders often put up walls. Unfortunately, your people do need to see something of who you are in order for them to trust you (and for you to inspire them). We just said that a part of establishing integrity is allowing people to see what you stand for and that you mean what you say. They're going to need to know you and what you stand for in order to trust you.

From a leadership standpoint, trust is granted to those who have proven, over and over again, that they are committed to what is right and what is in the best interests of their people and their organizations. They have shown that their "structural integrity" is strong and that it will enable them to resist any stresses or pressures. They can be counted upon to do what is right and to act in accordance with their values. Great leaders understand that it takes a leap of faith for people to trust, and they recognize the severity and impact of a betrayal. They treat the trust of their people as the invaluable gift it is. If your well-behaved, trustworthy son or daughter were suddenly caught in a lie, your trust level wouldn't drop just a little. It would drop significantly, and it could take months or years before they completely regain your trust. Stephen Covey likens trust to a bank account.[24] Leaders know that a "trust account" is built on small, $5 deposits, but they also understand that the minimum withdrawal is $1,000. One withdrawal can wipe out years of deposits, and so they work to protect each and every account they have established.

LOYALTY

We've just seen that trust requires a degree of vulnerability. It involves the decision to open oneself up to possible injury. Loyalty goes even further. Loyalty is a faithfulness or allegiance to a person, cause, value, ideal, organization or product. It is the result of a true bond and is borne out of a shared passion as well as mutual trust and respect. It marks an elevated level of engagement, caring and connection. It goes beyond trust in the sense that we are investing a piece of ourselves in a person or a concept. We are providing our endorsement on a very personal and emotional level. Although great leaders strive for loyalty to the organization and its vision, mission and values, leaders who focus on generating updraft do tend to garner personal loyalty as well.

In a sense, you can think of trust as a secret engagement. There's a history of experiences which have led to a strong connection, but it can remain private—just between the two of us. Loyalty, on the other hand, is more like a Public Display of Affection. People can see that a connection exists and that we are "in it together." It is more public and more apparent. While trust is a condition or judgment that can exist passively, loyalty manifests itself through action—like painting yourself in your team's colors or ringing doorbells to support a candidate. Oftentimes, it isn't until a situation arises that tests our loyalty that we begin to understand how acutely it is felt.

From a leadership perspective, loyalty, like trust and respect, is a two-way street. It is the idea that "I'm hitching my cart to your wagon. We're in this together. I'm watching your back, and I'm inspired and willing to follow you. At the same time, I expect you to remember I'm back here. I'm trusting you to navigate carefully, watch for obstacles and ensure my safety as well as your own. Both our fates are in your hands."

Unfortunately, it is not unusual for CEOs, directors and others in leadership positions to confuse military-style obedience with loyalty. They object when employees have a differing opinion, question a decision, or even refuse to engage in practices they deem to be inappropriate. These leaders don't "get it." They no more understand the true meaning of loyalty than they do the value and contribution of their people. With such an attitude, it is no surprise that these people do not engender trust, respect or loyalty because they really do not understand what it is, what value it provides, or how to get it. They will be forever trapped in a vicious cycle where their frustration with results leads to more command-and-control behavior, which, in turn, fuels an environment of fear, intimidation and blame. Instead of leading their organization through the clouds, their view of an organization is more akin to whipping the slaves because they aren't rowing fast enough.

Be aware that more than any other topic we'll address, this one is probably the most difficult. Attempting to understand and accept how you are perceived requires tremendous courage, determination and strength. Opening your mind to reconcile what you believe to be true with what others' perceive is intimidating and a bit frightening. It may be surprising and hard to hear what people truly think, and you may not like what you find. Something you see as a strength may not be interpreted the way you interpret it (being direct and getting right to the point, for instance, may be seen as abrupt and unfriendly). You may also be surprised at how difficult it is to get this information. People will need to be extremely secure and confident in order to tell the person who signs their checks what they think of them, and social convention dictates that we temper our responses so as not to rock the boat or upset someone.

> **It is not unusual for CEOs, directors and others in leadership positions to confuse military-style obedience with loyalty.**

But integrity, and all it implies, is crucial to your own aerodynamics. Since updraft cannot be created on the ground, you need to focus on your ability to take flight. To do that, you need to nurture an accurate self-image so you are comfortable with who you are and what you stand for. Only then will you be admired and esteemed, as both a person and a leader, earning the trust and respect of your flock.

STRETCHING YOUR WINGS...

1. Reflect on who you are as a human being. Choose five adjectives you think describe who you are. Do they differ from who you strive to be? Would others agree with the adjectives you've chosen? Find out by asking family, friends and coworkers for five adjectives they would use to describe you. How do they compare to your list? What do you need to focus on in order to become the person you want to be?

2. How does who you are as a person affect your ability to lead?

3. Are you truly comfortable with who you are and what you believe?

4. Do your people respect you or your title/position? Why do you think that is?

5. Think about a mentor, teacher or close friend. What is it about them that engenders your respect, trust and loyalty? Do they demand respect and trust, or is it given freely? How does this translate to you and your organization?

6. Select a few people who you trust and will be comfortable having a difficult conversation with (i.e., spouse, children, executive team member, friend, business associate, etc.). Ask questions to find out more about how you are perceived. Are you a person of your word? Are you "looked up to" and respected? Ask for specific examples that illustrate their perspective. (Prepare yourself—this is one of the hardest exercises as it can be surprising. Open your mind and put your ego in neutral—and no disagreeing, just listen and ask questions.)

CHAPTER 3

Are you airworthy?

There's more than one way to feel free as a bird, and one of those ways is to become a pilot. To do that, you need to log a certain number of hours, ace the written exam, and pass the check ride, a combination oral and practical test. The check ride involves taking an FAA (Federal Aviation Administration) Examiner on a flight and demonstrating certain maneuvers like stalls, straight and level flight, turning to a specific heading, emergency procedures and other important things…like landing and collision avoidance. (Note: if at any time during the flight, the examiner grabs the controls, you've probably failed.)

As you might expect, prospective pilots are required to have a thorough understanding of the theory and practical applications of flight, navigation and communications. They need to have a working knowledge of weather and other natural phenomenon, knowing, for instance, that you never fly through the smoke and dust from a volcano. They have to memorize all kinds of procedures and, of course, understand at a glance what the plane's instrumentation is communicating. What you might not realize, however, is that just about any related subject is fair game for the examiner, who can ask about anything he likes, even rattling prospective pilots by asking unexpected questions about the plane's performance or its maintenance history.

To journey safely across the skies, a pilot needs to know how to fly and how to get to where he's going, but he must also know all about the strengths, limitations, abilities and idiosyncrasies of the particular aircraft he is flying. For instance, he must know the following:

- The kind and amount of fuel the aircraft holds.

- How far he can glide if the engine fails.

- The maximum maneuvering speeds with and without flaps.

- The length of runway needed for takeoff and landing in a variety of situations.

- That the stick pulls slightly to the right.

- What the plane was built for—acrobatics, cruising, racing, etc.

- That the gas gauge doesn't work so well.

The more thoroughly a pilot knows his plane, the better he can prepare for any contingencies. In fact, if you had gotten your license while flying a Cessna 152 (a small, two-door plane, kind of like a Smart car with wings), you couldn't just decide to switch to a Cessna 172 (a very similar but slightly larger aircraft). To do so, you have to get "checked out" by an instructor, meaning they have verified that you know everything you need to know about *that* particular plane. The pilot and the plane need to work as a team. The more the pilot knows about how the plane will respond in a variety of situations, what it is best for, and how to get the best out of it, the smoother and safer the ride.

The same applies to you. As the lead bird, you are both pilot and plane, but before you can take your organization into the wild blue yonder, you need to be acutely aware of your own strengths, limitations, abilities, idiosyncrasies, fears and ambitions.

- What kind of fuel fills your tank?
- How do you respond when pushed to your limits?
- What kind of maintenance do you require to keep yourself at peak performance levels?
- What happens when your fuel tank begins to run low?

You need to understand how these things affect your performance and, therefore, your ability to lead. You need to know yourself like the pilot knows his plane so you can take advantage of your strengths, find ways to mitigate your weaknesses, and be on alert for anything that could compromise your performance. The more you know, the less likely you are to be influenced by beliefs and biases that unknowingly affect your decision making. Knowing yourself covers a broad range of issues. You need to be in touch with who you are, what you believe, how you function, and how all these affect you and, by extension, the performance of your organization.

I'm not sure if it has to do with pride, fear, insecurity or something else entirely, but I find many of the owners I work with (and human beings in general) often resist taking a long, hard look in the mirror. In an engineering firm, one of the partners became so agitated at the prospect of this kind of self-reflection, he lashed out at his partner and summarily refused to participate. Our perceptions are so closely tied to self-image and self-confidence that many people find it uncomfortable and even somewhat distressing to look at themselves objectively and attempt to accurately gauge their own performance. Maybe they are afraid of what they might see or afraid they won't like what they see. In any event, a leader who doesn't have this knowledge or is intimidated by this kind of self-reflection will be emotionally compromised, lacking the internal strength and confidence needed to be aerodynamic.

In addition, as the main architect of your organization's culture, you will be ignorant of the impact you make. Interestingly, researchers have begun using journals to document their thoughts and emotions during studies so they can monitor, assess and understand how they might be unintentionally influencing the results.[25] You need to do the same thing. One business owner I met with spoke extensively about the lack of accountability that permeated his organization. He was especially frustrated with his executive team who were delivering excuses rather than results. He was eager to enroll them in some kind of magical sessions that would eliminate the problem. When I asked him to talk about his own behaviors, my questions were quickly deflected or ignored. He was completely unwilling to consider or even discuss how his own behavior was relevant, which, it turned out, was the example others were emulating (as I discovered in discussions with other staff members). This leader will never have the organization he wants because he is unwilling to confront his own shortcomings, leaving him at the mercy of his weaknesses and blind to opportunities for improvement.

In another situation, I was facilitating a meeting of about 60 people for a large, pharmaceutical client; it was going quite well. Everyone was relaxed and enjoying the session, and most importantly, we were accomplishing exactly what we needed to. People were freely expressing their opinions and openly discussing some rather emotional issues. At one point, the director of the department walked in. I could see the change in body language immediately as people tensed up and quieted down. After he left, it took some work before I could reestablish the atmosphere we had been enjoying before he walked in. I often wonder if he is aware of the impact he has on his people and whether that is the impact he wants.

Part of knowing yourself includes being keenly aware of the fact that you have an impact on people and of what that impact is. What happens when *you* walk into a room? Even though you may be well liked and respected by your team, you are still the boss and your very presence can dramatically change the mood or tone of a situation—both for the better and for the worse. Be open to examining the effect you have. While you may think you know exactly how you are perceived, there's a good chance you are wrong.

So, what do we mean by self-reflection?[26] At its most fundamental, self-reflection is the process of consciously discovering more about who we are, what we want and why we act the way we do. It can include feedback from others, personal exercises, coaching and journaling, as well as other forms of personal expression like art and photography. Start simply by setting aside 30 minutes at a specific time every week (more often if you are going through a particularly difficult period in any aspect of your life). Find a quiet, peaceful setting where you can be comfortable, relaxed and undisturbed (no people, no phones and no computers). Feel free to talk aloud to yourself, asking questions like a coach might.

Having a place to jot down thoughts and notes is highly recommended but not required. Different sessions may focus on different areas:

- Take the time to look back over the past year and note achievements you are proud of. What did you learn from them?

- Keep a running list of things that occur to you that you'd like to do, both personal and professional.

- Reflect on what's truly important to you, using these thoughts to begin compiling a list of your values.

- In your mind, paint a picture of what you'd like your life to look like, spending time imagining each of your life's roles (i.e., leader, spouse, parent, coach, etc.). Once you can see it clearly, write it down.

- Any time you make a pivotal decision, Peter Drucker recommends that you write down what your expectations were and revisit those thoughts in nine months to a year later.[27]

- Identify any interactions or situations that didn't go as well as they could have, and think about why you reacted the way you did, what was influencing you, and how you might do it differently. Also look at events that went well, congratulating yourself but also analyzing why you were so successful.

- In preparation for a significant event, take the time to consider how you are feeling about it and how you'd like to handle it.

For some people, it will take time before they are comfortable sitting alone with their thoughts, but don't let that deter you. Such a concern is more common than you realize. Notice also that your objective is not to judge, discourage or diminish, but to further your understanding of yourself in order to enhance confidence as well as competence. If you are still feeling hesitant, keep in mind that research conducted at Cornell University's School of Industrial and Labor Relations found that while self-awareness is often ignored or overlooked, it was the "strongest predictor of overall success"[28] for executive positions.

YOUR INTERNAL COMPASS

Geese navigate using a combination of instinct and landmarks, returning to the same rest stops, watering holes and breeding grounds year after year. Pilots use a compass and navigational beacons to stay on course while negotiating difficult weather and challenging conditions. People stay on course by relying on their personal values to provide that same kind of guidance. In order to use your personal values in this way, however, you must know exactly what they are. What we are talking about here are passionately held convictions that stem from the very essence of who you are and how you define yourself. What do you, above all else, hold dear? What do you expect from yourself? What do you stand for? What behaviors are and are not acceptable? Needless to say, it's going to be rather difficult to ensure that your actions are compatible with your values if you don't know what those values are. Only a person who has invested time in self-reflection and analysis can easily and accurately articulate what his or her values are, as well as what they mean, and use them to guide behavior in a way that creates and supports his or her integrity.

> **Personal values are passionately held convictions that stem from the very essence of who you are and how you define yourself.**

This loyalty to your values and beliefs does not happen by accident. It comes from an honest, thoughtful identification of your ideals and a thorough understanding of what they mean. Personal values can encompass a wide variety of issues and often include both physical items as well as concepts. Personal values could include:

• Family	• Honesty	• Health
• Hobbies	• Fun	• Community
• Friendship	• Making a difference	• Justice
• Education	• Equality	• Spirituality
• Financial security	• Integrity	• Happiness

In addition to identifying personal values, such an exercise also includes prioritizing those values. Proactively considering and revisiting these issues keeps them top of mind and greatly reduces internal conflict. Personal and professional dilemmas become much easier to navigate because you've already deliberated, examined and considered—the "hard thinking" is already done. During the previous chapter's discussion of respect, I said we were going to talk about someone who left a high-level position rather than compromise his values. In this particular situation, this gentleman had recently made partner at his accounting firm, and as a result, the firm was putting pressure on him to work longer hours (he was already working 10- to 12-hour days, 6 days a week and taking work home on Sunday), to shed his smaller clients (some had been with him from the beginning of his career), and to step up his business development efforts. He struggled with these changes because they were in conflict with his values, which included his children (who were first and foremost on his list), the forging of strong personal relationships, and the opportunity to teach and mentor within the accounting field. Although financial stability was important to him, it didn't outrank these other issues. The firm wasn't willing to make any changes, and predictably, he left for a situation that allowed him to stay true to his values. Because he had already identified and prioritized his values, he was able to refer to them to make what was certainly not an easy decision, but was the right one for him.

Incidentally, don't approach this exercise thinking about what you should have on your list or what others might have on theirs. Approaching the exercise this way will not benefit you because it will not reflect what you truly feel. For instance, we just talked about the gentleman whose children were at the top of his list, and from working with him, I can tell you that rang true. However, that doesn't mean children or family should necessarily be in the top spot on your list. If the business meeting in Boston is going to trump your kid's soccer game, then so be it. It's not a matter of being right or wrong; it's a matter of exploring the issue and being honest and true to yourself.

DAVID VS. GOLIATH

As a leader, the importance of your personal values goes beyond you and impacts your decisions at a higher level. Imagine you are entering a big, beautiful conference room. You are there to meet and interview with the board for the position of CEO for a company that designs and manufactures packaging for the toy industry. You are, of course, brilliantly prepared, having researched and studied up on the organization. They've had a few quality issues in the past, but they have a lot of potential and you are excited about the opportunity. As the conversation progresses, you become aware of several comments that prompt you to ask, "Why is the position available?" They explain, "The previous CEO didn't understand our way of doing business." Your "Spidey" sense begins to tingle. You say, "And what way is that?" In and among a few platitudes, you hear someone say, "Don't get us wrong. We're all for quality as long as it doesn't affect cost." Suddenly those quality issues seem more significant. You press on, trying to understand what and how much authority you'd have to run the company, but you aren't feeling optimistic. Of course, cost is always important, but one of your values has always been quality. And the fact this product could end up in the hands of your 7-year-old isn't helping. Is this the company for you? As you contemplate taking on this leadership position, it is crucial that you be crystal clear about your own values so you can be sure there aren't any conflicts between your personal beliefs and those of the organization. This is important for two reasons. First, while great leaders are expected to focus on what is best for the overall organization even at their own expense, they never put themselves in a position of having to compromise their personal values. These values are absolute. They are sacrosanct and cannot be violated. Doing so would destroy personal integrity, along with sincerity, honesty and all the integrity-related attributes we discussed earlier. Only by knowing what is most important to you, can you make a sound judgment as to whether you are a good fit to an organization's beliefs and culture. Your personal values must be compatible with those of the organization you lead. Notice I didn't say identical, just compatible.

Second, beyond just avoiding actual conflicts between personal and organizational values, leaders must endorse and identify with the organization's values just as strongly as they embrace their own. Organizational values become an extension of the leader's values, and only through honest, ongoing introspection can the leader assess his or her passion and commitment to them. Earlier, we identified setting the standards for behavior and shaping the environment as part of the leader's job in creating and maintaining a positive culture. How will you effectively and persuasively spread the word and communicate about the importance of those values if you don't believe in them yourself? As Lyndon B. Johnson said, "What convinces is conviction. Believe in the argument you're advancing. If you don't you're as good as dead. The other person will sense that something isn't there, and no chain of reasoning, no matter how logical or elegant or brilliant, will win your case for you."[29] Only through self-reflection will you understand what those values truly mean to you and to your organization.

© Randy Glasbergen.
www.glasbergen.com

GLASBERGEN

**"The key to effective communication is sincerity,
even if you have to fake it."**

STRENGTHS AND WEAKNESSES

By now, I think it's safe to say this book has gone to the birds. So, in that spirit, I'd like to introduce into the cast of characters the barn owl and the gannet. While the owl may not seem so exotic, it harbors some amazing abilities. You might know the barn owl[30] is typically a nocturnal hunter, so its having the best night vision of all birds isn't terribly surprising. But take a look at its face. That circular pattern of feathers is a satellite that focuses sound to its asymmetric ears, providing some of the best directional hearing in the world, even allowing it to "hear a mouse stepping on a twig from 75 feet (20 m) away."[31] The barn owl can actually perceive whether a sound reaches his right or left ear first and uses this information to pinpoint the location of his prey, judging both elevation and location. On top of that, their wings allow for silent flight, helping them surprise their victim but also enabling them to make in-flight course corrections.

Barn Owl

The northern gannet,[32] on the other hand, is a large seabird with a wingspan over two feet. It is a snow-white bird accented with black wing tips, an almond-colored head, and eyes ringed in black. Unlike most birds, it has no external nostrils, and both of its eyes face forward, which allows it to accurately judge distances. These characteristics are notable because they enable the bird to employ a unique hunting technique called plunge diving. Unlike other birds in this category, the gannet can dive from heights as high as 130 feet, hitting the water at speeds exceeding 60 mph. And the chase doesn't stop there, as the gannet can pursue its prey by swimming with its large webbed feet and even its wings. Science has discovered that the gannet has an exceptionally strong skull and a system of air sacs in its face and neck which inflate during a plunge, protecting the bird from what should be certain death.[33]

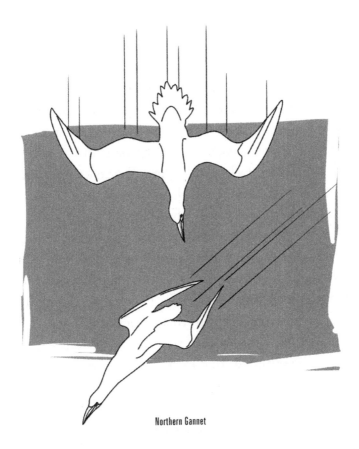

Northern Gannet

So, how does the owl feel about the gannet's ability to plunge into the ocean from 130 feet? I would imagine he doesn't give a hoot (sorry). And does the gannet complain to his flock that if only he had better hearing, he could catch more food? Probably not. Instinctually, animals take advantage of the unique abilities they possess, and they use those abilities for everything they're worth. Exploiting those strengths is the key to their survival—and the same idea pertains to you. Leaders who know themselves know their strengths and weaknesses. They gain confidence from their strengths and know not only *how* to leverage them but how to ensure they *are* leveraging them. In fact, research has shown that knowledge of your own strengths and weaknesses makes you less likely to "derail," the situation in which a promising executive reaches a certain level but then fails to advance or is asked to leave.[34]

Why is this so important? Well, we've identified you as the lead bird and discussed the fact that navigating the way, for instance, is an important part of your job. What if you had a terrible sense of direction? If you didn't know it, it poses a very real danger—ending up in Montana in winter when you are heading for Central America could put your entire flock at risk. But a deficiency, even in such a critical skill, isn't an insurmountable problem for you or your organization—as long as you are aware of it. Like the owl and the gannet, you want to exploit your strengths. Unlike them, however, you need to be just as aware of your weaknesses. Knowledge of your own weaknesses puts you in a position to manage and mitigate them. You may decide to target a specific weakness for personal development, or you may choose to hire someone with that particular expertise. Until you know where the gaps are between your current performance and the improvement opportunities that exist, the issue will remain invisible to your eyes and you'll do nothing about it. It is honest introspection that allows us to see what is as well as what is possible.

Knowing yourself also means you have invested time thinking about the issues we're covering throughout this book. It means you have tremendous clarity around your roles and responsibilities and how they translate to your strengths and weaknesses. Just identifying strengths and weaknesses isn't enough. Maybe you aren't the best negotiator. Is that important? Maybe. Maybe not. You can't really answer that question unless you've taken the time to thoroughly understand your specific role within your specific organization. Weaknesses (and strengths, for that matter) are only important for how they relate to success in a particular position.

During one search for an executive administrator, for instance, we came across a candidate who possessed extremely high potential in the areas of developing, evaluating and leading others. Based on the results from the benchmarking process we had used, we had a thorough understanding of the job and knew that those competencies did not correlate with success in the position. (We'll discuss benchmarking in more depth in Chapter 6. Suffice it to say this process begins with a discussion of why a job exists and results in a short list of the competencies that will lead to success in the position, making it much easier to evaluate and compare candidates.) However, because the business owner valued those traits, she was being drawn to the candidate, seduced by a list of strengths that didn't align with those required by the position; it wasn't a good match. Another client faced a similar situation but knew from the benchmarking sessions that while those skills were not required for their entry-level positions, they were indicative of a candidate who had the potential to grow into other roles—something they were looking for. In the first situation, the ability to develop, evaluate and lead others wasn't an advantage because it wouldn't contribute to success in the position. In the second, those same skills were deemed an advantage because they did correlate to success, albeit for more senior positions. Strengths and weaknesses cannot be evaluated in a vacuum; they must always be assessed against the requirements of the role and the needs of the organization.

> **Strengths and weaknesses must always be assessed against the requirements of the role and the needs of the organization.**

WHAT'S YOUR STYLE?

In addition to their contrasting strengths, the gannet and the barn owl display very different styles. Where the gannet is a gregarious, highly-social bird, the barn owl is a quiet, solitary, highly-analytic creature. Leaders also have their own styles. To me, leadership style refers to a person's most basic, underlying beliefs about how to create the spark that supercharges people. It is their guiding philosophy about how to enable people to achieve great things and is inextricably linked to the culture of the organization. However, much of the management literature promotes the idea that a leader should strive to develop as many leadership styles as possible in order to tailor one's approach to the situation. Such a concept contradicts much of what we've discussed about trust and the importance of consistency. A leader who is continually changing his or her leadership style would undermine that trust and the stability of the culture he or she has created. In addition, some styles, like commanding and autocratic, are anathema to things like engagement and will destroy any chance of creating updraft. Rather than shifting their *leadership style*, I think what we are really talking about is *communication style*.[35]

While significant at the leadership level, communication style is also important to understand at the operational level because it affects your management style. Unfortunately, most people don't think much about their own management style, so they manage people the way *they* would like to be managed. The Golden Rule, however, doesn't apply when it comes to people management. Rather than managing people the way *you* would like to be managed, you need to manage people the way *they* *need* to be managed. Of course, this will be impacted not only by information related to their communication styles but also by their levels of ability, expertise and enthusiasm. Choosing the right approach requires knowledge of their styles as well as your own, in addition to a basic understanding of behavioral style and how to use it to enhance communication and development. The important thing to remember is that communication style describes your preferences for how you go about getting things done. This means given the same task, the various styles will enlist different techniques, tools and approaches. The better you understand your style and your ability to adapt, the more techniques, tools and approaches you can choose from.

Have you ever met someone who was very outgoing and expressive? What about someone who was direct and forceful, almost confrontational? These are examples of different communication styles. While you might have recognized someone from one of these statements, they might have recognized you. Communication style is wholly observable and manifests itself in things like tone of voice, pace of speech, demeanor and level of eye contact, as well as a whole host of other behaviors. Once you know what to look for and understand its scope, you can see it in yourself and at play in the people around you.

COMMUNICATION STYLE			
D	**I**	**S**	**C**
Descriptors: • Assertive • Candid • Competitive • Decisive • Direct • Forceful	• Charming • Confident • Convincing • Emotional • Enthusiastic • Talkative	• Amiable • Cooperative • Friendly • Patient • Relaxed • Supportive	• Accurate • Careful • Conscientious • Logical • Reserved • Precise
Characteristics: • Authoritative • Big-picture thinker • Confrontational • Sense of urgency • Independent • Innovative • Loves a challenge • Problem solver • Results oriented • Risk taker	• Big-picture thinker • Encouraging • Impulsive • Inspiring • High need for interaction • Optimistic • Persuasive • Shows emotions • Very verbal	• Avoids conflict • Builds strong relationships • Calming and stabilizing force • Easygoing • Good listener • Helpful • Process oriented • Team player	• Analytic • Conflict averse • Conservative • Data gatherer • Detail focused • Methodical • Objective thinker • Quality focused
Look for: • Big gestures • Direct eye contact • Fast-paced speech • Leans forward • Strong, clear tone	• Animated • Expressive gestures • Fast-paced speech • Friendly eye contact	• Friendly eye contact • Relaxed pace • Warm, steady tone	• Business-like demeanor • Direct eye contact • Few gestures, if any • Precise, steady tone

These communication styles, or behavioral styles, describe how we act, and they are typically expressed by a four-factor model. To get a basic understanding of each factor, we look at it in its pure form, even though your style is a combination of the factors you exhibit as well as those you do not exhibit. A High D, for instance, would be described as direct, forceful and independent. High D's can be recognized by their strong, confident tone and extensive eye contact. An animated, friendly approach describes the High I, in contrast to the more laid-back, warm but non-emotional High S. Coming full circle is the quiet, reserved and precise High C. While most people have one or two factors that dominate, all people are some combination of the four factors, and most people have the ability to adapt their style—at least to some extent. A thorough understanding of one's own style, and its implications, is a truly fundamental piece of information every leader—and, in fact, every person—should have. Look at the chart to see which factors best describe you.

Communication style is applicable in a whole host of situations and is closely linked to our previous discussion about understanding the impact you have. In fact, I have found that a lot of so-called personality conflicts and team dysfunctions disappear once people understand how differences in communication style lead to conflict. While your communication style comes through in just about everything you do, I'm going to focus on just a few specific situations here.

I mentioned earlier that I believe it is the ability to adapt communication style, rather than leadership style, that is the key to effectively handling a variety of situations. For example, while the decisive, results-oriented approach (High D) *might* be effective for running a board meeting, it might *not* be the best approach for soliciting feedback or delivering a performance review. Similarly, an analytic, detail-focused approach (High C) might *not* be best for conducting a brainstorming session, but could be ideal for walking people through a process. (Please do not get the wrong impression. I'm not in any way saying or implying a High C, for instance, couldn't run a brainstorming meeting or a High D couldn't solicit feedback, just that there are times when certain styles may be more effective. We do not use communication style to put limits or restrictions on a person's abilities.)

An understanding of communication style also provides an abundance of information regarding a person's behavior and natural tendencies, and it contains reliable clues about their preferences related to work environment. In one case, two people actually traded jobs after I conducted a communication style session for their organization. One was a quiet, reserved, analytical person (High C) who was serving as a client support person, and the other was an outgoing, high-energy person (High I) who was predominantly handling administrative issues. Both were dissatisfied with their respective positions, but it wasn't until our discussion of behavioral style that the reasons became obvious. Once they switched places so their natural behavioral style corresponded to the needs of the position, they were much happier and far more productive.

Communication style also impacts delegation, the need for information and detail, decision-making style, time management challenges, team approach, general demeanor, communication preferences, and so on. As a result, people with different communication styles require different management approaches in order for them to develop and reach their potential. Have you ever had someone bird-dogging you after you've delegated a project to them? Most likely, they are highly detail oriented and methodical (High C) and are looking for more direction or details than you provided.

Sometimes the influence of your communication style isn't so obvious. In one firm, the owner came to me because he was frustrated that his people were overreacting to issues and hesitant to take action without his blessing. It turned out that his driving, goal-oriented approach (High D) was causing his people (who were predominantly

High S's and High C's) to become more and more fearful of making mistakes, leading right to the behavior he found so frustrating—and this was a well-intentioned leader who did care about his people. The next time you find yourself dissatisfied with a pattern of behavior your people are exhibiting, take a close look at how you could be affecting or even provoking that behavior.

Great leaders know their style and work on their ability to adapt it. This expands their repertoire, giving them a wider variety of responses and approaches that can be tailored to specific individuals or situations. In this way, their leadership principles and philosophies remain constant while they retain the ability to effectively manage a variety of situations and people. In words attributed to Thomas Jefferson, "In matters of style, swim with the current; in matters of principle, stand like a rock."[36]

THE TOTAL PERSON

When we say leaders need to "know themselves," we are referring not only to issues surrounding professional competence but also to the "total person." Like it or not, we all know it is almost impossible to separate what happens at work from what happens at home. We've all seen someone whose performance suffers when a problem at home saps their energy and focus, and we've all struggled to keep work issues from affecting our family life. To maintain high levels of performance, it is imperative you tend to all areas of your life and yourself.

Leaders (and top performers) know what they need to keep themselves healthy—mentally, physically and emotionally. They proactively make time for those pursuits that help them to recharge and stay focused. At a recent event, I had the pleasure to chat with a business owner who told me about his morning routine, something he had adopted a year ago at the advice of a friend who was also a business owner. Instead of getting up and rushing into the office, he gets up, meditates for 20 minutes and then checks his emails. After that, he exercises, showers, eats and then heads to the office. This is *his* time, and he protects it by turning off his phone. In fact, he often doesn't get into the office until 9:00 or 9:30 but feels that taking the time to take care of himself has profoundly affected his ability to support high levels of performance and achievement in all aspects of his life.

Leadership is a demanding job that requires a sharp, keen mind. Fatigue and burnout, in all its forms, will negatively affect your ability to lead by compromising emotional intelligence, optimism, confidence and motivation. The healthier the total person, the better able he or she will be to cope with the stress and challenges endemic to a leadership role. Knowing yourself means knowing what you need to stay healthy, but it also means recognizing changes in your own physical and emotional states. These changes are important in that they may signal an approaching problem that could jeopardize performance. High levels of self-awareness allow one to recognize these warnings and to take action before they become problematic.

Nurturing the total person is important for other reasons as well. Great leaders accept themselves for who they are, and they appreciate themselves simply as unique human beings. The ability to value themselves without the trappings of position, title and achievement gives them tremendous confidence and strength. This means they can see their own value, separate and apart from what they've accomplished, from their title, from who they married, and from how much they make. By seeing yourself as a total person, you can separate *who you are* from *what you do*. Your role does not define you, and as such, it becomes easier to step back, see things objectively and keep things in perspective. Imagine if all your self-worth and self-esteem was tied to the last project you did—either something work related or something you did at home. How well would you be able to take constructive criticism or even helpful suggestions? An attack on your project would feel like a personal attack, making you much less able to hear, no less accept, feedback. Your defenses would go up, and you would have tremendous difficulty hearing anything being said. A balanced, well-rounded person is more likely to hear feedback objectively and act on it appropriately.

IS IT EASY TO RUFFLE YOUR FEATHERS?

Aristotle said, "Any one can get angry—that is easy—...; but to do this to the right person, to the right extent, at the right time, with the right motive, and in the right way, that is not for every one, nor is it easy."[37]

Maybe you're overtired. Maybe you're frustrated or disappointed. Maybe you're having a bad day (or a bad week or a bad year!). And then someone cuts you off in traffic. Or your boss criticizes the project you've been slaving over. Or the nice cashier tells you that you just missed the 30-day return window. Suddenly, you are overwhelmed by emotion, and your entire system is flooded with rage, anger or frustration. You are no longer rational. You "lose it," and before you know it, you are yelling at the cashier or pressing "send" on that scathing email or shutting down and withdrawing. While we like to think of ourselves as intellectual and rational, human beings have emotions—lots of them—and as you are going to see, they are a much bigger part of who we are, how we act, and how we think than we'd ever want to admit.

Unfortunately, as the lead bird, your flock needs you to be unflappable. Overly emotional responses and reactions will have your people walking on eggshells, will undermine your integrity, and will destroy an atmosphere of respect and trust—so much for updraft. Problems and bad news need to roll off you like water off a duck's back. Like most businesspeople, you have probably heard the term emotional intelligence and have some idea of what it means, but I find few truly understand how critical it is to leadership and to the creation of updraft.

What you may not realize is that without emotional intelligence, your brain's go-to response is one of emotion rather than one of rational thought. Emotional intelligence is a foundational capability because "the power as well as the speed of an emotional response is infinitely faster than that of rational thought," asserts Dr. Izzy Justice, an authority on emotional intelligence in the workplace.[38] In other words, every time there is a race between rational thought and emotion, emotion wins—it has the "house edge." So, it takes effort to override that emotional response and instead behave calmly and rationally, tapping into your interpersonal skills, business knowledge, sales know-how, project management expertise, and all those skills and abilities you've worked so hard to develop.

To truly understand the role of emotional intelligence both as a leader and as a human being, it is helpful to know a little something about how your brain processes information.[39] Basically, information from your five senses comes in and is routed to both the thalamus and the amygdala (parts of the limbic system). The thalamus is like a traffic cop, and in an effort to keep things moving, it sends information to the cortex (the "thinking" brain) for processing. The cortex "thinks" about the information and then sends impulses out to execute the instructions. At the same time, however, a small portion of the information is sent directly from the thalamus to the amygdala. If a threat is perceived, the amygdala can trigger a response while the cortex is still figuring out what is going on.

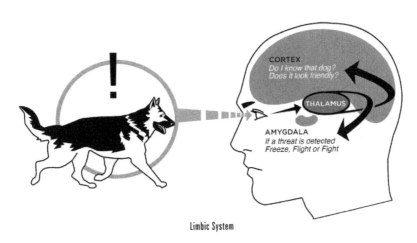

Limbic System

Imagine you are taking a walk through the neighborhood and suddenly a huge German shepherd comes running toward you. If you recognize that dog as friendly, gentle "Dexter" from down the street, the amygdala doesn't see a need to respond because no threat is detected. Your cortex might instruct you to call to the dog or to tell him to "go home." However, if you don't recognize the 90-pound dog with huge teeth racing toward you, then your amygdala (relying on your past experiences) will jump into action and trigger the survival reaction known as the freeze, fight or flight response. A part of that response includes the release of a whole bunch of hormones that prepare your body for the survival reaction.[40] The results of this are familiar: increased heart rate, increased blood pressure, dilated pupils, the tensing of muscles, and racing thoughts. Internally, other changes occur that are not as evident to us, including the redirection of blood to major muscles (getting you ready to run), the increasing of blood-glucose levels (giving you extra energy for the situation), and the shutting down of noncritical systems like digestion and the immune system. If you are in a survival situation, your body becomes less concerned with the flu it *might* catch next week and more concerned with just making it *to* next week.

Your limbic system registers danger and immediately kicks into gear, choosing whether to freeze you where you are, give you a sudden burst of speed to race out of the way, or give you the strength to fight. Interestingly, it is not yet well understood how your system chooses whether to freeze, fight or flee. I've seen this with two of my cats in how they dealt with the introduction of a dog into our home. One cat, Domino, would freeze at the dog's approach. His kitty eyes would dilate, and he would look as though it was taking every fiber of his being to remain still. However, this reaction was fairly boring to the dog, and it wasn't long until they came to an understanding. Then there was our other cat, Salem. She would hiss and flee, exciting the dog and enticing him to chase her. To this day, she maps routes through the house designed to avoid the canine and still hasn't forgiven us for ruining and complicating her life.

The limbic system enables us to react quickly to serious threats to our survival. But here's the problem: this system operates pretty much like it did for our caveman ancestors. So, you might think the limbic system doesn't activate very often because our lives have evolved so we rarely, if ever, need to run from a German shepherd, no less a saber-toothed tiger. You'd be wrong.

Remember the last time you were fuming because you got caught in traffic and were late for a meeting? Or the time your boss gave you a bad review? Or when your teenaged son totaled the car? All of these events, and millions more like them, can trigger the limbic system. And to make matters even worse, human beings are thinking animals, able to trigger the limbic system just by *thinking about* getting stuck in traffic or being late for a meeting (or writing a book). "Essentially, we humans live well enough and long enough, and are smart enough, to generate all sorts of stressful events purely in our heads," explains Dr. Robert Sapolsky, author, researcher and professor of biology, neurosurgery and neurological sciences at Stanford University. "How many hippos worry about whether Social Security is going to last as long as they will, or what they are going to say on a first date?"[41]

Luckily, not every negative thought or experience triggers the freeze, fight or flight response, but every stressor does produce some degree of stress response. What this means is while you may not have had a dramatic response to the flat tire you found on your car after your kids missed the bus, there was *some* degree of stress response. Exactly how that manifested itself will vary from person to person, but some physiological changes have occurred as a result of whatever hormones were released. The bottom line is you are not at your best and it will take some time before you return to a "normal" state, assuming another stressor doesn't occur in the meantime.

Knowing yourself means being aware of your own level of emotional intelligence. Just being cognizant of this process, and the implications thereof, raises your level of emotional awareness. Toward that end, there are five realities of this process we need to emphasize:

- *This is an automatic process.* It is not something you (or anyone else) have control over. Improving your ability to recognize and manage the effects of this process are your only lines of "defense."

- *This is a physiological process.* Actual chemical changes are taking place in your body, thanks to the release of hormones. These occurrences go beyond the idea of "a bad mood" or "negative attitude"—your chemical composition has actually been altered.

- *It can take hours for these hormones to clear out of the body* before you resume a completely "normal" state. Think about what happens if you have a minor car accident on the way to work. If you're like most people, the entire morning is shot as you tell the story, call the insurance company, and even go over it in your mind— all in an attempt to "shake it off" and regain your focus. What you probably didn't realize, however, is try as you might, it takes several hours for those hormones to clear out.

- *Continuous experience with smaller stressors has a cumulative effect.* Since it takes hours for those hormones to dissipate, a series of small events will pile up and can eventually result in a sudden and dramatic reaction—along the lines of the proverbial "straw that broke the camel's back."

- *When the freeze, flight or fight response kicks in, you actually lose your ability to access or use your thinking brain.* As the amygdala takes control of your brain, your mind is flooded with emotion and you become highly irrational. These episodes are characterized by a strong emotional reaction, sudden onset, and often, the eventual realization that the reaction was out of proportion and inappropriate. It's the adult version of a temper tantrum, and it can ruin careers, not to mention lives and relationships. Two famous examples include Mike Tyson's biting Evander Holyfield's ear during their 1993 boxing match, and Zinedine Zidane's head butting of Marco Materazzi during the 2006 World Cup Soccer finals. Tyson was fined $3 million and lost his boxing license, and Zidane was kicked out of the game. (Examples are certainly not limited to sports figures, but these were two particularly public instances.)

As you can see, emotion is deeply embedded in your thinking process; the two are inextricably linked. So, with thanks and acknowledgment to Peter Salovey and John Mayer[42] (two of the leading researchers on emotional intelligence) as well as Daniel Goleman[43] (who popularized the term and brought it into the realm of business), let's take a look at our definition of emotional intelligence and at how it impacts your ability to lead. I'm defining emotional intelligence as the ability to...

Perceive, experience, recognize, understand, communicate, analyze, tap into, use and manage emotions 1) to enhance one's own performance and growth, 2) to improve one's own relationships and interactions, 3) to help others understand, manage and regulate their emotions in order to aid their growth, enhance their performance and improve their relationships, and 4) to create socially and psychologically healthy environments.

At its most basic level, emotional intelligence refers to exactly what we are discussing here—how well do you know yourself? How accurately and openly do you assess and accept what you are feeling? Can you express your emotions without losing control of them? Think of this as the ability to have emotions without becoming emotional. On this first tier, you are striving for the skill to be aware of and sensitive to your own emotions so you recognize them, experience them and use them *without being excessively influenced by them.* Do other people know you are in a bad mood before you do? Do you find that you continue treating people badly even once you recognize that you are angry or annoyed? Such behavior isn't appropriate or acceptable; it will not only destroy your ability to create updraft but will also jeopardize your relationships. It's time to get a handle on this kind of behavior for the good of your organization as well as the people around you. (And if your behavioral style—i.e., your DISC—is a High D, pay especially careful attention to this.)

As with everything in this chapter, there are steps you can take if you are something of a slave to your emotions. Think back to a recent incident and examine what happened and how it could have been different had you been in better control of your reactions. To make progress on this issue, you need to recognize the impact this pattern of behavior is having on both your personal and professional relationships. Then, your next step is committing to giving this issue your full attention and beginning to monitor your emotional states. Pay attention to what triggers your emotions (particularly the negative ones) and how quickly your emotions escalate. Identify the emotion you are feeling, and notice how that emotion manifests itself for you. Does your breathing quicken? Do you feel tightness in your shoulders or your chest or your stomach? The key is gaining the ability to recognize when your emotions are starting to take over so you can interrupt the cycle, responding consciously and deliberately rather than emotionally. Some other methods that can be helpful when dealing with this include the following:

- Slowing down so your reaction isn't the automatic, emotionally laden one.

- Considering the effect you want to have on those around you, and understanding the damage your current behavior is causing.

- Recognizing and taking responsibility for the consequences of your behavior by apologizing, personally and sincerely, when you take out your frustration or anger on someone else.

- Working on being more empathetic to how others are feeling.

- Finding techniques for alleviating stress.

- Working on your ability to communicate calmly so you can have difficult conversations without upsetting yourself or other people.

- Writing or journaling about how you feel and what you are experiencing emotionally, which can help you get in touch with those feelings and reveal patterns you might not otherwise notice.

- Enlisting the help of someone who can give you honest, accurate feedback.

So many of the business owners I speak with want to suppress or ignore their emotions rather than recognize their power. But consider this scenario. You are on the golf course and you birdie the first hole (shoot one under par). But then, on the next tee, you slice the ball badly. This annoys you. Try as you might, your next shot is no better, and from this point on, your game deteriorates until you deposit the clubs, bag and all, into the next water hazard you see. Negative emotions have a huge impact on performance, and your ability to master this level of emotional intelligence helps you to maintain an even keel while dealing with the ups and downs of business, life and golf (in fact, emotional intelligence plays a huge role in sports). Emotional intelligence contributes to less stress, more personal growth, better relationships, more confidence, more professional opportunities...I could go on and on.

As you will see, each subsequent level of emotional intelligence requires a more sophisticated and highly-developed level of expertise, building on the level preceding it. While the first level dealt exclusively with you, the next component of emotional intelligence relates to your relationships. Can you sense what someone else is feeling? Are you looking below the surface to truly understand what is going on? Are you careful not to let your own reactions and emotions trigger a stress response in others? Now we begin using the knowledge we have about emotions to improve *our* relationships and interactions. By understanding the role of emotions and the way your emotions impact other people, you understand the importance of keeping a handle on your reactions in order to bring out the best in others. In addition, you enhance your ability to read people and situations more effectively, which allows you to sense and diffuse potential problems earlier and to maintain healthier and more productive relationships.

I've already mentioned how important it is for you to be aware of the effect you have on people. Occupying the top position in the pecking order means you have an inflated ability to arouse emotion. Using that power to trigger negative emotions and their resulting consequences is not productive and constitutes an abuse of that power. Think about what happens to the person who has to deliver bad news to you. If his or her anxiety over having to bring you the news doesn't trigger a stress response, you becoming as mad as a wet hen certainly will. Now neither of you is rational, and the situation quickly escalates into an interaction nobody will be particularly proud of.

Fear, intimidation, yelling and the like are anathema to creating updraft. These constitute not only an ineffective form of communication but also a quite damaging one. It is up to you to develop your emotional intelligence and control your own emotions so you aren't "infecting" people with negative emotions and undermining their ability to use the intellect and skills you hired them for. If you are constantly "losing it," you will be unable to inspire trust, and no one will be willing to fly too close to you.

The final levels of emotional intelligence go beyond our focus on knowing yourself, but are important to mention because of their role in the creation of updraft. Supporting, encouraging and helping others to understand the implications and importance of emotional intelligence is at the heart of the third level. Is emotional intelligence a subject that your team and staff understand? Do you encourage others to acknowledge and express their feelings? Do others feel safe expressing their emotions to you without being concerned they will be judged? There is no doubt that being surrounded by emotionally intelligent people is preferable to the alternative, no matter your situation. If you aren't yet sure of this, you'll have to take my word for it. But we've also just talked about how closely emotional intelligence is related to high levels of performance in so many areas. As a result, the higher you want your organization to soar, the more critical emotional intelligence becomes, so encouraging this kind of growth becomes absolutely crucial to your organization's success.

Supporting and encouraging growth in this area is important for another reason as well. As a leader, your team is an extension of you and of what you stand for. By tolerating even one executive or manager who exhibits behavior linked to low emotional intelligence (regardless of how good he or she may be in other areas), you are giving tacit approval of that behavior. As soon as you do that, you undermine your own integrity, trust and credibility and destroy any possibility of organizational updraft. Great leaders take responsibility for everything under their watch and recognize how important emotional intelligence is to the performance of each and every person in the organization.

The most advanced level of emotional intelligence links directly to one of the leader's most important jobs—creating the environment. What kind of culture are you nurturing? How do people treat each other? What is acceptable behavior? As we've seen, how a person treats and interacts with others is directly related to his or her own level of emotional intelligence. Low levels of emotional intelligence can result in highly-reactive, irrational behavior that can easily trigger the same behavior in others (remember, it is an automatic, physiological response). Great leaders know this is not conducive to the development of a high-performance organization. Simply put, the more emotionally intelligent you become, the less tolerant you will be of "emotionally unintelligent" behavior because you understand all too well the negative effect it has on the culture, the organization and your ability to succeed. By encouraging the development of emotional intelligence in yourself and others, you reduce the likelihood and impact of negative emotions. This, in turn, contributes to the creation of a psychologically and emotionally healthy environment that encourages growth and accountability, promotes cooperation and teamwork, and supports innovation and creativity—all behaviors that greatly support updraft.

Don't fear introspection, seek it out, starting with those subjects covered here. Learning to accept yourself and seeing your own intrinsic value goes a long way toward making you the kind of person who people are inspired to follow. As Lao Tzu observed, "He who knows others is learned; he who knows himself is wise."[44]

STRETCHING YOUR WINGS...

1. Schedule your first self-reflection session. Pick any subject we've covered or go back to the list on page 50 for ideas.

2. What are your personal values? Have you committed them to paper? (To jump start this process, go to www.DeltaVstrategies. com/Resources and download the Personal Values exercise.

3. Make a list of what you feel are your top four strengths and weaknesses. Then, think about how they relate to your position. Are there strengths you should be using that you're not? What should be targeted for development, and what should be "outsourced" to someone else?

4. Do you know your communication style? Review the chart on page 61. Which descriptors sound most like you? How about the styles of the members of your leadership team? Learn the fundamentals of communication style so, at the very least, you understand your style and its implications.

5. What stresses you out? What helps you to refuel? Do you proactively make time for those things that help you recharge? Choose something you enjoy that helps you to refuel, and put it on your schedule within the next two weeks (that is, do it within the next two weeks).

6. Reread the section on emotional intelligence paying particular attention to the five realities of the process (discussed on pages 70-71). Start accepting the power of your emotions, and make it a point to notice and acknowledge them rather than block them out. Begin working on the first level of emotional intelligence by identifying the emotions you experience and noting their intensity.

CHAPTER 4

Are you going the way of the dodo?

You've undoubtedly heard of the dodo bird. A relative of the pigeon, the dodo has been extinct now for over 300 years. Recent studies[45] suggest that this strange bird, at one time thought to be a myth, was a strong, resilient animal that survived despite some extreme local and climactic conditions. However, living on the island of Mauritius, off the coast of Madagascar, the dodo did not need to escape from predators as there were none on the island. As a result, the dodo actually lost its ability to fly—an ability that might have enabled it to escape from mankind as well as the foreign predators that man introduced.

While adding new skills and expanding thinking have always been essential for leaders, it is absolutely crucial in today's environment. If you stop stretching and testing your wings, you too will lose the ability to fly. Forget about updraft—you won't even get off the ground. And once *you* lose that ability, your organization will be unable to take off; you'll ultimately be sentencing it to the same fate as the dodos'. Unfortunately, the rate of change and the speed of information have made it a tougher and tougher challenge. Just trying to keep up feels like flying into a headwind. And if you aren't making an effort, then you're not just stagnating, you're falling behind.

Leadership is an organizational constraint. Like a houseplant whose growth and development will be obstructed by the size of its container, an organization's growth and development will be hampered by its leadership. So many times I'm invited in by the top executive to discuss how I might help with the development of his leadership team, only to find that he isn't including himself in that process. At one service organization, the president told me their last development efforts had been to bring in a few workshops for their executives about six or seven years ago; but he couldn't recall what the sessions had addressed, nor had he participated. He couldn't even remember the last time he had taken part in any kind of professional enrichment.

ARE YOU A CONSTRAINT?

Think about it this way. Let's say you speak a few words and phrases of Spanish and want your child to learn the language. Kids pick up languages fairly quickly, so before you know it, they'll be counting to ten and asking everyone they meet, "¿cómo estás?" (How are you?) At that point, however, their progress will come to a sudden stop. While you can teach them what you know, your child's learning is limited by your own. In the same vein, you can't develop your people past the point where you've developed yourself. We're not talking about hard skills or even expertise here, as great leaders are not afraid to surround themselves with people who know more than they do. But in the area of leadership, you must be leading your flock—both literally and figuratively. Earlier, we discussed the importance of engagement to the creation of updraft, and not surprisingly, trust in executives is a primary driver of engagement.[46] If you do not continue to hone and develop your skills as a leader, you jeopardize your organization in several ways.

First, you undermine the confidence your people have in you as they begin to realize that you are not up to the task. Please don't make the mistake of thinking they don't or won't notice—they will. And it isn't just their confidence in you that will take a hit. Trust, integrity and credibility will erode as well, leaving your people questioning your ability and hesitant to follow you. In fact, at that same service organization, the president assured me this wasn't the case. And yet, in discussion after discussion with executives and staff, the same sentiments were expressed—as much as they liked the president, they felt he was "in over his head." While no one condemned him, they were acutely aware of how much things in their industry were changing, and they couldn't understand why he wasn't doing anything. If you see yourself here, start challenging your own thinking. Reaching out for guidance and counsel is a *strength*, not a weakness—remember Phil Mickelson and all his coaches? In this organization's case, several people even indicated that if the situation didn't change, they would start "looking around." This leads us to the second danger. Your organization will lose its ability to recruit and retain top performers. These kinds of people crave new challenges and covet the opportunity to work with a great leader. However, they will just as quickly recognize when they have nothing left to learn, and it won't take long before they start investigating other options.

> **You can't develop your people past the point where you've developed yourself.**

Goslings, with their instinct to imprint, illustrate yet another danger. Imprinting, as you probably know, is when a young duck or chick forms a strong bond to the first moving object it sees, typically its mother. However, if presented at the right time, researchers have seen goslings imprint to a human, a ball and even an electric train.[47] Once that bond is established—and it happens very quickly—that piece of information becomes permanent and cannot be "unlearned," despite how seriously it threatens the gosling's survival. For all practical purposes, the gosling is blind to the options around him.

As soon as you stop proactively expanding your thinking and seeking out new ideas and perspectives, you can easily become blinded by what you already know, just like the gosling. And if you allow what you already know to impede your ability to acquire new knowledge, it may well threaten your survival as well. By operating and making decisions based on old and outdated information, the very existence of your organization will be at risk. You must realize that if you remain stagnant while the world around you changes, you will no longer be competent to lead. Your ability to see opportunities and be a visionary will be compromised if your information, perceptions and frames of reference are out of date. The business landscape is littered with stories of executives who couldn't or wouldn't see how dramatically their world was changing.

Blockbuster, for instance, who revolutionized their industry and became the world's largest movie-rental company, filed for bankruptcy in September 2010.[48] Its demise has been attributed to several factors[49] but none more interesting than the fact that as late as June 2010, then CEO Jim Keyes was still denying that Netflix (founded in 1998) was their competitor[50] (and one, by the way, they could have purchased for just $50 million in 2000).[51] Or what about Kodak, celebrated for decades as an industry leader and an outstanding example of American innovation, who filed for bankruptcy in January 2012. Once again, many circumstances contributed to this development, and you may be thinking it was inevitable as digital cameras wiped out the need for film, Kodak's highly profitable cash cow. But what you might not know is that Kodak[52] was actually the first to invent the digital camera— and way back in 1975. At the time, however, Kodak executives were so busy trying to protect the status quo, they couldn't see that the future of photography was right in front of them. Engineer Steve Sasson and his team estimated it would take 15 to 20 years to bring the product to market. Imagine where Kodak would be today had they not been holding so tightly to the past. Leadership is an organizational constraint; if an organization's leadership stops growing, learning and listening, so does that organization.

At its most basic level, continuous learning refers to exactly what it sounds like, and it starts right where knowing yourself leaves off. Self-reflection allows us to comfortably and confidently look for questions as well as answers and provides the opportunity to revisit experiences and to learn from them. And maybe most importantly, self-reflection provides the opportunity to discover what we don't know that we don't know, uncovering potentially dangerous gaps in our skills or knowledge that we're unaware of.

> **If an organization's leadership stops growing, learning and listening, so does that organization.**

Once we move an ability out of our blind spot and realize we don't know something, we can address it by putting ourselves into learning mode if it is found to be relevant. If you judge it to be irrelevant, that's okay too. I know I do not know advanced physics, and I am totally fine with that. Continuous learning means pursuing development that will have an impact on your performance, either personally or professionally.

Any of the topics we discussed in the previous chapter are a good place to start. Comparing your strengths and weaknesses to those that are most relevant to your performance as a leader will expose potential areas for development. I certainly hope reading this book will provide new perspectives and make you aware of areas that might need to be addressed. I'm sure many people didn't even know they had a behavioral style or how much emotional intelligence impacted their daily lives. Now that these concepts have been brought to your attention, you can target those that are most relevant to your performance and begin to map out a process for your ongoing development.

Start by keeping a growing list of topics, skills and abilities you've identified as important, and choosing just one (maybe two) that you're going to focus on. Let's say public speaking is a challenge for you. If you do a little research (or have someone else do it), you'll find a huge variety of books, videos, coaches, classes and online seminars on the topic. Maybe you decide to start with a book and your local Toastmasters International® club, with the idea that you'll reach out to a coach before your next presentation. Select the resources you'd like to use and get them on your calendar by scheduling the time for them, whether attending a class, meeting with a coach or setting aside time to read.

While most of the business owners and executives I've met have a natural love of learning, especially for topics they enjoy or feel will be useful to them, their own development and growth falls to the wayside as they attempt to juggle the demands of their positions. Don't allow this to happen. Join a peer group. Reach out to organizations and leaders who you admire and meet to share best practices (consider including your leadership team). Remember, what's good for the goose is good for the gander. You can't tell your people growth and development are important but that the concept doesn't apply to you. Make these development activities a priority—they are not to be neglected or constantly rescheduled.

As a discipline, leadership encompasses any number of subjects. Although we said leaders look to address issues that are relevant to performance, exemplary leaders define that very broadly. As lifelong learners, their passion for learning will draw them to a tremendous diversity of subjects and challenges—some mental, some physical and some spiritual. They are the very epitome of well rounded, and they are usually working to acquire some new skill—anything from improving facilitation skills to speaking Japanese to learning how to ski. They may stumble across a topic they find fascinating and throw themselves into learning all they can about it. They recognize that although a subject may not appear to be related to job performance, anything that stimulates thinking or expands confidence and comfort zones will ultimately result in personal growth and development. Continued learning helps us to embrace the new rather than fear it. It gives us a chance to process and question and analyze so what is new is not completely foreign and unknown to us, allowing us to react with curiosity and interest rather than fear.

Another reason leaders don't restrict their learning and self-development to so-called work-related topics is they recognize thinking and problem solving to be anything but linear, logical events. They know preparation, study and research culminate in "Aha" or "Eureka" moments that occur when the brain is allowed to relax and process information on a subconscious level. That's why the answer to 26-Across suddenly pops into your head while you are driving or in the shower. The idea for Velcro® came to Swiss engineer George de Mestral when he and his dog returned from a hunting trip with burdock burrs stuck to them,[53] and Art Fry's annoyance with the little scraps of paper he used to bookmark his hymnal led him to suddenly see a use for fellow 3M scientist Spencer Silver's removable adhesive (which became Post-It® Notes).[54] Answers and ideas can be sparked by the most seemingly irrelevant information or trivial thought that causes a synapse to fire and suddenly, clear as day, connects two previously unrelated ideas. Carl Ally, an American advertising executive, understood this:

> The creative person wants to be a know-it-all. He wants to know about all kinds of things: ancient history, nineteenth century mathematics, current manufacturing techniques, flower arranging, and hog futures. He never knows when these ideas might come together to form a new idea. It may happen six minutes later or six years down the road. But the creative person has faith that it will happen.[55]

CHALLENGE YOUR THINKING

You may have noticed that our definition of continuous learning includes developing skills, expanding thinking, and seeking out new ideas and perspectives. There is a plethora of honking, tweeting, quacking and hooting going on within your organization, and if you aren't listening to it, you are missing out on opinions, information, assessments, criticisms, concerns—some of the most valuable information you can get your hands on. Your ability to soar is dependent not just on your skill set but also on an intimate knowledge of your own organization. Too many restrictions on what kind and how much feedback you choose to receive will impede your ability to learn about yourself, your performance, your organization, your clients, your industry and so on. To create updraft, it is imperative that you consider every interaction and every discussion as an opportunity to learn something new and that you consider these situations to be an integral component of your continuous learning.

Cartoonresource/Shutterstock.com

"Sometimes it's good to get a
different perspective."

As a person in a position of authority, getting honest, accurate feedback can be a challenge. Even with the advent of 360s and other tools designed to gather feedback, common sense and organizational politics will tend to soften language and result in less than candid comments. For a leader who is committed to self-improvement, this inability to get to the truth is deadly to self-development. We've talked about how challenging it can be to assess ourselves objectively. Some of the people who audition for *American Idol* sound like screeching crows and yet are shocked to find that the judges don't believe they have talent, even though it is extremely obvious to the rest of us. Just because *you* think the meeting went well doesn't necessarily mean it did. While introspection and reflection are significant components of the self-development process, leaders must be able to reconcile what they observe with what others perceive so they can identify any gaps and further focus their improvement efforts.

As an officer of the organization, you also need an accurate picture of the organization's health. Most executives spend a lot of time concerning themselves with operational and financial issues. They are aware of what progress has or hasn't been made against goals, objectives and metrics. They carefully watch profit and loss, and cash flow, as well they should. But most executives stop here. While I can't blame them for preferring to focus on these nice, objective measures, stopping here is problematic for two main reasons.

First, they are missing the bigger picture.

- What is morale like?

- Is the culture reflecting the vision, mission and values?

- Is leadership functioning as a team?

- Is the turnover rate higher than it should be?

- Why is client retention slipping?

Without addressing these, and a myriad of other issues, they miss getting a true understanding of the emotional health of their organization and they will be blind to potential problems. It's like the husband (or wife) who is shocked when their spouse announces they are seeking a divorce. Everything seemed fine on the surface, but they never chose to look any deeper, essentially ignoring the indications that something was wrong.

Second, by focusing exclusively on financials and operational metrics, they are looking at what the organization accomplish*ed* (past tense). Of course, we all use this information for forecasting, budgeting and looking at trends, but in reality, these numbers do not accurately predict the future or even reflect the present, for that matter. For a time, a company can appear financially viable even when it is emotionally compromised, so it is absolutely critical you look beyond the numbers to get the full story. Without the passion, engagement and innovation that an emotionally healthy organization possesses, the company will eventually flounder. The decline may take weeks, months or decades, but without an internal spark, the organization will lack the ability to create or sustain a competitive advantage, making long-term growth and prosperity all but impossible.

> **Without the passion, engagement and innovation that an emotionally healthy organization possesses, the company will eventually flounder.**

In order to assess the organization's true health, people who serve at the executive levels need to be aware of the dangers of isolation and of how dramatically it will obstruct their ability to learn. Whether by design or by accident, alienation will render a leader ineffectual. Many executives have been accused, and rightly so, of being out of touch—with customer needs, stakeholder concerns, and organizational realities. While commonly used to refer to academicians whose theories or research are so disconnected from reality that their work is considered useless, the so-called "ivory tower" generically refers to a secluded area, reserved for the elite, where they are sheltered from practical concerns and the complications of everyday life. But it is those daily complications and challenges that make up organizational life (and life in general, for that matter). As such, it is the responsibility of the leader to ensure those issues are addressed in such a way that the organization's mission, vision and values are upheld and that people receive the support they need to rise up and overcome those challenges. Never forget that problems, opinions and commentary need to pierce through several layers and will often be diluted on the way up. As a result, leaders must surround themselves with people who can be trusted to "tell it like it is," but also to acquire as much direct feedback as possible. No matter how massive your company, recognize that losing touch with the realities of everyday existence is lethal to your ability to lead.

© MARK ANDERSON, WWW.ANDERTOONS.COM

"The good news is we're getting a lot of feedback.
The bad news is we're getting a lot of feedback."

Make it a point to walk around your organization looking for opportunities to interact, discuss and even just observe what is going on. We are going to talk about this in more detail in Chapter 12, but don't make this more complicated than it needs to be. Start by taking a stroll through your enterprise, understanding that if your presence is unusual, people may be reticent to speak up and even suspicious of your motives. Your first few times out, just seek to connect with people on a personal basis. Work issues will crop up; listen carefully and without judgment and you'll find each successive trip will be easier and easier. A good rule when encouraging others to speak is to restrict yourself to clarifying questions so you don't inadvertently dominate the conversation. But, and I cannot emphasize this enough, you must be sincere, authentic and genuinely interested in what your people are saying. You must recognize that your experience of your organization is not typical, and so you need to make every effort to be objective. It can be a hard pill to swallow—not only do things look very different from your employees' perspective, but their experiences and impressions are undoubtedly a more accurate reflection of reality.

I remember an accounting firm that had recently acquired a smaller organization in order to expand its offerings. I had been brought in to work with several of the partners and to run some training sessions for the general staff. While the president characterized the transition as smooth and indicated they were "one big, happy family," all operating under the new, larger umbrella (but admittedly struggling to create updraft), my discussions with other executives and staff members revealed a very different reality. It turned out that people from both sides of the merger were struggling with how they fit into the new organization. In addition, an atmosphere of resentment was growing as managers from the acquired company handpicked which policies they would or wouldn't follow. As a result, a person's experience of the firm was heavily dependent on who they reported to. Had the president made it a point to be in touch and available to her organization, she would have realized that her bird's-eye view was not giving her an accurate picture of the situation. While we spoke at length about this issue and how to address it, this leader's highly conflict-averse communication style prevented her from moving forward, and the situation continued to deteriorate.

Successful leaders truly believe they can and should be open to learning from anyone at any time, so they seek out feedback from all levels of the organization. Search for diverse opinions. It's easy to listen to the opinions of those with whom we agree, but it takes a special effort to hunt for those with whom we disagree—even though we can learn far more from them. These efforts to swoop down and personally check in with people will also garner respect and strengthen relationships. As Mao Zedong said, "We should never pretend to know what we don't know, we should not feel ashamed to ask and learn from people below, and we should listen carefully to the views of the cadres at the lowest levels. Be a pupil before you become a teacher; learn from the cadres at the lower levels before you issue orders."[56]

STRETCHING YOUR WINGS...

1. Is continued growth and development something you encourage within your organization? How do you encourage it? Have you considered how it applies to you?

2. What is the last development effort you've undertaken? How long ago was that?

3. Create your own development objectives that dictate what your efforts should look like on an annual basis. Begin mapping out your plan for the year.

4. In a self-reflection session, review your last week or two. Was there a situation you could have handled better? Was there a topic you felt uninformed about? Use that to start your ongoing list of potential development subjects.

5. Go back to the list of strengths and weaknesses you created from the last chapter (you did that, right?), and review the subjects we've covered so far. Choose two topics to focus on, and create development plans for them. Do it.

6. Reflect on leaders and organizations you admire. Reach out and connect with at least two every year. Get together with other leaders through networking, peer groups, or coffee meetings. Consider hosting a luncheon for the leadership teams from both organizations to share best practices or to discuss issues and challenges.

PART II:
LIFTOFF

To create updraft, your organization must get off the ground. We need to look at those factors that are foundational to creating a culture that can fly.

CHAPTER 5

What kind of woodpecker are you?

In my line of work, difficult conversations are par for the course. We have to dig deep in order to understand what is truly going on, and I am fortunate and very thankful so many leaders are comfortable sharing their ambitions as well as their challenges and frustrations with me. Some conversations, however, are difficult in a different way. Rather than profound and emotional, they are complicated because we are not necessarily speaking the same language—along the lines of Abbott and Costello's *Who's on First* skit.[57]

Me:	"Does your organization have a mission?"
Leader:	"Yes," they answer, handing me a short paragraph that talks about quality and customer service and respect. *Ahhh. Their values.*
Me:	"How about your values?" And I get a bulleted list that includes innovation and caring and excellence. *More values.*

Me: "And what about a vision?" Most often, they don't have a vision, but sometimes they'll hand over a couple of sentences that talk about being "the best" or "the leader" or "the premier provider." A vague marketing gimmick, at best.

Values. Mission. Vision. These three words are among the most misunderstood and misused concepts in all of business. If you do a little research, you'll make some headway. If you do a lot of research, you'll end up right back where you started, mostly because the definitions often overlap and the terms are constantly interchanged. To make matters worse, people frequently use examples that contradict their own definitions. And yet, I'm going to tell you that creating and communicating vision, mission and values is one of the most fundamental tasks a leader performs. These three things shape your culture and are essential to the creation of updraft. The mission, vision and values provide three distinct pieces of information about your organization, and the absence of any one clips your organization's wings, making it unable to generate lift. We will look at values here in Part II, while mission and vision will be addressed in Part III.

GUIDING BEHAVIOR WITHIN THE FLOCK

Earlier, when we discussed the job of leadership, we touched on the fact that Canada geese teach their young about the rules of conduct which guide behavior within the flock. But with about 10,000 species of birds, it shouldn't come as too much of a surprise that what constitutes "acceptable behavior" varies from species to species. For instance, despite being two of only four woodpecker species that store food, the behavior of the acorn woodpecker[58] and the red-headed woodpecker[59] couldn't be more different. The red-headed woodpecker is a solitary bird that can be very aggressive, going so far as to destroy the nests and eggs of other birds that have the misfortune to live in its territory, the central and eastern United States. On the other end of the country, along the western coast of the United States and Mexico, lives the acorn woodpecker, whose complex social behavior has made it a favorite for researchers. These birds live in family groups that work together to raise their young and to gather, store and guard their food—sort of an avian commune. So, while cooperation and collaboration would be important for an acorn woodpecker to learn, it wouldn't even make the curriculum for a red-headed woodpecker.

Most animals teach their young what constitutes acceptable behavior in order to promote their survival and reduce conflict within the flock or group. Different standards of behavior are not exclusive to the animal kingdom, however. Like most children in the United States, I was taught to eat soup quietly using a spoon, a lesson which prompted me to send my mother a photograph from Japan where I was drinking soup directly out of the bowl. At an early age, we begin teaching our children about our rather complex culture, which requires different behaviors in different situations—i.e., the classroom versus the playground, or when eating at home versus eating out at a restaurant. Much of what we teach are manners, social conventions, and that tailgating is appropriate before a football game but not so much before the opera. To some extent, we are simply striving to raise socially well-adjusted children who can move seamlessly from situation to situation. But because we want our offspring to thrive and not just survive, there is a deeper meaning to these lessons.

We teach our children to "behave in school and be good for their teacher" because we value education. We teach them to "play nice with the other kids" because we value friendship, cooperation and respect. We teach them to "tell the truth" because we value honesty. We teach them not to "throw their brother out of a moving car" because we value family. As they get older, we hope that they begin to understand the deeper meanings behind these lessons and that they embrace many of the same things we see as important. As they internalize these concepts and make them their own, they begin to understand not only *what* behaviors are valued and appropriate but *why*, creating a framework for their own decision making. As that framework develops, we recognize their increasing responsibility as well as their capacity to make independent decisions—ones we desperately hope will lead not only to responsible behavior but to confident, self-sufficient adults. At some point, even the most protective bird in the avian kingdom must let its children fly solo.

Cartoonresource/Shutterstock.com

"Let's try it without the parachute."

Inside your organization, values serve a similar purpose. They keep us true to ourselves and provide limits on the kinds of behaviors that are acceptable, making them inextricably linked to the culture. They remind us that the ends do not justify the means and that how we achieve results is as important as the achievement itself. A strong set of values protects against the very issues we see every day in the news, where companies cross the lines of ethics, morals and legality. They are the very essence of who we are as an organization and enable us to guard against "Machiavellian" behavior that can quickly and easily lead to the destruction of morale, culture and the organization itself.

Back in Chapter 1, we talked about how the creation of updraft frees you from monitoring the day-to-day and allows you to spend your time on leadership issues. In the same way values provide a framework for our children to make decisions, they enable your people to make decisions within the context of the organization. Without established values, you clip both your wings and theirs. Instead of soaring overhead, you will need to hover close by, making or monitoring every decision and every step because you won't know what's guiding, driving and influencing your people's actions. This level of distrust and micromanaging is sure to make your people feel, well, henpecked. But once your organization has committed itself to a set of powerful, clearly-communicated values, you can encourage independent decision making, knowing the organization's values will provide the necessary guidance. A leader who has created an environment where all people are using similar standards, measures and benchmarks in concert with their expertise, experience and passion, can be very comfortable pushing decision making further and further into the organization.

Values allow you to leave the nest, and if they did nothing else, that alone would make them an indispensable tool for leadership as well as management. Not only do they do much more, but they profoundly affect your organization's ability to create updraft in other ways as well. As I've said, strong values provide guidance and structure, which reduce the need for a command-and-control approach to management, but they do that while simultaneously encouraging independence and initiative. Their existence supports an environment of engagement by fueling trust, providing security and empowering action. The very same decision-making framework that gives you confidence in your people, also gives your people confidence in themselves. They know they have a strong foundation upon which to base decisions, and one that transcends the short-term influences of events, the press, investors, competition, financial results and other similar pressures. They know what the organization's priorities are, and they can act accordingly, feeling safe in the knowledge they are surrounded by others who will support actions and decisions based on that same foundation. Having a supportive culture that "has your back" is very empowering and pushes people to take appropriate risks, expanding their comfort zones and allowing them to feel the wind under their own wings.

> **Values support an environment of engagement by fueling trust, providing security and empowering action.**

By identifying what's important to us, we set expectations and limits on behavior. Our values are a constant reminder of what we, as an organization, represent. They define what we hold dear and what we won't tolerate. People know exactly what is expected of them as well as what they can expect from others. Remember the accounting firm that was "one, big, happy family?" If they had had a strong set of values and had appropriately integrated the acquired company, then I would not have heard so much anger and resentment from people frustrated by the inequities in treatment. This is a common reason mergers and acquisitions fail; the two organizations don't take the time to compare and integrate their values so they can move forward as one organization. Organizational values set the standards across the entire company, contributing to a positive, uplifting environment for everyone.

Powerful, pervasive organizational values also help you to attract the right people—something critical to updraft (and a topic we will look at in the next chapter). Admittedly, an organization with a strong, pervasive culture will not be a good fit for everybody. However, you don't want to attract just any people, you want the organization to appeal to those whose passions and values are aligned with those of the organization. In just a moment, we're going to look at Ingram Micro's organizational values, which include accountability and integrity. If you are the kind of person who has trouble following through and is somewhat unreliable, then this isn't the place for you and you are unlikely to seek employment there. Considerable time and energy will be saved when candidates recognize that the values (or mission) don't resonate with them and that they aren't a good match. Those people who are drawn to the mission, value and culture will be strongly and strategically aligned with the goals of the organization. They will have a much greater likelihood of integrating into the organization and becoming engaged, inspired performers. In fact, it's not at all unusual for organizations to see a certain amount of turnover as they strive to create updraft; there will be a small percentage of people who don't resonate with what the "new" organization is all about, and that is perfectly okay.

A CLOSER LOOK

So, what do organizational values look like? Typically they are a word or short phrase followed by a sentence or two of clarification (as always, the more concise, the better). Since the idea is to focus everyone on those specific concepts and beliefs that are most important to us, there shouldn't be too many—ideally between three and six. By definition, we want people to focus, and you can't ask people to focus on ten things at once.

Wegmans (the grocery store we discussed earlier), for instance, has five core values:

1. We **care** about the well-being and success of every person.

2. **High standards** are a way of life. We pursue excellence in everything we do.

3. We **make a difference** in every community we serve.

4. We **respect** and listen to our people.

5. We **empower** people to make decisions that improve their work and benefit our customers and our company. (emphasis theirs)[60]

Ingram Micro, a wholesale distributor of technology, has six.

VALUES

We commit to these values to guide our decisions and our behaviors:

Innovation

We constantly look for better ways to deliver value to our customers, shareowners, suppliers and fellow associates. We anticipate change and create the solutions before we are asked to.

Accountability

We say what we do and we do what we say. We consistently produce results that meet or exceed the expectations of our customers and suppliers. We accept our individual and team responsibilities to meet our commitments.

Integrity

We abide by the highest ethical standards, demonstrating honesty and fairness in every action that we take, everywhere, all the time.

Teamwork and Respect

We honor the rights and beliefs of our fellow associates, partners and community. We treat others with the highest degree of dignity, equality and trust, leveraging diversity to meet our common goals. As a team, we deliver more than as individuals.

Learning

We continually acquire new knowledge to improve performance and enable growth for the Company and for ourselves.

Social Responsibility

We partner with our customers and suppliers to minimize our joint impact on the environment. We are responsible, active citizens in our communities through involvement, volunteerism and charitable giving.[61]

By reading their values, it is easy to see what these organizations care about. You know what they expect from their people and the other organizations they deal with, and you know what others can expect from them. You understand what unites them as well as what behaviors they celebrate and what they condemn. If these companies truly live their values, then we can assume that a manager who mistreated people would not last long at either organization. A company's values become its soul and conscience and are one of the driving forces behind its culture.

Despite my passion for organizational values and their importance to the creation of updraft, I must ask you to resist the temptation to immediately commit words like "teamwork," "integrity," "innovation," or "excellence" to a piece of paper you bring to the next executive meeting or hang up in the conference room. Do not treat this subject lightly. A set of values that we feel we should have or that sounded good elsewhere won't

> **A company's values become its soul and conscience and are one of the driving forces behind its culture.**

103

be beneficial and won't be reflected in the culture. In fact, they'll do more harm than good. If you aren't doing it for the "right" reasons and aren't willing to wholeheartedly commit to your values, don't do it at all. You certainly won't fool your employees. Regardless of whether you are starting from scratch or revisiting this concept, everyone in a leadership role must participate in the process; they must be onboard and fully committed.

I remember one business owner lamenting that his executive team was not embracing the organization's values. When I asked about how those values came about, he said he had come up with them during a recent session with a consultant and then had brought them to his team. No interaction. No discussion. Just, "Here they are." In addition to overlooking the importance of the executive team's passion and buy-in, the owner failed to truly educate his team about the real meaning of these values. Only when everyone has a thorough understanding and appreciation for the values will they be in a position to effectively use and communicate them. Every interaction, every discussion, every decision, even every memo will either model, support and reinforce those values or undermine them. Consistency is the key to getting the message across and to ingraining it into the culture and the organization.

As a leader and an executive, it is crucial that you and your team approach this issue honestly and sincerely, fully exploring the implications of what you are doing. To be effective, organizational values need to ring true. They need to be a genuine reflection of what the organization believes; otherwise, they won't serve any purpose. In one session with the executive team of an engineering firm, the concept of "honesty" was thrown out early in the discussion and was immediately met with nods and cries of, "Oh, yes," and, "Absolutely!" The conversation continued for a little while until one of the quieter members of the group spoke up and asked, "Are we truly ready to commit to honesty as a value? I'm not suggesting we conduct ourselves dishonestly, but sometimes we shield our clients from issues that come up. And we don't always tell our employees everything." You could hear the proverbial pin drop as his words sunk in. After a few moments, discussion resumed, but it had taken on a very different timbre as the group began looking at the proposed values on a much deeper level.

It will take some time to achieve consensus on the values and how they are stated. Don't get caught up in the wordsmithing; it isn't important. What is important is the connection between those concepts and the behaviors, beliefs and attitudes of leadership. After all, Enron's leadership created a culture of greed and unethical behavior despite corporate values that espoused "Respect, Integrity, Communication and Excellence."[62] The platitude "Do what I say, not what I do" won't cut it when it comes to organizations; the culture will always reflect leadership's example.

VALUES IN ACTION

Once you've identified and communicated your values, they must take on a life of their own. The more they are shared, discussed, cited, referred to, analyzed and debated, the more ingrained they become inside the organization and its culture. One such story involves Dr. P. Roy Vagelos, Merck & Co.'s former CEO, and the river blindness decision.[63] This story begins back in the 1970s when William Campbell's team of research scientists discovered they had a drug that was showing promise against the worms that cause river blindness—a very nasty parasitic disease, common to Africa and parts of the Middle East, that is carried by tiny black flies that breed along rivers. When the flies bite humans, they transmit the larvae of the parasitic worm, and when the worms reproduce, they send millions of tiny offspring through the body's tissue. This causes a severe itching reaction (so severe some victims commit suicide), disfigurement, and once they invade the eye, blindness. In some areas, the majority of those over the age of 45 were blind due to the disease.

Right from the beginning, Merck knew that the people who needed the drug would be unable to pay for it. Despite that, Dr. Vagelos, the Senior Vice President of Research at the time, approved Dr. Campbell's request to continue developing the drug. The company went ahead, spending a decade and $200 million not only to develop the drug but also to conduct the human clinical trials, which harbored several additional risks. Merck continued developing the drug in the hopes some third party would come forward to help with the effort, but no help materialized. What would eventually be called Mectizan® was proving to be a wonder drug against river blindness, requiring small annual doses and causing very few side effects. Dr. Vagelos, who by this time was serving as Merck's CEO, said, "We faced the possibility that we had a miraculous drug that would sit on a shelf."[64] So, on October 21, 1987, Merck announced to the world that it would provide the drug, free of charge, to anyone who needed it, for as long as necessary.

But the story doesn't end here. Merck knew there was no way to get the medicine to the people who needed it. Forget about pharmacies, many of these isolated villages were accessible only on foot. To solve the distribution problem, the Mectizan® Expert Committee was formed as an independent organization charged with establishing the guidelines and processes that would ensure the drug Mectizan® was distributed and used responsibly. Today, distribution is accomplished through the Mectizan® Donation Program (MDP), which provides and distributes the drug through partnerships with public and private organizations. MDP is the largest, ongoing medical donation program of its kind. It reaches over 200 million people annually[65] and has made tremendous strides, virtually eliminating the disease in some areas.

Photo credit: Merck & Co., Inc.; Kenilworth, N.J. USA

The Gift of Sight—Displayed in Merck's lobby, "This statue depicts a young boy leading
a blind man… a common scene that is disappearing as a result of Merck's decision,
in 1987, to control this ancient scourge," explains the commemorative plaque.

While an unusual and unprecedented decision, it seems less so when viewed within the context of the company's values, so eloquently expressed by George W. Merck several decades earlier:

> We try never to forget that medicine is for the people. It is not for the profits. The profits follow, and if we have remembered that, they have never failed to appear. How can we bring the best of medicine to each and every person? We cannot rest until the way has been found with our help to bring our finest achievements to everyone.[66]

Leadership's commitment to their philosophy of placing "people before profits" is what allowed Merck to even entertain such an option. There is no question that a whole host of circumstances contributed to Merck's ability to propose and implement such a solution, but it was their values that opened the door for such a discussion to take place. In 2012, Merck observed the 25th anniversary of the decision, celebrating the success of the program and the tremendous progress they've made against this devastating disease.

While not all stories will be quite so dramatic, the impact on the organization will be. Over time, stories that embody your values will become a part of the organization's history and will be told over and over again, in an effort to reinforce, educate and celebrate what you stand for and what you've accomplished.

STRETCHING YOUR WINGS...

1. Do you see how a strong set of values enables you to fly by encouraging and guiding independent decision making (among other things)? (Mission and vision will be discussed in Part III but if you'd prefer some clarification now, go to www.DeltaVstrategies. com/Resources and download our Immune System Infographic.)

2. Do you use a consistent set of values for your own decision-making? Can you identify them?

3. Does your organization have a set of values? If not, why not? What guides decisions? If so, are they actively discussed and referred to on a daily basis or just given lip service?

4. Can you think of a recent issue where having a set of values did make or might have made a decision easier? Can you think of a recent decision where you and your executive team discussed a situation using your values as the framework?

5. Envision the organization you're striving to create. Make a list of the attributes you'd like to see in your organization. Have each member of your executive team do the same.

6. Get even more input. Reach out to the organization and ask people what they think the organization values today and what they'd like to see it value. This can be done through meetings or submitted via email or paper responses.

7. Hold a leadership team meeting. Start by having each member of your team present their list of the organizational attributes they'd like to see (from #5 above). Then, review and analyze the input from the organization as a whole, focusing on the following:

- Which adjectives were used most often? Are they positive or negative?

- If we were starting over, are these the characteristics we'd want for the organization? What do we want to stand for?

- How do the team members' perceptions differ from each other and from those of the organization?

CHAPTER 6

It's all about the flock

When you get right down to it, an organization is but a group of people working together to accomplish something—make refrigerators, write software, design buildings, repair cars—for the most part, to deliver a product or provide a service. As we've discussed, it is that group of people who differentiates you from your competitors, the other inputs being pretty much the same from organization to organization. Ultimately, it is your flock that takes wing, not your buildings or your equipment or your capital (despite the fact that money does seem to fly out the door).

In order for you to soar, you need a team of engaged, motivated and passionate people. But having a team of engaged, motivated and passionate people depends on you—i.e., leadership—more than any other variable. So, there's a bit of the "which came first, the chicken or the egg?" conundrum here. And there's no gentle way to put this—while you may be frustrated because you feel your people are impeding your ability to soar, there's a very good chance they are just as frustrated waiting for you to step into your role and lead the way.

For just a moment, in your mind's eye, picture a group of birds flying in a v-formation. Which position in the 'v' do you think is the least important to creating updraft? While certain positions require more strength and experience than others, this is basically a trick question. If each bird relies on the updraft created by the bird preceding it, then no bird is unimportant to the formation. What about those in the trailing positions, you ask? There's nobody behind them. True, but while the lead bird works the hardest because she is flying into undisturbed air, the trailing positions are challenging because there is no one behind them to dispel the downdraft coming off their wings.[67] It turns out the trailing positions, like the lead position, are particularly strenuous. So, each and every position must be occupied by a bird that has the strengths and abilities to support and further the flock, not just for takeoff but for whatever will be needed 10, 100 and 1,000 miles into the journey. There are no unimportant positions in the formation, and there are none inside your organization; without the right people in the right spots, your goose is cooked.

YOUR MOST IMPORTANT ASSET

I'll say it over and over until I'm hoarse as a crow—more than anything else, it is the caliber and dedication of your people that has the greatest impact on your success. But until you truly understand and embrace this idea, you will be unable to create the organization you wish for because you will be unable to create updraft. While you often hear "people are our most important asset," more often than not, it is just a platitude bandied about by executives and companies who think it sounds good and don't seem to realize that just saying it isn't enough. Without a culture that truly values and appreciates people, that statement is nothing more than a cliché.

"Our employees are our greatest asset. I say we sell them."

I remember a presentation where I had just finished discussing how essential it is for leaders and managers to understand that their people are not just cogs in the organizational machine and that such an attitude is incompatible with a culture of engagement. A female executive stood and asked, "But what if they really are cogs? How do we engage them?" Wow. She couldn't see that they were caught in a vicious cycle where leadership's beliefs brought about the very behaviors they condemned. Treating people like mindless, interchangeable cogs is sure to suppress initiative, smother creativity, and stamp out any vestiges of enthusiasm, thereby creating the mindless, interchangeable cogs leadership complained about. Leadership just didn't get it. And guess what it says on the career section of their website? "People are our most important asset." The people who work there know only too well that it just isn't so.

I've probably just drunk too much of my own Kool-Aid®, but I'm not really sure why this is such a difficult concept for people to grasp. Who sells your product? Who talks to clients? Who develops new products? At this point in the growth of your organization, much of what gets done doesn't get done by your hand. Don't get me wrong, most of the executives I speak with appreciate their people and think highly of the vast majority of them. And most of the people I speak with are relatively happy at work. What you need to understand, however, is that being relatively happy or satisfied isn't enough for updraft. It's a good start, but we don't want to confuse a truly engaged workforce with a merely satisfied workforce.

Engaged Workforce	Satisfied Workforce
• Actively looks for opportunities where they can contribute • Voluntarily goes the extra mile • Brings high levels of passion as well as commitment • Is an advocate for their company • Is constantly innovating • Supports and collaborates with colleagues • Regularly achieves and surpasses company goals • Focuses on the achievement of the organization's vison and goals and their role in achieving it	• Works hard • Performs the requirements of the job • Has good working relationships with colleagues • Takes care of customers • Focuses on issues like compensation, environment, workload and security

To create updraft, you need an engaged workforce and they need you. It is a symbiotic, give-and-take relationship, and to fully understand this, we need to take a closer look at both sides of the updraft equation.

How did you feel when we talked about letting go of the day-to-day, leaving you free to spend your time on all those leadership-y issues you've always wanted to address? Consider two business owners I've worked with. One of them is able to take off on a three-week vacation and attend industry conferences. The other one cannot even meet me for a quick lunch without being interrupted several times with questions and problems. Yes, they are in different businesses, but not as different as you might think. And while the second business owner does have a good group of people, there's no updraft. I'm simplifying the situations, of course, but it is the engagement level of the people behind you that determines how your day will be spent. If you need to be supervising and overseeing operational issues, then no matter how hard you flap your wings, you'll be unable to generate lift and will have to sacrifice not only your "true" responsibilities but also any chance of work/life balance. Your people don't make you aerodynamic, but they are key to getting you off the ground. We've been talking a lot about engagement; it's time to look at it from an entirely different perspective.

DISENGAGEMENT AS A COPING MECHANISM

Let me tell you a story. Once upon a time, in an organization far, far away (well, not that far away), lived a young lady who was the epitome of a top performer—just what every executive hopes to find. She was bright. She was intelligent. She was intuitive. She was an expert in her field, and she was a snappy dresser. Every day, she packed her picnic basket lunch and went into work, passionate about her organization's potential and determined to make a difference.

It didn't take long before word of her wisdom and insight spread throughout the kingdom, I mean organization, and people at all levels sought her counsel, bestowing upon her an acute awareness of the challenges they faced. She counseled a Director of Sales concerned his team wasn't going to meet the sales targets. She met with members of the customer service department who were unhappy with the treatment they were getting from their new manager. She watched as a layoff destroyed morale and tried to assist a management team that didn't really know how to manage. To the best of her ability, she attempted to address these issues on her own, providing coaching, arranging training and finding resources. Over and over, she brought these concerns to the attention of leadership. But it was to no avail. Leadership responded by burying its collective head in the sand, essentially ignoring the issues that were plaguing the organization.

More than five years later, the young lady is not sure if leadership doesn't want to confront these issues or if they don't know how, but it really doesn't matter. She has finally accepted that nothing is going to change, regardless of how desperately change is needed. So, every day, she packs her picnic basket lunch and goes into work, and although nobody realizes it, she's become a disengaged worker.

Why did I tell you this story? Well, think about how maddening it is for you as you squawk and flap, fiercely trying to get off the ground. Now imagine what it's like to be the third or fourth bird back in the formation working feverishly to create an updraft that will lift those positioned in front of you, despite the fact it doesn't work that way. Our young lady's passion, commitment and expertise drove her to take on the organizational issues she saw, even though leadership didn't want to. After years of caring and commitment, it pains her more than you know to admit that she's lost the ability to convince herself she can make a difference or that things are likely to change. She's exhausted from banging her head against the wall, but she's still a top performer who holds herself to very high standards. So, what does she do? The only thing she can for right now—she disengages.

The vast majority of people in your building want to do a good job and make a difference for their organization. Yes, there are low performers complete with bad attitudes, but they are far fewer than you think. Most of the people you would characterize as "low performers" or "disengaged" didn't walk through your door that way. But at some point, they are going to say, "I give up. If leadership doesn't want to or doesn't care about (fill in the blank), then why should I?" Disengagement is actually a coping mechanism that allows people to stop banging their heads against the wall. It is their way of stepping back and trying to accept things the way they are. Sometimes, like with our young lady, it is a conscious decision to let go, and sometimes it isn't. And you know the old joke about how good it feels when you stop banging your head against the wall? For these people, it doesn't feel good at all because they are hardwired to give it their all and are uncomfortable and unfulfilled doing anything less. In fact, disengaging is a constant struggle for them, because caring and passion and engagement come more naturally than the alternative. If you feel that you have an organization of "cogs" or disengaged people, it's time to stop blaming them and start looking in the mirror. Their engagement depends on you.

If you want to feel the wind beneath *your* wings and see your organization soaring through the clouds, you need to create the wind beneath *their* wings. For every CEO or business owner I meet, there are dozens and dozens of executives (not to mention the rest of the organization) who can't do their jobs because they are waiting for you to step into your role as leader. (Please be aerodynamic by keeping an open mind—the "that may be true, but not here" reflex will ground you. Remember, the North American engagement level is 29 percent. If these situations were the exception, it wouldn't be so low.) Don't put your people (and your organization) into a holding pattern. Are strategic decisions holding up plans for the pursuit of a new sales channel? *Then get a bona fide strategic planning process underway.* Is your organization working around the problems caused by a leadership team member? *Then stop accepting poor performance. Start developing your executive team and holding them accountable; it's high time for them to straighten up and fly right.* Have you told an HR executive who's worried about engagement and morale to "handle it?" *Then recognize how destructive disengagement is to your organization and begin identifying and discussing the factors that are causing it.* Neglecting to address even the smallest decision or situation leaves someone dissatisfied, waiting and unable to act. By failing to provide the leadership your people and your company are craving, you force them to hover rather than enable them to fly.

And what are the implications of hovering? It turns out that hovering flight is the most energy-intensive way to move,[68] and nothing demonstrates this better than the hummingbird, one of the world's best at hovering. Some of the smallest birds on the planet, their size, coupled with their incredibly high activity levels, results in the highest metabolic rate of any bird or animal.[69] As a result, hummingbirds live on the edge of starvation, having to eat one and one-half to three times their weight every day (sometimes more) just to survive.

> **By failing to provide the leadership your people and your company are craving, you force them to hover rather than enable them to fly.**

Hovering requires a tremendous, nonstop expenditure of energy, far more than ordinary flapping. Just imagine how quickly energy levels deplete in something the size of the average human being. Forcing your people to hover pushes them to their physical and emotional limits and accomplishes nothing. There's no forward progress; in fact, there's no movement in any direction. And that exhaustion, frustration and burnout lead straight to disengagement. There's no question in my mind that not a single executive realizes the full implications of what happens when they choose to bury their head in the sand. It's time to stop hovering and take your place at the front of the v-formation; just by stepping into your role, you begin leading your people and encouraging engagement as well as updraft.

A CULTURE OF ENGAGEMENT

Like an individual's personality, organizational culture is extremely complex, difficult to define, and yet, crucial to understand. Everything we're discussing in this book is in some way related to culture. Your culture is inextricably linked to engagement and engagement is inextricably linked to updraft. What many executives don't realize is that culture, like leadership energy, is one of those rare black and white issues; either it's working for you or against you. (Hint: if you think it is neutral at your organization, then it is working against you. Take my word for it.) Regardless of whether your culture is a liability or an asset, like air, it permeates every office and every corner of your organization. If your air is clean, filtered and oxygen rich, then a deep breath is healthy and energizing. But if it contains mold, chemicals, bacteria or radon, then every moment spent there makes a person sicker and sicker. And a sick person doesn't focus on creating updraft, but focuses on just making it through the day.

Do you remember coming across Maslow's Hierarchy of Needs, a theory that provides a framework for what motivates human beings? Abraham Maslow proposed a hierarchy where basic physical needs like food, water and sleep are on the bottom. As these needs are met, people move up through the hierarchy to higher-level needs like independence, achievement and self-fulfillment. The loss of a lower-level need, however, causes a person to retreat back to that lower level until the need is fulfilled. According to Maslow's theory, for example, a group of galley slaves living in deplorable conditions, being whipped and beaten, would not be focused on whether they might be recognized as "Rower of the Month" or whether they were realizing their personal potential. Instead, they would be more concerned with those lower-level issues like food and safety. In the same vein, people are not going to focus on innovation, customer service, personal development, fun or honesty (high-level organizational values) if they are distracted by poor treatment or conditions. At its most basic level, culture dictates how people are to be treated—by leadership, by management, by clients, by vendors and by each other. A culture of disengagement feels like subpar working conditions for those subjected to it.

I know this is a tremendous paradigm shift for many executives. While it may feel as though I am beating a dead chicken, I can only hope you are beginning to see how critical you and your leadership and management teams are to creating (or destroying) engagement. The reason I've devoted so much time to examining engagement and its link to leadership, is that until you sincerely believe and internalize this concept, you will be unable to create updraft. Updraft, like engagement, requires a healthy, positive culture. Like a pitcher "telegraphing" to a hitter or a poker player with an obvious "tell," the way you truly feel about people will be reflected in your actions, reactions, decisions and behaviors—and intentionally or not, will become the foundation for your culture. Any incongruities between what you say and what you do will become part of the culture—either energizing performance or becoming just another reason the engagement level is a mere 29 percent. And, if you think you have time to address this because you haven't yet hired anybody, surprise—your culture begins taking shape before you even add your very first staff member.

> **The way you truly feel about people will be reflected in your actions, reactions, decisions and behaviors— and intentionally or not, will become the foundation for your culture.**

Of course, an organization's culture reflects an infinite and unique combination of characteristics, eccentricities, principles, ideals, philosophies and values. At this point, I hope you can see how every one of your actions, attitudes, decisions and behaviors sends a message that either supports an inspiring culture or creates a toxic one. But we need to take this idea a step further, understanding that your organization's processes and policies are a direct reflection of the attitudes and beliefs of leadership. As such, we need to examine them to see how they impact your culture's ability to generate lift. So, we're going to focus on just a few common organizational processes in order to illustrate their effect on updraft. And having just discussed the importance of every member of your flock, we're going to start with your hiring process.

DON'T FILL POSITIONS, STRIKE A MATCH

You want bright, talented, passionate people—that's a given. But did you know Robert Redford was rejected for the part of Benjamin Braddock (played by Dustin Hoffman) in *The Graduate?*[70] That Robin Williams, Adrien Brody and Steve Carell all publicly expressed interest in playing the Joker (ultimately played by Heath Ledger) in *The Dark Knight?*[71] Or that Elizabeth Taylor wanted to play Eliza Doolittle (played by Audrey Hepburn) in *My Fair Lady?*[72] In all these cases, and many, many more, it wasn't a lack of talent that led a director to say no—it was their determination that it wasn't a good fit. You need to see yourself as a casting director. You're not just looking for talent; you're trying to match a candidate to a role in order to get the best performance possible.

Think way back to the very beginnings of your organization. Somebody, maybe you, had an idea for a product or service. And while the organization was still a fledgling, there's a good chance you were very involved in the development, production and delivery of that product or service because you had a vision for how things should work and what they should look like. But as your efforts were rewarded with increased demand, you got to the point where you couldn't do it all. It's an important crossroads in the development of a company and marks the first time you entrusted another person with some aspect of your process. I find many owners remember their "first time." How exciting and nerve-racking it was. How they pored over candidates, determined to find just the right person. How they took them under their wing until they were sure the gosling was ready to go solo. Something must have worked because growth continued. Now you rely on your organization to carry out the production and delivery of your product, while your specific role is determined by the particular strengths you bring in conjunction with your leadership responsibilities.

That very first time, you were so focused on getting the right person into that position. You knew the job because you had been so close to it. You also knew that in order for you to be truly free to take on the changing responsibilities of your organization, you would have to be confident in this person's abilities. But as the organization grew, one of two things happened. Either you remained extremely involved in the hiring process or you began to delegate most of it to others, staying involved only with positions that report to you. Neither of these situations is ideal. Being overly involved in the process may not be the best use of your time and, depending on your availability, you could easily become an obstruction to the process. At the same time, being too removed from the process suggests you don't fully recognize or acknowledge the strategic importance of each person and his or her relationship to the creation of updraft.

It turns out, getting the right person into the right position is key not only to great performance but to engagement as well. People want to enjoy what they do, excel at it, and make a difference within the organization—all things that occur much more naturally when you are put in a position for which you are well suited. When we discussed the role of leadership, we said you were ultimately responsible for making sure the organization has all the resources it needs, including people, and yet I've just told you that you shouldn't be too involved or too uninvolved in this process. So, what are you supposed to do?

Although there are lots and lots of processes throughout your organization, your hiring process is a little bit different. Even if your organization's process for sending out invoices, receiving materials or picking an order isn't as efficient as it could be, you can be reasonably sure it achieves the desired result. The same isn't true here, and that's why your involvement is so crucial. You need to ensure that your organization has a reliable and repeatable process that gets the job done—and while duck, duck...goose is reliable and repeatable, it's not quite what I have in mind. In fact, what I'm alluding to probably isn't what you have in mind either. The issue starts with the phrase "hiring process," which right away puts the emphasis on the wrong activity. It puts the focus on hiring—getting an offer out and striving to put a body into a position, sometimes even when the candidate's greatest attribute is their ability to convert oxygen into carbon dioxide. In this situation, a bird in the hand is not worth two in the bush. For engagement and updraft to happen, we aren't looking just to *fill* positions but to identify great candidates who are an excellent *match to* the position. Very few organizations have a process that supports this goal, and even fewer realize it.

Cartoon by Mike Lynch. Used with Permission.

"It's not the best way to make a hiring decision,
but I love the look on their faces when the wheel spins."

Most likely, your process is similar to everyone else's. You advertise, collect résumés, arrange one or two rounds of interviews, and then select a candidate. Some organizations improvise, creating an ad hoc procedure each time, and some are much more formal; but in either case most of the process is focused on getting and assessing candidates. But what about the position itself? It's like picking up a square peg and saying, "I wonder to what extent this will fit into the round hole," instead of starting with an analysis of the hole (How deep is it? What is its diameter?) and then comparing it to all the pieces available until you identify one or two that fit well without forcing or whittling the piece. It is up to you to make sure your organization has a matching process rather than a hiring process. The difference is this alternative approach starts not with candidates but with a thorough and holistic understanding of the position.

Hiring Process	Matching Process
Write and advertise the job description ↓ Collect résumés ↓ First round interviews ↓ Second round interviews ↓ Fill the position	Identify and bring together people who know the job well ↓ Through a facilitated discussion, thoroughly understand the job and create the key accountabilities ↓ Create a benchmark ↓ Using the benchmark, write the copy and advertise the position ↓ Compare candidates to the benchmark ↓ Interviews* ↓ Fill the position ↓ Use the accountabilities and the benchmark for training and development purposes (*Some people compare candidates to the benchmark after the first round of interviews, and some do it before any interviews take place.)

My clients are always amazed at the difference this approach makes. While some subjectivity will always exist, this process reduces the likelihood of mistakes because it provides decision makers with a significant amount of objective criteria, helping to reduce both unconscious and conscious bias. Decision makers love it because it establishes the criteria for success in the position, allows them to target training and coaching efforts to the needs of the person, and helps them to identify talent by separating the superstars from the competent performers. (Note that assessing your top performers to create a benchmark, a common approach, isn't as effective because results are artificially bound by your current crop of people.)

Others involved in this process benefit as well. Using the benchmark, they can write ads that actually attract the "right" people by accurately communicating the roles, responsibilities and expectations of the position, going beyond the job description to identify the soft skills that will contribute to success—things like emotional intelligence, problem solving and interpersonal skills. In one situation, just by editing their advertisement for an operations manager to include the phrases, "highly accountable," "on-the-spot decision making" and "need for assertiveness," we targeted the position to attract candidates who would be naturally comfortable with those situations. Having had difficulty filling the position, the client was thrilled to be able to choose from four extremely qualified candidates. And, while all this groundwork is helpful to you, it helps the applicants as well. While you can more accurately assess someone's fit to the job, so can they, drastically increasing the likelihood of getting an enthusiastic, engaged performer while simultaneously decreasing the massive pile of submitted résumés.

Understanding the job also helps people conduct useful interviews that provide genuine insight into the candidate's suitability for the position as well as their immediate and future potential. One client told me she had never felt so prepared or realized how productive an interview could be. We mapped out the interview and created questions designed to explore those competencies emphasized by the benchmark rather than general questions about strengths, weaknesses and past positions. In the matching process for the operations manager position, for instance, we asked the prospective operations managers for examples of when and where they had to make on-the-spot decisions, and then we probed for information about how that felt and how the decisions panned out. This made it far easier to compare candidates and their responses. In addition, the ability to reuse the benchmark the next time you need to fill the position makes it less likely you'll slip back into old habits.

Even in industries and positions that traditionally have high turnover like food service (44 percent and up to 50 percent at fast food restaurants),[73] retail (67 percent part-time and 24 percent full-time),[74] sales (25.5 percent)[75] and retail call centers (26 percent),[76] high turnover often indicates you are missing the mark on what the position truly requires. A national retailer in a market where turnover had been at 50 percent utilized a benchmarking approach, and after ten months turnover in store management was reduced to zero.[77] And NetSuite,[78] a large, fast-growing software company, lost 100 of their 450 new hires before they could celebrate their one-year anniversary with the company. A large percentage of these new hires were in the sales area. NetSuite incorporated a benchmarking approach, and three years later, only five salespeople left before their one-year anniversary.

Although it may seem counterintuitive, deep down you know it is better to leave a position vacant than to fill it with the wrong person—no matter how difficult or inconvenient that may be. How much extra time, energy and money do you spend trying to transform an underperformer? And how successful are those efforts? At one manufacturer/distributor, a revolving door of production managers was leaving the owners overwhelmed and exhausted. Their focus on just getting the position filled resulted in less than stellar performers who required constant supervision. At that point, they were essentially doing the job themselves anyway *and* having to deal with the damage left in the underperformer's wake. And as problematic as this is for businesses to grasp, it can be a particularly diffi- cult concept for nonprofits who feel that if someone volunteers, they shouldn't be turned away. But the same principle holds true. Don't take a body just because it's warm. Find a way for people to contribute, but don't put them into a position that isn't a good fit—they will do more damage than you realize.

> **It is better to leave a position vacant than to fill it with the wrong person—no matter how difficult or inconvenient that may be.**

Any time you are tempted to just fill a position, think about the chicken and the egg and remember that your success is dependent on having the right people behind you. Your role is not necessarily to review every résumé or sit in on every interview but to understand how important this process is to the creation of updraft and to determine at what level and to what extent you will be involved:

- Some leaders meet every candidate before the organization makes an offer.

- Some organizations include a social component in their process (i.e., lunch, coffee or drinks with a group of employees) and the leader participates.

- Some leaders sit in on the candidate review sessions that occur after a round of interviews.

- Some leaders are heavily involved in the onboarding process, even meeting every new hire on their first day.

It is up to you to educate your organization about the tremendous damage done to (deep breath) morale, performance, engagement, operations, customer service, quality, sales, the culture, etc., when a warm but unqualified body is put into a role *for even a short period of time.* And if you're thinking that your organization is so large you can't possibly be involved, know that Zach Nelson, the CEO and president of the $400[79] million software provider we just spoke about, reviews every job offer NetSuite makes.

ORGANIZATIONAL PROCESSES—UPDRAFT OR DOWNDRAFT?

I've discussed the selection process in some depth due to the enormous impact it has on updraft, both for you and for your people. Getting the right people into the right positions allows them the opportunity to do what they are good at, which, all by itself, creates updraft. But you can't stop there. Once you are attracting top performers, you need to keep them. In the same way continuous learning contributes to your aerodynamics, great people want opportunities to learn and be challenged in order to keep themselves sharp and current. One sure way to address this is with career development and growth opportunities, which just happen to be another significant driver of engagement. And like selection, this process supports both sides of the updraft equation.

The last thing you want is for those bright, enthusiastic, talented people to get bored. Instead, you want them learning and growing. You want to provide new challenges as well as opportunities for advancement, both of which support their ongoing engagement. And from your standpoint, supporting growth opportunities ensures the following:

- You will have the expertise and experience you need as the organization changes and grows.

- You will be able to promote from within the right way (without encountering the Peter Principle).

- You will be able to guide development efforts so they align with the organization's future plans, strategies and needs.

- People won't be afraid or unwilling to stretch their wings and leave their comfort zones because they will be constantly learning and taking on new challenges.

Culturally, encouraging development says that the organization cares about its people and is eager and willing to invest in them. Although people are expected to take the helm when it comes to their growth and development, the organization shares in this responsibility. Unfortunately, organizations often forget they have a vested interest in the continuing development of their people. Just encouraging and supporting the *idea* of development isn't enough. Managers must be able to provide concrete guidance so development efforts are aligned with the current and future needs of the organization, ensuring a strong, healthy bench of up-and-coming players. Notice that having benchmarks for all the organization's positions will come in very handy, since you can use that information to groom people for new positions. In fact, one organization found a candidate in an unlikely place by comparing all existing staff to their sales benchmark. After investing in some training and coaching, this former warehouse person has become their top salesman!

The organization also needs to support development efforts by providing resources and guidance, but the traditional one-size-fits-all concept no longer fits the bill. Such an approach ignores the specific needs of each individual and hampers the creation of productive, thought-provoking development plans tailored to each staff member. In addition, there is so much wonderful content in today's world that restricting development efforts to a finite set of resources is counterproductive. I remember working with a director and one of his people to create a year-long leadership program. They put considerable effort into the plan, thoroughly researching and ultimately using a mix of in-house and external options. However, when they submitted the final plan, instead of approval, they were told they should stick with the organization's in-house resources, despite the director's explanation that the in-house offerings didn't deliver what was needed. As a result, the program wasn't nearly as effective or as engaging as it could have been, and the organization severely damaged both the director's and the employee's engagement.

It's time to accomplish this process a little differently. Think of it more like a college curriculum, where there are course requirements (i.e., 30 credits, 5 electives, etc.) but students have the freedom to choose many of the classes. In the organizational setting, the benchmark combined with the up-and-coming needs of the organization will provide the course requirements, identifying the specific topics to be addressed. Then, the individual, with their guidance counselor's input (i.e., their manager), will go out and find the "classes" that provide the required content (in much the same way you did for yourself back in Chapter 4). The organization may have an extensive array of offerings like the following:

- Classes on subjects with a broad appeal (i.e., time management, effective meetings, etc.) available on a quarterly or monthly basis.

- Arrangements with local colleges/universities.

- Organizational memberships to online education options. (The number of elearning sites is increasing rapidly. To get an idea of what's out there, look at www.skillsoft.com, www.curious.com and www.coursera.com.)

- Organizational memberships to a variety of associations and organizations.

- Access to coaches or specialists.

- An organizational library of books, videos, etc.

Or an organization may have very few offerings, opting instead to rely on external resources. By providing direction to the development efforts and access to the needed resources, organizations hold up their end of the bargain, giving the issue more than just lip service. I've even seen programs that assign a budget for each individual and then track spending as well as progress. I know times are tough, but you have to consider what it says to your people if you say professional development is important but you won't authorize any time or expenditures. Either it's important to the success of the organization or it isn't. And remember, it is fuel for an engaged workforce, so the costs should easily be offset by the increases in productivity and reductions in turnover. Not only that, but if you don't develop the people "below you," you create obstacles to your own growth and inhibit your ability to fly.

If you are serious about updraft, these are not the only processes that need careful attention. Every policy and every human resource-related process either supports the positive, energized culture and engagement levels you want—or they don't. One by one, these programs need to be audited to ensure they are not compromising updraft by undermining engagement efforts. Everything needs to be reviewed in a new light. Think about your onboarding process. A person's first day on the job is typically one of their most exciting. They can't wait to meet their coworkers, get the lay of the land, and start to understand the culture and the business and their position. And the higher the caliber of the person, the more he or she wants to jump right in and make a difference. So, what do most organizations do? Many do not have any formalized process at all, but if they do, it frequently includes lots of paperwork and forms. These things need to be attended to, but can you imagine a less engaging first day than sitting around and filling out paperwork? (And what about their first week or month? How do you keep tabs on your newest recruits?)

And what about compensation issues? A lot of executives don't believe me when I tell them that money doesn't translate to engagement. Yes, people want to be fairly compensated, but more money doesn't make up for a lack of resources, poor treatment or low morale. Ironically, it's often the other way around: people want more money in order to compensate themselves for what they have to put up with. What, if anything, does your bonus program say, and is it supporting engagement or undermining it? One large corporation uses a "normal distribution" approach for the performance review and bonus process at their so-called high-performance organization. The system requires that people be categorized into top, satisfactory and unsatisfactory so a manager who has put together an outstanding team will be forced to put some of them into the unsatisfactory category—even if that doesn't reflect their performance. How would you respond to, "You don't belong in that category, but I had to put someone there because that's how the system works"? I don't think there is any way to explain this to an employee without their engagement taking a serious hit.

And what about your performance review process? Most are not designed to boost engagement and, in fact, are amazingly disengaging. Looking at all these processes and procedures from an engagement perspective will provide tremendous insight into how your organization may be unintentionally undermining engagement and what you can do to reverse it. Some of these processes are still serving the needs of the organization, some will need to be phased out, and some will need to be stopped cold turkey. (Remember, fostering an environment of engagement has far less to do with what you do and far more with getting out of the way.) Every year, waterfowl molt, going through a period when they regrow their outer wing feathers, replacing those that are torn or missing. Unable to fly during this time, the birds are very vulnerable, but it is vital to their survival that they replace what is no longer working for them. The same holds true for you.

© Randy Glasbergen.
www.glasbergen.com

"Your productivity this quarter has been outstanding, your performance has been impeccable, and I'm someone who believes in rewarding perfection. Too bad about that speck of lint on your tie."

While I believe it is never leadership's intention to block the flow of updraft, our discussion has illustrated how easily and inadvertently that can occur. Remember—it's all about your flock. Your job is to ensure it has what it needs, including leadership that's leading and a culture that's supporting updraft and engagement. Toward that end, I'd be ducking my responsibilities if we didn't take a moment to touch on just a few concepts that are central to creating an aerodynamic culture. These concepts are fundamental to creating a culture that can fly.

Integrity, respect and trust...for all.

We talked at length about integrity, respect and trust as characteristics that are essential to making you aerodynamic, but they are just as significant for your people. Remember, we are working to get everyone into a tight formation so they are close enough to take advantage of the updraft created by the bird in front of them. In order to be comfortable flying so close together, each person needs to have the utmost confidence in themselves as well as in each member of the team. It is up to you to make sure that you are aerodynamic and worthy of being followed, but it is also up to you to inspire the confidence and passion that contributes to the aerodynamics of your people. An environment that strives to make people feel valued and respected will go a long way toward fueling their confidence.

Loyalty goes both ways.

Early in my career, I was responsible for taking customer complaint calls until I was able to return this responsibility to the customer service department. I created reference materials for them and trained them on how to handle irate customers. Most importantly, though, I let them know it was not appropriate for someone to yell and curse at them, and that if a person wouldn't calm down, it was okay to tell them they were going to hang up—and then to do so. Since I couldn't be on every call with them, they needed to know that they didn't have to subject themselves to abuse and that they could stand up for themselves in an appropriate manner, knowing we would back them up. The client isn't always right, and while clients may come and go, you want your top performers to stay put and to stay engaged.

Loyalty means standing up for your people no matter what. If your culture will include concepts like respect and courtesy, then it is up to you to ensure those standards are upheld—by everyone—both internally and externally. Being abused by clients, vendors or board members is just as demeaning and damaging as being mistreated by managers, leadership or peers. People who deal with the public—like cashiers, waiters and customer service people—are sitting ducks for this kind of treatment and need to know that you don't condone such behavior under any circumstances. People will pay close attention to these kinds of situations because they quickly reveal whether you are committed to your people, your values and your culture or if it all becomes chicken feed in the presence of, say, an important customer.

Earlier, we likened loyalty to a Public Display of Affection because both require action that is proactive and observable. We also discussed how high levels of respect, integrity and trust, in conjunction with a passion for our values, mission and vision, often create a strong bond of loyalty to the leader. That loyalty must go both ways. Your culture must also reflect the fierce loyalty and intense commitment you have to your people. While leadership connotes visions of being in front, it often requires taking a stand behind someone, backing them up. If they can't be sure you (leadership/management) have their back, they'll start to second-guess themselves. And that insecurity will erode their confidence, weighing them down like an albatross around their neck.

Loyalty also means giving people the benefit of the doubt. It means your first instinct is to back up your people—no matter the situation. Rather than assume the worst or accept information at face value, you need to call on your integrity and emotional intelligence so you do not react or make judgments until you get all the facts. This is a very concrete way of demonstrating trust because it says that people are "innocent until proven guilty," and that you assume your people to be in the right until you discover otherwise.

In one organization, the HR manager was constantly complaining to the president about the organization's finance manager. The president would respond by confronting the finance manager in an accusatory manner. And typically, once the finance manager was able to explain, the president would discover she hadn't heard the entire story. Not only was the president failing to back up the finance manager, she was contributing to an atmosphere of blaming and finger-pointing. Ironically, she was disappointed with the way her leadership team functioned, and yet, she couldn't see she was at least partially responsible. High levels of emotional intelligence, coupled with an understanding of your communication style, help you to calmly and objectively listen to people without jumping to conclusions. Be careful to slow down and remain neutral until you get all the facts.

I remember a situation from very early in my career when, as an assistant director of catering for a large hotel chain, I made a call to cut off alcohol service at an event. The group's four-hour party had already been extended for an additional hour, and I was concerned that another hour of drinking was not advisable since they were not staying at the hotel. Needless to say, the somewhat inebriated host was not pleased with my decision and insisted on talking to "my boss." He even followed me into the kitchen area where we found the Food and Beverage Director, technically my boss' boss, who allowed the gentleman to speak and then assured him we would be right out. I explained the situation. He nodded and indicated that I should walk out with him. We went back out to the party where he reiterated what I had told the host, informed him we would be closing down the bars, asked me if I needed anything else, and then left me to take care of the remainder of the event.

This was my first job out of college, and to this day, I remember how empowered and confident I felt. If you have the right people in the right positions being guided by a strong set of values, then you'll be able to trust their judgment and expertise. In fact, constantly overruling your people will not only destroy engagement, but will eat away at their initiative and confidence, ultimately "teaching" them to go to you for every decision.

Newsflash: People are human beings.

Human beings make mistakes no matter how hard they try not to. Sometimes, it will take every fiber of your being to avoid flying off the handle, but how you react to mistakes will have huge implications for your culture. Everything we've discussed—emotional intelligence, integrity, trust, respect, loyalty—will be put to the test as you force yourself to focus on solutions and teaching opportunities. Anger, blame and guilt are not constructive and create a culture of people who are indecisive, hesitant and unwilling to act (more on this later). And, since engaged performers tend to hold themselves to high standards, you may notice that you are becoming more of a coach or mentor, helping them forgive themselves for an error, learn from it and move past it.

In the workplace, we sometimes forget human beings are multidimensional. We forget they have families, interests, and other commitments and concerns. They have children who get sick, basements that flood, and all the other challenges of everyday life. Expecting people to walk into their offices and leave all those other concerns at the door is unrealistic. Life is not that easy to compartmentalize, and there will be times when the demands of private and professional lives overlap. Managing all those competing priorities can result in stress and fatigue, which can jeopardize performance and lead to poor decision making. Beyond that, what does it say to people when they are expected to stay late or work weekends when the need arises but they can't leave 15 minutes early to get to a doctor's appointment? Cultures that adopt a holistic view of their people are sending a strong message: "We appreciate that you are here when we need you, and we are going to be here when you need us." Treating people like adults reinforces trust and respect. Organizations that are sensitive to the realities of life, and develop cultures that help people deal with life's more challenging moments, tend to garner tremendous feelings of appreciation and loyalty. Acknowledging and supporting work/life balance goes a long way toward being a great place to work.

Silos are for farmers.

Organizations are no longer made up of independent silos of functional experts who interact only when necessary. Instead, they have evolved into synergistic groups where people collaborate, cooperate and support each other, creating the kind of "magic" that produces brilliant insights, breakthrough innovations and game-changing strategies (and, of course, updraft). Like an orchestra, you need every chair to be filled by someone who can shine as a soloist thanks to his or her technical excellence and passion, but who can just as easily harmonize and blend with others. As Babe Ruth said, "The way a team plays as a whole determines its success. You may have the greatest bunch of individual stars in the world, but if they don't play together, the club won't be worth a dime."[80]

STRETCHING YOUR WINGS...

1. How do you truly feel about your people? Are they a necessary evil, or do you enjoy working and interacting with them? Carefully consider these questions during one of your self-reflection sessions. Look for ways you can express your appreciation for their efforts. Implement two of these right away.

2. Think about someone you consider to be disengaged. Reflect on their time with the organization. Did they start out disengaged? What circumstances, processes or people might have led to the current situation? Meet with this person's manager to discuss how they became disengaged and what could be done to reverse the situation.

3. Get an overview of your organization's hiring process. Did you know what it looks like? Is it effective (that is, does it result in low turnover and happy, engaged employees)? Are you appropriately involved? Form a team tasked with reviewing the process and making recommendations. You should participate, at some level, on this team.

4. To get a better idea of what turnover could be costing you, take a look at "The Costs of a Revolving Door" at www. DeltaVstrategies.com/Resources.

5. Can you think of any decisions that are pending? How long have they been under consideration? Start a list of issues that are up in the air and begin addressing them.

6. Think about your compensation process. Performance reviews. Onboarding. Can you see how they might contribute to disengagement? Start analyzing and discussing these issues with your leadership team, looking at them from an engagement perspective.

CHAPTER 7

Can you hear the honking?

I t's a pretty safe bet to say that if you've seen geese fly by in their glorious v-formation, you've undoubtedly heard them as well. Geese are considered to be one of the most talkative animals—after humans—and as many as 13 different Canada goose calls have been identified. On the ground, their squabbling is just as lively. According to Ducks Unlimited Canada, there's even evidence that "baby geese begin communicating with their parents while still in the egg,"[81] which may explain how newly hatched goslings are immediately able to distinguish among the different calls and respond appropriately to their parents.

Their distinctive honking reverberates across the skies for miles, announcing their arrival long before you can see them. While all that honking may sound the same to us, the geese are actually making a variety of in-flight announcements. Like humans, geese form strong family bonds, and they honk in order to keep tabs on the location of family members so they don't get separated. They are also greeting each other, warning of danger, indicating their position in the flock, encouraging the lead goose, and even expressing excitement.

At first blush, it appears that the geese are expending an awful lot of energy communicating. For such a large bird, that energy might be better spent on flapping their wings and generating the wingtip vortexes responsible for updraft. But it turns out that a goose's honk occurs during the downbeat[82] of its wing stroke, which is when it contracts its chest muscles to exhale. So, you might say their anatomy makes communicating with each other as natural as breathing—and, in this case, almost makes it a part of breathing. As a result, the geese are able to converse during flight using very little excess energy.

In order to create updraft within your organization, communication within your flock needs to be just as lively and as natural as breathing. Interestingly enough, while geese have a wide variety of vocalizations covering everything from aggression, takeoff, mating, parenting and greeting, on the ground they do not have an alarm call. Instead, a goose becomes silent.[83] As others notice that behavior or become aware of the danger themselves, they too become silent. The same holds true within the walls of your organization—silence is a sure sign of impending danger. And because communication is critical to so many aspects of updraft, its absence is a warning not only that danger is imminent but also that it is encroaching on several fronts. To create and maintain updraft, you must be keenly aware of not only *what* you are communicating but also *how* you go about it.

WHAT'S GOING ON IN THE COCKPIT?

While geese are in flight, their communication seems almost non-stop—an extremely relevant lesson for those whose in-flight communications occur over an airplane's intercom system. If you fly, I'm sure you've been on a flight where the pilot got on the speaker and informed you there was turbulence up ahead. It didn't make the turbulence any less, well, turbulent, but somehow it made the experience less scary. There is tremendous comfort in knowing the leader—in this case the pilot—knew what was coming and was prepared for it. And since the pilot informed the rest of us, we can prepare as well, finishing our drinks and stowing away any possessions we might have taken out. That one quick announcement makes a world of difference to the people sitting behind the cockpit.

I'm a bit of a nervous flier. Aside from the whole turbulence thing, I'm constantly straining to see where we are, where we're headed, how we're doing, and how far along we are. Every announcement and every update provides just a little more information and assurance that we are on track to get to our destination safely and on time. Just like the passengers on the plane, the people in your organization want that same information. Most of them can't see firsthand where they are or what obstacles lie in their path. Even those people whose roles put them at a window seat can't see the whole picture.

We haven't yet covered the importance of a vision, but in an upcoming chapter we're going to discuss how an appropriate vision stimulates progress and promotes action by giving us a destination. But what if my job takes place in the "back" of the plane, where the majority of your people sit? High levels of engagement will depend on your ability to communicate not only what the vision is but how important each person is to its achievement and how well we are progressing. Even though I may have taken to the air with this information, I can't really see how we are doing from my vantage point because I don't have access to the cockpit or even a window. Will this diminish my drive and enthusiasm? You bet it will—engagement will suffer, and I will be less and less convinced that what I'm doing matters. Updates are inspiring and motivating because they enable me to see our progress and reinforce that my efforts and updraft are making a difference.

In addition, at the first sign of turbulence or a detour due to bad weather, less reliable sources of information will fill the silence if open, honest communication is not forthcoming. It's no secret that information, especially negative or "juicy" information, will travel through your organization almost instantaneously. While no one wants to be the bearer of bad news, hearing the truth straight from the cockpit is preferable to allowing rumors and gossip to undermine integrity, destroy morale and corrupt the culture. Besides, the information is going to creep out no matter what you do. Face it, "secrets" in your organization are about as safe as a canary in a coal mine. I remember one large corporation about to lay off a considerable number of people. While they didn't tell anyone what was coming, a few people noticed that human resources had booked every single conference room for two days, and before the first meeting had occurred, the news had spread throughout the organization like wildfire, creating angst, anger and anxiety.

Ensuring your people know what is going on enables them to have confidence in you as their leader—another essential component for updraft. It is comforting to know that those who chose our destination and mapped out our route are aware of where we are in the journey and of what obstacles lie ahead. The rest of us can be encouraged and reassured by the knowledge that our pilots are paying attention. We can feel confident that alternate routes and contingency plans are being formulated before they are needed and that unforeseen developments are less likely. It means those of us in the "back of the plane" can focus on doing our jobs the best we can, secure in the knowledge we are safely headed in the right direction. And let's not forget our discussion of self-organizing systems. We said the agents of these systems perform activities based on their own judgment and on the information and feedback they receive. If you and your team are blocking the flow of information, progress will slow as people become hesitant and insecure, concerned they could be blindsided by unforeseen circumstances affecting their ability to make good decisions.

And remember the discussion about trust, respect and loyalty? We talked about the idea that we're supposed to be in this together. "I'm watching your back, and I'm inspired and willing to follow you; but at the same time, I expect you to remember that I'm back here." Ongoing, effective communication reinforces the idea that you are committed to the people sitting aft of the cockpit doors; that you remember they are back there. This approach goes a long way toward maintaining an atmosphere of trust. It says you respect their contribution and you want the organization to function as a team and work together to address any problems or obstacles that appear on the horizon.

Think of it this way. We said earlier that engagement translates to "caring" and that this emotional connection extends beyond functional areas to the organization as a whole. While your people are responsible for staying current and relevant (just like you are), they do not usually have up-to-the-minute information on everything going on both inside and outside the organization. Only a subset of your organization is directly involved in all phases of the strategic process or all aspects of the business' operations. Customer service doesn't know what finance just discovered about overhead costs, and R&D doesn't know what feedback sales just received from your biggest customer. Without this information, your people are flying blind—you are compromising their ability to make great decisions within the context of the organization. They *want* to see beyond the confines of their job; it is up to you and your leadership team to make sure information flows freely so people are working with as complete a picture as possible.

> It is up to you and your leadership team to make sure information flows freely so people are working with as complete a picture as possible.

At the organizational level, progress isn't the only thing that needs to be included in your communications; mission, vision and values are just as important. Like a marketer promoting the brand, it's all about number of impressions, frequency and reach to make sure you are getting your message across. Keeping vision, mission and values in the spotlight means referring to them like an architect refers to a blueprint, using them to answer questions and make decisions—and the more public, the better. (Remember Dr. Vagelos and the river blindness decision?) Over time, the mission, vision and values become a living, breathing part of the firm, whose influence becomes almost palpable, like one of those TV characters you hear about but never see (like Howard's mother from *The Big Bang Theory* or Norm's wife, Vera, from *Cheers*). They shape attitudes, management styles, expectations, behaviors, beliefs, norms and perceptions, and as such, they have a profound impact on your culture. Human beings, though, tend to have short memories and sometimes get sidetracked. If you aren't advocating and promoting and keeping your organization focused, who will?

If you are thinking to yourself you've got this covered because you religiously conduct a quarterly company meeting, then you've missed the point. First of all, as we've just said, communication needs to be happening on an ongoing, everyday basis. Secondly, when we say "communication," we mean an exchange of information. Presentations and speeches have their place, but to create updraft, communication must be the proverbial two-way street. Organizations that prefer to rely on top-down communications are sending a pretty clear signal they are not interested in the issues, opinions, thoughts and ideas of their people. These organizations are not likely to be encouraging empowerment, initiative or inspiration, but then, they aren't trying to. How you choose to communicate sets the tone for the entire organization and has a huge impact on your culture, affecting everything from relationships to innovation.

"I want to open up better lines of communication with my employees. Plant these listening devices in all the washrooms."

The key to the kind of communication we are after is to find ways to incorporate interaction in order to promote as much two-way communication as possible. Planning a state-of-the-organization presentation?

Follow it up with smaller, informal meetings where people are encouraged to ask questions and discuss the issues. Start a monthly coffee or lunch with the president. (Other executives can do this as well.) Maybe have a "question of the month" the executives discuss throughout the organization, and then bring that feedback to the leadership team meetings. When you're in the office, make it a point to walk through different areas and departments, checking in with people and saying hello. And here's a thought: ask your people how communication could be improved, keeping in mind suggestions may be scarce at first, if an open, collaborative culture is new to them.

"HOW" IS JUST AS IMPORTANT AS "WHAT"

I remember a friend telling me about an interview she went on. It was going quite well when the executive excused himself and walked out of his office to where his administrative assistant sat. Through the open door, she could see and hear the executive yelling and screaming at his assistant because she hadn't left enough time before his next appointment. While my friend was shocked and vividly remembered how badly she felt for the poor admin., she was thankful she had seen the interaction as it stopped her from even considering employment with that organization. No salary or weeks of vacation could have enticed her to join them—she had just gotten a sneak preview of what she could expect.

We just talked about the dangers of silence within your organization and the importance of all the honking to the creation of updraft. We discussed how essential communication is to keeping people apprised of progress and ensuring that mission, vision and values stay top of mind, looking at communication from a big-picture, macro level. However, we must also take a look at communication on the micro level, concerning ourselves with the quality and tone of personal interactions within the organization. The way people interact is a direct reflection of the culture and goes right to the heart of trust and respect.

It is the very embodiment of how people are treated and how they can expect to be treated. However, creating an environment where people feel safe, secure and encouraged to speak up isn't easy. It can be especially stressful and awkward to deliver bad news or criticism, and some people will get nervous just having to speak with someone higher up on the food chain. The standards and behaviors you model will set the tone for everyone.

Hearing is passive; it occurs when sound waves cause your eardrum to vibrate. Listening, on the other hand, is active; it requires focus and concentration. Being accessible and encouraging people to come to you is not only worthless but potentially counterproductive unless you have the ability to truly listen. Although some of the honking within your organization is very loud and hard to ignore, you must listen very carefully. Otherwise, you will never hear the more subtle vocalizations coming from the goslings still in their eggs or pick up on the vast repertoire of body language that speaks volumes but doesn't make a sound.

> **The way people interact is a direct reflection of the culture and goes right to the heart of trust and respect.**

Think about how you feel when someone asks your opinion and then completely ignores what you've said—or even worse, doesn't even acknowledge your existence. Asking and ignoring is far worse than not asking at all. This is a common mistake people make with both internal and external surveys. How do you feel when you take time out of your day to respond to a survey or questionnaire but then never receive acknowledgment, see any results, or hear about how the information was used? Making people feel invisible and unimportant doesn't enhance relationships.

Instead, you want to engage and empower people. When we truly listen to someone, he or she feels valued, respected and important, and this gives him or her tremendous confidence. To do this, you must give people your full attention. It is not only a powerful sign of respect but also reinforces the idea that you value what is being said. You will need to put down whatever you are working on, turn away from your computer screen, and face your visitor head on. You'll have to be sure your eyes are focused on the person and not roaming around the room or trying to peek at the message on your phone. Take into account his or her body language, and if he or she seems stressed, acknowledge it: "Bob, you look upset. Have a seat and tell me what's going on." Once the person begins speaking, be careful to "park" your own thoughts and concentrate not only on what is being said but also on how it is being said.

I remember one discussion with the sales manager of a large commercial bank and his sales team. The manager was adamant that supporting his team required him to have an open-door policy so he would always be available to his people. I was trying to help him see it was okay for him to set aside time for his own work but I wasn't really making much headway until one of his people spoke up: "It's true you always make time for me whenever I come to you, but you seem so distracted. You're looking at your screen or what's on your desk, and I know that I've interrupted you and that I don't have your full attention. I think I'd rather you ask me to come back when you're able to focus on what I have to say." The manager was shocked at the message he had sent and by how much he had communicated without saying a word.

You want to be present in such a way that you are embracing (figuratively) and encouraging the speaker. Your ability to do this will speak volumes and will foster trust, respect and confidence. To be an effective listener also requires that you cultivate the ability to suspend judgment so you are open and receptive to what is being said. During our discussion of continuous learning, we talked about the dangers of isolation and how important it is that complete and uncensored information reach you. Being receptive to all kinds of incoming communications supports your efforts to be aerodynamic. It provides you with new perspectives, furthering your efforts to build trust and bringing issues to your attention. Great leaders (and listeners) approach every interaction as an opportunity to learn something new. As Larry King, often referred to as the "king of the listeners," said, "I never learn a thing while I'm talking. I realize every morning that nothing I say today will teach me anything, so if I'm going to learn a lot today, I'll have to do it by listening."[84] The strong sense of self and purpose we discussed in Part I helps to protect the ego, making objective, unbiased listening much more likely. However, you'll still need the ability to put aside your own prejudices, biases and agendas; otherwise, you'll never hear me over your own thoughts and self-talk. What if I came to you and said I had some concerns about a decision you made recently? Would you be able to hear me out without becoming defensive and judgmental, or would you be constructing your own counterarguments inside your head while I spoke? It takes tremendous self-awareness and discipline to turn off all the voices in our heads so we can be truly present.

And while you've undoubtedly heard this before, it is too serious to neglect; effective communicators are as aware of body language as they are the content and tone of the message. We just talked about the salesperson whose boss' behavior revealed he was distracted and not truly paying attention. As somebody who often facilitates sensitive, highly-charged meetings, it's not unusual for me to be approached by people afterward and asked, "How did you know I disagreed with that statement?" or, "How did you know I had something to say right then?" The looks of amazement are always amusing when I glance around a room and announce that it seems like time for a bathroom break. People don't even realize they begin to lose focus and get fidgety in their chairs. To be a great communicator and an effective listener, you must recognize that communication is far more than just the spoken word and that the nonverbal component of a message may tell you far more than the words themselves.

If your people are carefully chosen for their talents, passion and potential and are committed to the vision, mission and values of the organization, then you must do everything possible to get their perspectives and their input. You cannot create an organization of engaged, empowered individuals without creating a culture of listeners. You can't fake this because people recognize when they are being patronized or placated, and they won't be fooled. If you dismiss me, ignore me or demean me, you can be pretty sure I'm not going to approach you again. You can also be pretty sure I'm going to share that story with coworkers and other people who will now think twice about approaching you. So much for updraft. On the other hand, if you are attentive and supportive, I'm going to walk away from the interaction feeling good about myself as well as our relationship. Either leadership (and management and each individual) cares what people think and wants their input—or they don't. It isn't easy for people to open up and put themselves and their opinions on the line, so leaders must work hard to master the art of listening, encouraging others to speak confidently, appropriately and passionately.

> **You cannot create an organization of engaged, empowered individuals without creating a culture of listeners.**

DIFFICULT SITUATIONS

Many of the concepts we just discussed, in conjunction with the attributes we covered in Part I (i.e., integrity, respect, trust, emotional intelligence and self-confidence), support your ability to be a great communicator as well as a great listener. For the most part, if you are guided by a sincere desire to treat people with courtesy, patience and respect, then you probably will treat them that way. And if you have an organization full of top performers, then many of your interactions will consist of providing feedback, guidance and suggestions in a way that facilitates and encourages initiative and problem solving. There are, however, a few communication situations that have particular importance to updraft, so we'll mention them here.

Defending values

In Chapter 5 we discussed organizational values, establishing what they are and how critical they are to updraft. How you choose to respond to behavior that is in conflict with accepted norms and stated values will determine your success in establishing, maintaining and protecting your culture. If you ignore behavior that undermines or challenges your organization's values, your lack of action will be perceived as tacit approval of the behavior. You'll run the risk that similar episodes will become more frequent, leading to conflict, confusion, resentment and damage to the organization's values and culture.

Let's say one of your organization's values deals with treating people with respect. If you witness someone berating an employee and do nothing about it, for all intents and purposes you have sanctioned that behavior. By addressing the situation, you kill two birds with one stone. You stop the behavior in its tracks, and you send a clear message that the behavior is not tolerated. However, you need to do this while still maintaining high levels of respect, or you'll end up in violation of the very thing you are attempting to protect.

Getting bad news

Receiving feedback or bad news with poise and composure can be difficult for even the best of us, but it is imperative your immediate reaction be constructive. Remember, a verbal assault or a perceived attack on the self can easily trigger the stress response we talked about earlier, and a burst of anger or defensiveness is likely to result in the following:

- Cause some level of stress response in the messenger (making both parties irrational and useless).

- Trigger destructive fault finding and blaming which takes the focus away from the search for solutions.

- Break down a culture of trust and respect (if it existed).

- Ensure people become more and more reticent to bringing you bad news, until you only hear about things once they are completely out of control.

Know that the way you react to unpleasant information has more to do with who you are than with the message or the messenger. An understanding of emotional intelligence as well as your communication style will be very helpful in mitigating the probability of an excessively emotional response and the damage it can cause.

So, how does this play out in your organization? Think back to a situation where bad news needed to reach you and consider these questions:

- Was there a time lag between the incident and when you heard about it?

- From whom did you hear the news? Did it work its way up the hierarchy (as opposed to having the people involved bring it to your attention)?

- Did the details come from different sources until you put all the pieces together (rather than hearing the whole story all at once)?

If you answered yes to any one of these questions, then there's a good chance your people are not completely comfortable bringing you bad news. To reverse this trend, pay close attention the next time someone comes to you. Be prepared to monitor your emotional response, making sure you listen without getting angry, judgmental or playing the "blame game" (more on this in Chapter 8). Gain a thorough understanding of what the problem is, and then focus your immediate response on getting the person's thoughts as to how the issue can be resolved and what, if any, assistance they need from you. Concentrating on the resolution rather than the problem will encourage everyone to remain calm, searching for and discussing possible solutions. If the news doesn't come to you from those involved, make it a point to go to them, utilizing the same agenda. (Note that we're not going to ignore any related performance issues, we're just going to deal with them later, after the situation has been resolved and emotions are completely under control.)

Giving feedback

If you've ever spent time with young kids, I bet you've seen this: they've finished something, tried something new or gotten something to work, and they immediately run over yelling, "Did you see me? Did you see me?" And they don't let up until you've told them how great it was or what a terrific job they did. Attention and feedback nurtures our confidence and helps us to learn and to grow. As children, we are praised for everything from washing our hands to putting away toys. But as we grow up, the quantity of feedback diminishes (when was the last time someone told you what a great job you did washing your hands?) even though our need for it does not.

Fast forward to the work environment. While everybody walks around like mature, confident adults (well, at least a few do), the reality is that everybody is really dying to run over to coworkers and managers and yell, "Look what I figured out!" and to hear somebody say, "That's great! Good job." Research by Gallup, Inc. has shown that feedback affects productivity across all the job types they studied,[85] which included office and production workers, managers and salespeople.

While many managers believe "no news is good news," employees interpret a lack of feedback as evidence they are unimportant and their performance, ideas and feedback don't matter. Just like kids who misbehave in order to get any kind of attention, Gallup[86] also found that even negative feedback increases engagement because any feedback is better than none at all.

Copyright 2007 by Randy Glasbergen.
www.glasbergen.com

"If I walk past your desk without stopping to criticize your work, that counts as a compliment."

While managers who focus on the positive engage about 60 percent of their people and those who focus on the negative engage 45 percent, only 2 percent of those in the ignored category saw themselves as engaged. Not surprisingly, feedback has a strong, positive correlation with engagement, and that, in and of itself, makes it an indispensable tool for you as you strive to create updraft. We've talked at length about how much people want to be valued and to feel as though they are contributing. Getting feedback reinforces the message that people, as well as performance, matter, and that somebody cares about them and what they are doing.

Feedback should be seen as central to the learning process for your people and your organization, as well as for yourself. Note that by feedback, we're not talking about annual performance reviews. We're talking about ongoing discussions that touch on strengths, progress, appreciation, etc., and that help people to develop and learn. With the exception of more serious transgressions, like the ones we just discussed involving values and culture, feedback is a process designed to foster continuous development. Its purpose is to guide, mentor and engage, not to assign blame or guilt. And it is delivered with the highest levels of respect, sensitivity and emotional intelligence.

Tactically, you've heard it all before:

- Feedback should occur as soon as circumstances allow. (This a great example of a situation in which knowing your communication style is vital as it may inadvertently deter you from having a potentially difficult discussion, or it may spur you to have it when you are angry or frustrated—neither of which is ideal.)

- Timing must take into account the idea that applause should be public (and private) while a slap on the wrist should remain private.

- Feedback should be proportional—neither overreacting to nor minimizing the issue. This is true for positive feedback as well. While it is important for a leader to be generous with their thanks and appreciation, its impact and sincerity is diminished if it is too easily earned or not commensurate with the difficulty or importance of the task.

- Feedback should be tailored to the needs of the individual as well as the situation.

Feedback is another part of the investment you make in your people. It is, of course, a form of communication, and its relationship to engagement makes it crucial to updraft. Never underestimate the power of an encouraging word for its ability to energize, inspire and elicit great performance. Knowing someone is going to notice and appreciate your efforts goes a long way in the office as well as on the playground.

STRETCHING YOUR WINGS...

1. Jot down the communication tools being used within your organization. Are there a lot? Is there a wide variety? Are the majority of them one-way or two-way modes of communication?

2. Do the avenues of communication follow the organization's hierarchy, or do they flow freely between levels, departments and functions?

3. Think about a recent, positive situation—closing a new client, a product development breakthrough, a cost savings. Does everyone in the organization know about it? Plan a celebration for this achievement, but also think about how this information should be handled. Design a simple, low-bureaucracy way (announcements, emails, signs, quick celebrations, etc.) to quickly and easily let the organization know about good news. (Bad news often needs to be handled carefully and more gently, so you'll need a separate process for it.)

4. Pick a time (consider making this a weekly event) where your entire leadership team fans out and just walks through the organization, saying hello while expanding comfort zones for both your team and your organization. Keep it fun and light— maybe hand out lollipops or lottery tickets.

5. Does everyone in your organization have access to someone at the executive level? Does everyone in your organization feel welcome and comfortable approaching you? Talk to your executive team about starting "Coffee with the president" or "Lunch with the VPs"—meetings that encourage two-way communication and help your organization become more comfortable with this level of communication.

CHAPTER 8

What is the rooster's job?

Responsible for nature's wake-up call, the rooster takes his job very seriously. Every morning as dawn approaches, his internal alarm clock[87] prompts him to strut around his territory crowing the familiar "cock-a-doodle-doo" (or should that be "clock-a-doodle-doo?). The rooster crows, and then the sun rises. But this is not cause and effect; the rooster is not taking responsibility for the rising of the sun. Instead, he is simply getting our attention and demanding that we pause to acknowledge the beauty and promise of a new day. As a leader trying to create updraft, you need to understand this distinction.

Imagine this. You're an engaged person, committed to the work of the organization, and in the course of playing your part, you discover an issue. Maybe you noticed that rework from a particular department had increased, or maybe you realized there was a more efficient way to process invoices, or maybe a client's comment triggered an idea for a new product feature. You took it upon yourself to research the issue further, and you proposed a solution, which was implemented. You were very excited to have made such a contribution, and you're flying high. Next thing you know, you're reading the company newsletter or attending a corporate update where they mention the results of your efforts—but your name is nowhere to be found. Instead, your department head is waving and smiling, strutting around as proud as a peacock in response to the applause. Demotivating? Disengaging? Let's just say it's a good thing your feeling of achievement had propelled you to such heights, or you'd never have enough altitude to maneuver out of the tailspin such an incident would cause.

AND NONE OF IT GOOD

Taking credit for someone else's work achieves several things—and none of them good. Just look at what happens to the reputation, status and position of people who borrow a few words or paragraphs that were written by someone else. Jayson Blair, a reporter for *The New York Times* who plagiarized the work of another journalist, was forced to resign, putting a quick end to a promising career.[88] Kaavya Viswanathan, a 19-year-old Harvard sophomore whose first book was getting great reviews until it was discovered there were "striking similarities"[89] between her book and several others, had her book pulled off the shelves, her contract with the publisher cancelled, and her movie deal with DreamWorks Studios reduced to a dream. And then there was the $5.4 million Michael Bolton was ordered to pay due to similarities between his song "Love is a Wonderful Thing" and the The Isley Brothers' song of the same name.[90]

Copyright and legal issues aside, taking credit from those who deserve it flies directly in the face of updraft. We want people to see that what they do matters and, by extension, that they matter. Stripping them of their accomplishments is the antithesis of that. Instead of making people feel important, we're making them feel invisible. It's definitely not consistent with the creation of updraft. Like the rooster drawing attention to the rising sun, it is our job to crow as loudly as we can, highlighting and publicizing contributions and efforts.

An environment of gratitude, thanks and celebrating achievements is a powerful motivator. It fuels engagement and reinforces to people how they are making a difference to the organization. Getting genuine appreciation from "higher ups" not only boosts confidence but also communicates that leadership is paying attention and is aware of the hard work and contributions being made. People feel they are not being taken for granted, and that, in turn, creates a great, big "feel good" ripple effect. To paraphrase, Dolly Levi from *Hello, Dolly!*, "[Gratitude], pardon the expression, is like manure. It's not worth a thing unless it's spread around, encouraging young things to grow." (The quote is actually "Money, pardon the expression, is like manure...," but I think the concept works perfectly well for gratitude.)

Taking credit is all about "I," "me" and "mine." Leaders striving to create updraft, however, focus as much as possible on "we," "us" and "ours." Concentrating on the team and the organization as a whole maintains the focus on the bigger picture—our collective mission and goals. Individual achievements are celebrated for how they contribute to the team's success and/or the individual's growth and development. When one of us "wins," we all "win." If we begin to reward individuals without considering how they strengthen the team and contribute to our progress, we lose sight of our purpose. We run the risk of encouraging personal agendas and competing priorities (like the situation that can occur with a superstar player who scores lots of points but is undermining confidence, ignoring team values and destroying morale).

Taking credit for someone else's work also says a lot about the person taking the credit—and none of it good. This kind of behavior smacks of insecurity and a lack of confidence and is unforgivable in a leader. Rather than encouraging and enabling one's people to flourish and grow, it exposes a person who is threatened by the accomplishments of others. It doesn't bolster relationships, and it demonstrates a lack of integrity, honesty and respect. It also sends a clear message that the culprit is more interested in himself and his reputation than the team's, a development that will instantly ground even the highest flying organization.

© MARK ANDERSON, WWW.ANDERTOONS.COM

"Don't forget, I need to be taking credit for that report by three."

At its most basic level, your job is to achieve things through the work of others. Great leaders enjoy this process. They aren't in the game specifically for recognition or the expectation of rewards, but for the satisfaction that comes from developing people and helping them to achieve something beyond their own expectations. A leader takes pride in the work the team achieves and basks in a kind of reflected glory. The leader gets credit for the success of the organization, but never takes that credit for himself, and rightly so. It's not about you; it's about what you can inspire people to achieve. Ultimately, everything that comes out of your organization is a reflection of your leadership. However, you are not judged on the accomplishment of a single task but rather on the growth of the organization and the progress made toward its vision, mission and goals. If you keep your eye on the big picture, then it becomes obvious that it is far more important to updraft that people see their own contributions as vital to the success of the organization. Sharing and giving credit demonstrates integrity, respect and a true commitment to creating a team, while still maintaining the focus on mission, vision and goals. "A man may do an immense deal of good," said Father Strickland, a Jesuit Priest, "if he does not care who gets the credit for it."[91]

> **Ultimately, everything that comes out of your organization is a reflection of your leadership.**

THE CREDIT/BLAME COROLLARY

So, if our rule is "leaders never take the credit," then our corollary must be "leaders always take the blame." This does not imply people aren't held accountable (please note, blame is not the same as accountability). But updraft, as well as trust and integrity, requires the leader take full responsibility and hold himself accountable to those higher up the food chain. The ultimate responsibility sits with you. Like the sign on President Harry Truman's desk,[92] you need to believe that "the buck stops here" and that you are 100 percent responsible for what goes on within your organization.

You may say, "Wait a minute. I cannot possibly be responsible for every behavior, action and decision taking place within this organization." You may argue that even in a smaller company, the leader cannot be expected to weigh in on every decision. And besides, you're thinking, didn't she say that updraft requires people be empowered to make their own decisions and carry out the necessary actions? Yes, I did. We are not talking about a leader being directly involved in each decision or situation—we've already talked about the dangers of micromanaging and how it negatively affects engagement. Instead, we're looking at the big picture. Have you established powerful values that create a decision-making framework and guide behavior? Have you identified a direction as well as a destination that the entire organization is committed to reaching? If you have focused on leadership's most fundamental tasks, then your guidance and influence are always present. And if you haven't, whose fault is that?

Because I believe everything that happens in your organization is ultimately your responsibility, the Sarbanes-Oxley Act of 2002 (Federal legislation enacted to protect investors and prevent accounting fraud by imposing a variety of rules and processes and by making senior management responsible for the accuracy of their organization's financial statements.) has always mystified me. Taken in context, of course, it was a knee-jerk reaction to the developments of the time. To my mind, however, upper management has always been responsible for the accuracy of their financials since it is the behaviors and attitudes at the top that create an environment that either condemns or encourages fraudulent and dishonest activities. In a similar vein, consider a governor who got in trouble for something his staff did that he claimed to know nothing about. The ensuing investigation turned into a he said/she said, finger-pointing fiasco. Putting politics aside and looking at the situation strictly from a leadership perspective, it doesn't matter if the governor was in the loop or not. The pertinent issue is that he created an atmosphere, intentionally or not, where his messages and behaviors led an aide to make a bad decision. I don't care how far down the hierarchy the questionable or the unethical or the illegal or the bad decision was made, if someone in your organization made it, then your message didn't reach everybody. And that, comes back to you. (We'll give the benefit of the doubt and say the message didn't get out rather than wonder what message was sent.) Ultimately, everything that comes out of your organization is a reflection of your leadership.

**"We've got to draw the line on unethical behavior.
But draw it in pencil."**

And while more studies are needed, research has begun to establish a link between a "blaming" mindset and low emotional intelligence.[93] Such an attitude smacks of a lack of self-esteem, self-worth and confidence, and it will negate those attributes we discussed in Part I, destroying your aerodynamics. Certainly, it undermines credibility, trust and integrity. But maybe more importantly, when you blame people or circumstances outside of yourself, you undermine your own self-esteem and confidence, making yourself a victim. I remember a lovely woman I worked with both professionally and as a volunteer. I don't think she hit a single deadline she committed to, and it was never her fault. The kids got sick, her car needed service, her boss kept her late, her husband had to go out of town…and on and on. Ironically, she was always asking for productivity tips and ideas, but then she would explain why they wouldn't work.

You see, when you push the blame onto external forces, you give away power and relinquish your control. If your actions didn't create the situation, how can your actions resolve it? If she had acknowledged that she had the power to fix the situation, she would have had to take responsibility for it. But remember, people don't follow victims. They sympathize with them, they console them, sometimes they offer to help them—but they don't follow them, and they certainly aren't inspired by them.

Not surprisingly, a blaming mindset is the enemy of updraft and has a devastating effect on culture. In fact, Nathanael Fast of the University of Southern California and Larissa Tiedens of Stanford University have shown that "blame is socially contagious."[94] As a result, you must stop such behavior before it starts. By emphasizing your own accountability, you garner tremendous respect from people both above and below you. You strengthen integrity, credibility and trust through such a demonstrable commitment to your people. Your willingness to take the blame sets a clear example and does more to establish a culture of accountability than anything else. You are sending the unmistakable message that not only are you part of the team, but also that if the team has failed, then you have failed them in some way. By taking the blame, you are also running interference and shielding your team. While it would be ideal if your board members and investors understood the updraft concept and shared the same values as the organization, that won't always be the case. It will be up to you to protect the organization from overreactions, unproductive behaviors and less emotionally intelligent responses that could jeopardize performance as well as updraft.

Culturally, the "blame game" focuses us on who did what and on what happen-*ed* (emphasis on the past). But once someone comes forward and takes responsibility, we shift to the search for solutions, which has us looking forward and making progress. Consider the comments of Sanjay Jha. In June 2011, the CEO of Motorola blamed third-party application developers for many of the performance problems on Motorola's Android devices.[95] "Unlike most other mobile app stores," he explained, "the Android Market is totally open, meaning anyone can upload an application to the store."[96] Jha asserted that, as a result, the applications had not been fully tested for their effects on Motorola products. So, it's not us, it's them. And yet, this was the reality of the space in which they competed, and it was unlikely to change. Instead of taking ownership and focusing the organization on the hunt for solutions, Jha relieved the organization of any responsibility. Motorola could sit back and busy themselves in a round robin of finger-pointing, undoubtedly alienating the very developers who might have been solicited to help.

Or what about Oracle president Safra Catz who publicly blamed their drop in revenue on their sales force?[97] (Remember, we're all for accountability, just not for blame.) As soon as you begin placing blame, you create an "us" versus "them" mentality that obliterates the team concept and is deadly to updraft. First, those team members you throw under the proverbial bus get caught in a powerful downdraft, making them fearful, angry, resentful and defensive, putting them into survival mode, and making them feel like those galley slaves we mentioned earlier. Second, as we've discussed, you destroy their trust in you. Third, by absolving parts of the organization, you encourage "it's not my job" thinking, which leads to an insular and functional focus— another enemy of updraft. And lastly, instead of inspiring the entire organization to work together to overcome the obstacles standing in the way of our vision and mission, you destroy the collaborative, "we're all in this together" culture. Now, rather than creating updraft to support each other, we're intentionally blocking the flow of air. Focusing on blame distracts us from what is really important. Not only does the company not make progress but it opens the door for competitors who may choose to take responsibility, see the issue as a challenge and get to work on it. The only way to ensure forward progress is to redirect attention on where we want to go, not on where we've been.

ANOTHER CASUALTY OF THE CREDIT/BLAME GAME

So, great leaders easily and happily give away the credit but hold onto the blame. We've just seen that the credit/blame conundrum destroys updraft on several levels, impacting your aerodynamics as well as the aerodynamics of your people, destroying cooperation and jeopardizing forward progress. But there is another issue adversely impacted by the credit/blame game and is important because it, too, impacts updraft and progress in several ways. I'm referring to the related issues of creativity and innovation. "What is the difference?" you ask. At their most basic, creativity is the process of coming up with a new idea while innovation is the practical implementation of that idea. Creativity leads to innovation, but creativity can also exist for its own sake (i.e., the arts). In a sense, creativity is thinking of new things while innovation is doing new things. Of course, there are subtler distinctions, but this will serve for our purposes.

Organizationally, a lack of creativity is an indication something is wrong. Very wrong. In the same way that the silence resulting from a lack of communication indicates danger, so too does an absence of innovation. Like many of the issues we've discussed, creativity and innovation impact updraft at the individual level, but they also have broader implications regarding the health of the organization and its ability to fly (i.e., updraft at the organizational level). The presence (or absence) of creativity speaks volumes about leadership, management, the culture and the people. The level of innovation in an organization can be a very accurate barometer of its emotional state as well as its financial health and future prospects. Without new ideas, progress ceases, and without progress, there is no forward motion, leaving your organization about as aerodynamic as a rock. New products are not developed, processes are never improved and perspectives never change. In Chapter 10, we're going to talk about how a powerful vision spurs progress and growth by forcing us to find solutions

> **The level of innovation in an organization can be a very accurate barometer of its emotional state as well as its financial health and future prospects.**

to the obstacles and challenges that arise on our journey. Without creativity and innovation, we will be unable to overcome those issues.

A steady stream of ideas, comments and suggestions also serves as evidence that people care about what they are doing—that they are engaged. And, as we know, engagement is a prerequisite for individual updraft. Those ideas and suggestions tell you that people are not just robots carrying out instructions but are interested parties who are on the lookout for what is "better." Someone who doesn't care doesn't devote his or her own resources (time, energy, thinking) to contemplating and researching an issue and considering solutions.

But in an organizational setting, we need to go further. Most ideas will need to be shared with others in order to be implemented. I call this "collaborative creativity" because it requires that people work together to analyze, perfect and implement an idea. However, when we share our thoughts and ideas, we feel exposed and vulnerable. Seeing something in a new way is both illuminating and a little frightening, and the prospect of sharing it can be even more frightening. In order for collaborative creativity to flourish, people must be confident in themselves and in their ideas and must have the utmost faith in the people around them—bringing us right back to culture and leadership. While credit grabbing and the blame game will severely impact creativity, there are other issues that will block creativity, and you need to be aware of all of them.

WHAT'S BLOCKING INNOVATION?

In "Barriers to Creativity and Creative Attitudes," Gary Davis[98] identifies six barriers that inhibit creativity and block implementation—all of which are probably already at work in your organization. The first barrier is resources. You may remember back in Chapter 1, we discussed how performance and engagement are compromised when people don't have what they need to do their jobs. As the person ultimately responsible for getting the organization what it needs, you must understand that a lack of resources also has a profound effect on creativity. People who are stretched so thin they can barely accomplish what they need to, won't have the time or the energy to contemplate issues from a bigger-picture perspective. And they certainly won't have the bandwidth to implement solutions, regardless of how much more efficient the solution might be. In fact, in Adobe's *State of Create Study: Global benchmark study on attitudes and beliefs about creativity at work, school and home*,[99] they found that 80 percent of U.S. respondents (and 75 percent globally) indicated "there is increasing pressure to be productive rather than creative at work." Respondents also identified time and money as being the most significant challenges to creativity.

If you want improvements and suggestions to be a part of everyone's job, you need to provide them with the time and other resources they need in order to be creative. While you may not be able to implement 3M's Fifteen Percent program, which encourages employees (all employees, not just the scientists) to use 15 percent of their salaried time on whatever creative pursuits they want,[100] you can talk to your staff and take an objective look at their workload. It is very possible creativity and innovation have been put on the back burner by an understaffed organization that is overwhelmed and just trying to get through the day.

The next barrier, learning and habit, come from behaviors and approaches we have internalized to such an extent they've become unconscious—we forget they are there. Do you put on both socks and then your shoes, or do you put on a sock and then a shoe and repeat on the other foot? There's a good chance you aren't even sure what you do. These habits become so ingrained we don't even realize they exist. On a daily basis, they save time and help us get through everyday situations. But they also limit our creativity because they allow us to do things automatically, without thinking about them, and this closes our minds and can blind us to alternatives and opportunities. Make an effort, every so often, to shake up your habits and those of the people around you—take a different route to work, eat lunch out if you usually eat in (or vice versa), hold a meeting outside, try a yoga class instead of heading straight to the treadmill, and even switch the way you put on your shoes. Just experiencing new things at this everyday level will open your mind and help you to see other possibilities.

Rules and traditions, the third barrier to creativity, are like habits in that they help us to accomplish things without reinventing the wheel each time the situation arises. You certainly wouldn't want to create a new order entry and fulfillment process for each order coming into the organization. However, for most organizations, these policies, guidelines and processes become cemented in place. One of my favorite stories is about the woman who always cut off both ends of the ham before putting it into the oven. When her husband asked why she did this, she said her family had always done it that way. When they asked her mother, she replied that *her* mother had always done it that way. At a family dinner, the opportunity arose to ask the grandmother why she prepared the ham that way. "Why it's simple," she explained. "Our oven was very small, and the ham wouldn't fit unless I cut off the ends."

As your organization develops, you need to be sure your processes, procedures and practices haven't become so ingrained that people feel they *can't* question them. An organization soaring through the air has no room for sacred cows (they can't fly, and they don't fit in the overhead compartment). What worked for the organization early on may not work as you grow. When an organization stops challenging its own thinking, it stops growing. Go back to your organization, find out what people perceive to be off-limits, and make it clear to everyone that the shield protecting those issues has been lifted. Get a cow-shaped piñata to represent those sacred cows, and let your organization have at it. As

John Maynard Keynes said, "The difficulty lies, not in the new ideas, but in escaping from old ones."[101]

Perceptual barriers are next, and they involve our inability to see things in different ways and from different perspectives. Think about the move to repurpose items. Perceptual barriers have us see a spoon as an implement for eating, but spoons can be rings, bracelets, wind chimes, cabinet pulls, hooks and decorations. Perceptual barriers can also impede our ability to see solutions that are right in front of us. I'm sure you've seen the optical illusion drawing of the faces and the vase. If you see the vase first, it is hard to change your perceptions in order to see the faces and vice versa.

These perceptual barriers also prompt us to jump to conclusions because we assume we know the answer based on a limited amount of information. For instance, here in New Jersey, if you visited your doctor in January and told him you were experiencing fatigue, fever and chills, he might diagnose the flu. His perceptual barriers would lead him down a particular path. However, if he probed further, he would have found that you just returned from a golf vacation where you may have been bitten by a tick which could have given you Lyme disease—something that could manifest itself with similar symptoms. Perceptual barriers can be difficult to identify and even harder to break. Slow down and take the time to get the full picture before you start looking for solutions.

One executive I worked with made terrific progress in her development efforts. She accomplished many of the objectives that had been set out for her, and her employees saw a difference in her performance, reporting growth in several areas. Her boss, however, could not see the progress she was making; his perceptual barriers were preventing him from seeing her differently. Organizationally, perceptual barriers may prevent you from seeing an employee in a new role, a new market for an existing product, or a new layout for the manufacturing area. Our discussion in Chapter 3 about making an effort to get different perspectives will help with this, but listen carefully to your own language and responses when people come to you with ideas that challenge perceptions. If your knee-jerk reaction includes phrases like "we've always done it this way" or "I don't see that working," recognize that you may be a slave to your perceptions. Then, make it a point to hear them out, intentionally giving the idea additional consideration in order to broaden your perspective.

The fifth barrier to creativity is cultural barriers, which have to do with conformity—doing things "right" so we fit in and feel accepted. Creativity and innovation, however, are all about originality and bucking convention. But a rejection of our thoughts and ideas is tantamount to a rejection of something in ourselves and can feel very personal, making us hesitant to share. Maybe it's a stupid idea. Maybe I've missed something. Maybe it won't work. Nobody wants to feel stupid or that they are making waves, but within an organization, collaborative creativity is going to be required most of the time. If there is any chance an idea will be met with personal attacks, malicious criticism or any negative reaction, people are going to chicken out. And a company whose people have a lot of great ideas that are never articulated is no better off than a company without creative ideas.

"Thanks, Brian, for your thoughtful and constructive proposal. Without further ado, we'll now dive into malicious, envy-based criticism, character assassination and petty bickering!"

While peer pressure is usually associated with getting someone to do something they might *not* normally do (smoking or drinking, for instance), cultural barriers may well inhibit people from expressing their ideas. As a leader, you need to nurture a supportive environment that minimizes those cultural barriers. Concerns about "standing out" or "being different" never really disappear, so reward those who speak up, and encourage diversity, in all its forms, within your ranks. Don't let birds of a feather make up your teams; instead, include a variety of people with varying expertise, communication styles and approaches. Be sure everyone understands the concepts behind brainstorming (i.e., no judging, shoot for quantity, "crazy is good," etc.) so ideas and people aren't abandoned before their time. Maybe create a "Making Waves" award that highlights particularly unique ideas and approaches, or give out a "Crazy like a fox" statuette at each brainstorming session for the most outlandish idea. And, needless to say, be sure to communicate and celebrate these awards throughout the organization.

Our last barrier to creativity is emotional barriers, which refer quite simply to emotions and emotional states that can interfere with creativity as well as with implementation. While a "bad mood" can impede creativity temporarily, high levels of emotional intelligence can help. The danger is that emotional barriers can go even deeper, embedding themselves into the fabric of your culture and impeding the generation of ideas. Creativity and engagement go hand in hand; anything that jeopardizes engagement is going to negatively affect creativity. We just talked at length about how credit grabbing destroys updraft, but we also need to talk about how it inhibits creativity. While top performers typically have healthy doses of internal motivation and self-esteem and do great work because they want to, knowing you'll never get the acknowledgment and recognition you deserve tends to discourage and demoralize even the most dedicated among us. Being a team player is one thing, but watching someone get compliments and accolades for something you did, while your contribution is ignored, is difficult to forgive and fosters feelings of anger and resentment—emotional barriers to creativity to be sure.

More examples may help to illustrate this connection between emotional barriers and engagement (or more accurately, disengagement). We've already talked about the importance of feedback to engagement and updraft, but think about how it affects creativity. For every business owner I speak with who laments the lack of creativity and innovation at his or her organization, I hear three or four stories from people who submitted a suggestion or spoke with their manager about an idea and never even got a response. Not even simple acknowledgment for the effort. Apathy and indifference on the part of supervisors, managers and executives is a contagious emotion that will lead to a "if they don't give a damn, why should I?" feeling, an emotion that certainly won't elicit creativity.

Or consider the blame game we just discussed. You can't tell people you value initiative, innovation and risk taking and then blast them for anything that doesn't work out perfectly. Regardless of the outcome, if my efforts are unappreciated or I am left feeling belittled and humiliated, I'm not going to be in the appropriate state of mind for creative pursuits. The same emotional barriers that will block creativity will also destroy updraft. If you've discerned that engagement isn't where it needs to be in your organization, then it is very likely creativity and innovation are suffering as well.

Thus far, we've talked about how emotional barriers to creativity impact ideation, but I mentioned they can also affect implementation. The most dangerous aspect of this is a desire to protect the status quo. Such a mindset can indicate that leadership and management are feathering their nest and have become overly invested in the current situation. When this occurs, fear, anxiety, stress and uncertainty can lead executives to delay or impede implementation, worrying that the "new" could precipitate change and threaten the present state of affairs. When you are at the top, you understandably want to stay there. However, you and your team must realize that by protecting the status quo, you are putting the entire organization into "hover" mode where progress ceases and updraft cannot be created. As Pablo Picasso said, "Every act of creation is first an act of destruction."[102] No matter how much you think you have to lose by changing, you will lose more by trying to stay where you are (remember Kodak?). The biggest threat to what "could be" is the fear of losing "what is."

This commitment to the status quo is also indicative of leadership that has forgotten its *raison d'être*. Outside the bounds of values, accepted behaviors and the like, leadership's focus should be on what we are achieving and the amount of progress being made. Once leadership and management become inappropriately focused on how things are done, they have misplaced their commitment to the vision and mission and lost their bigger-picture perspective. Leadership and management shouldn't care whether something is different but should be open to anything that furthers the goals, mission and vision of the organization. Becoming overly involved or concerned with the tactical also increases the risk of microman-

> **No matter how much you think you have to lose by changing, you will lose more by trying to stay where you are.**

aging and getting in the way of engaged performers. And without that bigger-picture perspective, the alignment between innovation and strategy disappears. This reduces focus and opens the door to the misuse of resources as the organization pursues ideas that don't advance the mission or vision.

ENCOURAGING CREATIVE ATTITUDES

Now that we've eliminated the barriers to creativity, we need to take a look at the other side of the equation. In Gary Davis' article, he discusses not only the barriers to creativity, but how to encourage what he calls "creative attitudes." While kids spend their childhood waiting for the benefits of growing up (i.e., driving, having a glass of wine, picking out their own clothes, qualifying for a mortgage), an unfortunate side effect is a decrease in creativity. Research by Darya L. Zabelina and Michael D. Robinson (2010), Elizabeth Rosenblatt and Ellen Winner (1998), Kyung Hee Kim (2011), E.P. Torrance (1967)[103] and many others continues to document a reduction in creativity, especially during the school years when logic, skill and the desire to conform increase. For how long and at what stages this occurs is still being studied, but coupled with Adobe's finding that just over half of U.S. respondents see themselves as creative, the challenges of encouraging creativity become apparent. In truth, every time you try a new combination of spices, think of a more efficient pattern for mowing the lawn, or string a few words together to create a memo, you are being creative. Most people don't consider these everyday accomplishments to be acts of creativity, so they dramatically underestimate their creative potential.

As a leader who wants to encourage creativity, your focus needs to be in three areas: resources, culture and direction (isn't that convenient?). We've already identified time as a required input and discussed how overwhelmed, overworked people are unlikely to be concerned with improvements and innovation. Let people know that thinking is a part of their job and that it is okay not to "look busy" at every moment.

- Create a process (either internally or with external assistance) that tracks ideas and suggestions and keeps them moving forward. Assign a budget to this process, signaling that the organization is serious about investing in creativity and innovation.

- Run a repurposing contest on everyday items or your products, prompting people to change their perceptions and see them in a new light.

- Encourage "outside" creative interests by having a rotating gallery of art or photographs by staff members.

- Inject humor and fun—they stimulate thinking and creativity.

- Bring in speakers on all kinds of topics (being sure to tap your own people for ideas and as potential presenters).

- Arrange for training on creativity-related topics and tools, giving your people what they need to be creative.

Notice I haven't listed any contests or games focused on eliciting ideas or submissions. We don't want creativity and innovation to be a one-time event triggered exclusively by the desire for rewards or awards; we want it to be a way of life motivated by passion, commitment and engagement. Engagement has to do with what people can sow, not with what they reap.

Culturally speaking, you now know about the barriers to creativity and can focus on removing them from your organization's environment. The way your organization treats ideas is synonymous with the way it treats its people. The good news is you are already in the catbird seat because much of what you are doing to create updraft will also encourage creativity. Make sure to pay particular attention to those barriers related to rules and traditions (slay those sacred cows), culture, and emotions, as these impact innovation and creativity at the organizational as well as the individual level. Lastly, remember that innovation needs to be aligned with strategy. It is up to you to ensure creative efforts are supporting your mission and vision.

As much as I enjoy facilitating brainstorming meetings, teaching creativity tools, and helping organizations to organize and administer continuous improvement processes (performance improvement), I know that these efforts cannot be implemented in a vacuum. Remember, innovation starts with creativity and creativity starts with people—engaged people. Success in these endeavors requires a leader who understands both the connection between updraft, engagement and creativity and the importance of new ideas to the future of the organization.

If the environment supports creativity, in all its forms, the organization will be blessed with a steady stream of new ideas. And a stream of new ideas is a good indication that an organization is getting a whole lot of things right—and that's definitely something to crow about.

STRETCHING YOUR WINGS...

1. Think about a few of your organization's latest achievements. How were they celebrated? What did you and your executive team do? Did the congratulations and celebration occur at the top of the hierarchy or closer to where the work got done? Just like you did in the last chapter, schedule a celebration, being sure the festivities celebrate those responsible.

2. Think about a recent mistake. Was it handled as constructively as it could have been? Did the "guilty" parties walk away feeling guilty or refocused on the search for solutions? Revisit this specific issue. Find out the issue's current status with the goal of ensuring that the organization is focused on moving forward.

3. Are you happy with the levels of creativity and innovation within your organization? Do you have a process for vetting ideas? Talk to your team about how ideas are handled. Start developing a process for quickly and efficiently reviewing improvements and suggestions, making sure bureaucracy is kept to a minimum.

4. Involve the entire organization in creating a list of "banished" phrases (i.e., "We've always done it that way," "We tried that before," "That won't work here," etc.) that are common in your organization but hamper creativity and innovation. For more creativity-killing phrases, get a copy of Roger Von Oech's *A Whack on the Side of the Head: How You Can Be More Creative.*

5. Involve the entire organization in a hunt for sacred cows, and celebrate as they are destroyed.

PART III:
HEADING

Your organization has taken to the skies, but without sufficient forward motion it won't stay there for long. The higher you soar, the faster you must fly in order to maintain lift, so you need to know how to inspire the kind of forward motion that spurs progress and generates thrust.

CHAPTER 9

Just surviving isn't enough

In Part I, we started with a frank and potentially uncomfortable focus on you, as a person and as a human being, and we talked about how who you are translates into you as a leader. We hammered home the idea that like it or not, what's going on inside your organization starts with you; you are the lead bird, and if you aren't generating updraft, there's not much hope for the rest of the organization. Then, in Part II, we looked at what it takes to get your organization off the ground, identifying those elements that generate updraft by supporting engagement and creating a positive culture. Our focus here in Part III is to look at the primary drivers of forward motion, which are critical for making progress and keeping your organization aloft. The good news is that you and your organization have finally taken to the sky. You are in the lead position, guiding your organization higher and higher. As you continue to gain altitude, however, there are other considerations affecting your ability to remain airborne.

All the way back on page 1, we discussed the four forces that act upon an airborne object: lift, thrust, gravity and drag. Lift, it turns out, is affected by several factors including weight, wing size, angle of attack (the angle of the wing) and air density. As you may know, the higher you go, the thinner the air becomes. Skiers, hikers and mountain climbers are acutely aware of this and watch carefully for throbbing headaches, loss of appetite, dizziness and other symptoms of altitude sickness.[104] What you may not realize, however, is as air density decreases, so does lift (everything else being equal).[105] So, the bad news is the higher you soar, the faster you must fly in order to maintain lift. For instance, when the air density is one-quarter of what it is at sea level, you need to fly twice as fast in order to generate the same amount of lift.[106]

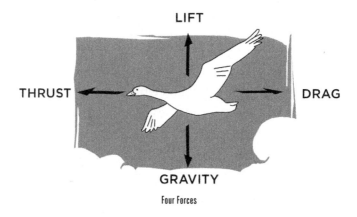

Four Forces

The low levels of oxygen at higher altitudes affect the geese as well, forcing them to work harder, flapping their wings faster as well as more deeply in order "to stay airborne and make progress."[107] But bar-headed geese, whose migration path takes them over the Himalayas, surprised scientists who expected them to make their impressive journey like an airplane does, gaining altitude and then maintaining it. Instead, researchers found that bar-headed geese "actually fly close to the ground, going up and down through the mountains like a roller coaster."[108] It turned out that the reduction in drag associated with staying at the higher altitudes wasn't nearly enough to offset the massive energy requirements needed to maintain lift (as measured by the geese's exponentially increasing heart rates).

What the bar-headed geese know and you need to remember, is that while your organization may need the ability to scale its own towering obstacles from time to time, flying continuously at high altitudes isn't required; it will exhaust your flock, compromising their ability to fly and, therefore, to generate updraft. Like the geese, once you've gotten off the ground, it is forward motion that enables you to stay airborne. We've addressed aerodynamics as well as what needs to happen for takeoff. Now we need to look at how you inspire the kind of forward motion that supports lift and enables you to remain aloft.

We've already touched on the confusion surrounding values, mission and vision, emphasizing that each one provides a specific and extremely important piece of information about your organization. But we only addressed values. We looked at the concept of acceptable behavior in the avian kingdom and how that translated to acceptable behavior inside your organization. We explained what values are, looked at some examples, and then discussed how they affect liftoff. Hopefully, that discussion left you with some clarity around values. Now, in an effort to continue chipping away at the mountain of confusion out there, this chapter will address mission, while the next will take a look at vision—both of which provide the kind of inspiration that stimulate forward motion (i.e., progress).

WHAT'S IT ALL ABOUT?

Unlike our avian friends whose lives revolve around survival and the perpetuation of their species, humans often ponder the meaning of life. *Avenue Q*, a clever, irreverent, adult-themed musical, takes up this very issue. Performed by a combination of puppets and live actors, the play includes puppet sex and lyrics like "it sucks to be me" and "the more you love someone, the more you want to kill 'em." At its heart is the coming-of-age story of Princeton, a puppet and recent college graduate, who is desperately trying to answer questions like "what is my purpose in life?" "why am I here?" and "what do you do with a B.A. in English?"

A corporate mission statement answers these very same questions (well, not so much the one about the B.A. in English). Why do we exist? What is our purpose? What business are we in? Your mission is a declaration of what you are here to achieve—from a strategic, big-picture perspective. It is an enduring pronouncement of what you do, and it provides your "larger purpose" beyond producing a product or making a profit. It is your organization's calling, if you will, and you and your people are mission-aries, devoted to championing that cause (which is why I prefer mission for this concept). Your mission connects with people on an emotional level, infusing passion and energy into the organization. And because it is intangible, it is enduring, outlasting changes in product, strategy and technology.

> **A mission provides your "larger purpose" beyond producing a product or making a profit.**

One of my favorite quotes is from Peter Drucker, who said, "Profit for a company is like oxygen for a person. If you don't have enough of it, you're out of the game. But if you think your life is about breathing, you're really missing something."[109] Looking back on all the business owners and founders I've met with, very few of them started a company exclusively to make money. Of course they wanted the company to prosper, but it was much more than that. The vast majority of them saw something unique they could bring to prospective clients, to their industry, to their field, to their community or to the world. Your mission provides that very perspective, and as such, it is focused outward, not inward. Your mission is not about who you are, what you do or how you do it. It's not about what you physically do but rather focuses on the impact you have on the world, helping to differentiate you from others in your industry. And it is inextricably linked to not one, but two of leadership's most important tasks—culture and direction. As much as I'd like to jump right in to our discussion of how a mission supports updraft, I think that conversation will be much easier once we've looked at mission in a little more detail.

You've probably heard of Dyson. Categorizing them as a manufacturer of small household appliances feels almost like an insult to their highly-innovative, sophisticated product line, which can be found not only in stores but in *museums* all over the world, including New York's Museum of Modern Art and Zurich's Design Museum.[110] The company was started by Sir James Dyson (invent a cool vacuum and you too can be knighted) in 1993. His revolutionary design for a vacuum cleaner had been rejected by all the major manufacturers (who were undoubtedly desperately clinging to the status quo). While Dyson's engineers work on a wide variety of problems, product introductions have included fans, hand dryers and motors.

In commercials, James Dyson says, "Our mission is simple; solve the obvious problems others seem to ignore." That's it—an eight-word mission. (As a general guideline, good missions are no more than 25 words, and the very best are a dozen words or less.) It doesn't get much simpler or more elegant. Of the 2,950 people employed by Dyson, Ltd., one-third of them are engineers or scientists.[111] I can only imagine how much they look forward to spending their days "solving problems." Doing work they enjoy and making a difference to their organization and its mission results in high levels of morale, creativity, initiative and passion—in a word, engagement.

How about the mother of all search engines, Google? Their mission is "to organize the world's information and make it universally accessible and useful."[112] They need a dozen words to define their business.

CORPORATE MISSION STATEMENTS	
Organization	**Mission**
Merck & Co., Inc.	Our business is preserving and improving human life. We also work to improve animal health.[113]
Mary Kay Cosmetics	Help women achieve personal growth and financial success.[114]
Nike	To bring inspiration and innovation to every athlete* in the world. *If you have a body, you are an athlete.[115]
Microsoft	To help people and businesses throughout the world realize their full potential.[116]
Wawa	To simplify our customers' daily lives.[117]
Nokia	Connecting people.[118]
Girl Scouts	Girl Scouting builds girls of courage, confidence, and character, who make the world a better place.[119]
World Wildlife Fund	Preserve the abundance and diversity of life on Earth.[120]
Monster	To inspire people to improve their lives.[121]

I know what you're thinking: *These examples are from large organizations, so this doesn't apply to me.* Please don't make this mistake. The inspiration, guidance and focus a mission provides is invaluable to any size or type of organization, including for-profits as well as nonprofits and even government. A mission is critical for any organization that wants to create updraft, giving the phrase "mission critical" a whole new dimension.

MISSION STATEMENTS	
Organization	**Mission**
Revolution Foods Oakland, CA	To build lifelong healthy eaters by making kid-inspired, chef-crafted™ food accessible to all.[122]
Trentham Construction Fayetteville, TN	To transform your dreams into reality.[123]

MISSION STATEMENTS	
Organization	**Mission**
Virginia Commonwealth University Police Department Richmond, VA	To provide a safe and secure learning, living and working environment for the students, faculty, staff and visitors of Virginia Commonwealth University.[124]
Bloomington Photography Club Bloomington, IN	The Bloomington Photography Club explores the connection between the eye, the camera, and the spirit by fostering the growth of artistic vision and technical knowledge.[125]
Aurora Photography Bethel, CT	To help you celebrate the special moments in your life, from the quiet ones that go on daily without fanfare to the big, emotional, important moments that change your life forever, and everything in between.[126]
Cypress, LLP Los Angeles, CA	To transform how people experience working with lawyers.[127]
Zach Theatre Austin, TX	Creates intimate theatre experiences that ignite the imagination, inspire the spirit, and engage the community.[128]
La Porte Insurance Agency La Porte, IN	Committed to helping you manage the risks that arise in everyday life.[129]
Seneca Physical Therapy, Inc. Rockville, MD	To ensure a safe and comprehensive transition from injury or illness to overall fitness and well being.[130]
Oasis Landscapes & Pools Las Cruces, NM	To create livable and luxurious outdoor living environments, regardless of your budget.[131]
New York Public Library New York, NY	To inspire lifelong learning, advance knowledge, and strengthen our communities.[132]
Planning Commission Saratoga, CA	To maintain the unique character of Saratoga by ensuring that the physical development of the City is consistent with the environmental, social and economic goals as set forth in the City's General Plan.[133]
Fire Department Chanhassen, MN	To minimize loss of life, property, and the environment from fires, natural disasters, life threatening situations, and to assist other emergency agencies.[134]
While the examples here are all on the right track, most of them would be even more powerful if they were more concise, editing out the extraneous. For example, the Chanhassen Fire Department's mission could be "to minimize loss of life, property, and the environment," or "to protect lives, property and the environment." The Saratoga Planning Commission's mission could be "to maintain the unique character of Saratoga."	

(While these statements were fairly easy to find on websites or in company information, we have no guarantee these organizations are using their missions. As always, the power is in the implementation.)

Notice that if you weren't already familiar with these organizations, you might not deduce what they do, operationally, from their mission statement. The mission is more strategic than operational; it doesn't tell us anything about how the mission is fulfilled—and that is a good thing. By focusing on the "what" but not on the "how," the mission can stand up to significant changes in technology, the industry, the political environment and the economy because the "larger purpose" (i.e., focus) can remain consistent even if the way it's achieved changes drastically. It is the absence of the specific "how we do this" that provides the flexibility. If your mission needs to be changed when you add a product, adjust your strategy or target a new market, then you are on the wrong track. Look back at some of the examples. Microsoft can continue to "help people and businesses realize their full potential" regardless of how business and technology change. Mary Kay could ostensibly leave the cosmetics industry completely and still be in the business of "helping women achieve personal growth and financial success." These concepts and ideas won't become irrelevant. In fact, if done right, your mission should be able to outlive your organization. And since the mission is part of the very foundation of the organization and its culture, any change would mark a significant departure from the organization's current direction. The exception here would be for many nonprofits that are essentially in business to put themselves out of business. Susan G. Komen for the Cure works to "create a world without breast cancer,"[135] but I think it is safe to say they would be happy to live in a world where their mission became obsolete.

If everyone out there truly understood the power of a mission, there wouldn't be an organization alive without one. It is essential to engagement and updraft, providing the proverbial wind beneath your organization's wings while also lifting each individual. More than anything else, the mission inspires. It engages people with the prospect of contributing, in a meaningful way, to the achievement of something greater than themselves. It reminds them that what they do changes the world. Which is more inspiring to you?

"We manufacture pharmaceuticals."	Or	*"We preserve and improve human life."*
"We sell cosmetics."	Or	*"We help women achieve personal growth and financial success."*
"We sell athletic apparel."	Or	*"We bring inspiration and innovation to athletes."*

Even Alfred Hitchcock had a bigger picture understanding of what he did. When asked by a French customs inspector, "What do you produce?" he responded, "Goose flesh,"[136] (i.e., goose bumps).

A powerful mission changes the way you see what you do. By connecting everyday activities to the mission, it elevates the importance of that task—no matter how mundane it is. There is a parable about three men who were cutting stones from a block of granite. A man approached the three hardworking individuals and asked each one what they were doing. The first man, looking grateful for a break, replied that he was making bricks, while the second wiped his brow and replied that he was laying a foundation. The third man, however, cheerily replied that he was building a cathedral. Rather than filling out paperwork, cleaning offices, writing code or doing any one of the millions of activities that takes place within your organization, the answer to "what are you doing?" can be "improving human life" or "inspiring athletes" or whatever your mission is.

> **A mission engages people with the prospect of contributing, in a meaningful way, to the achievement of something greater than themselves.**

When people feel that what they are doing makes a difference, changing the world in even the smallest way, they feel good about themselves and their contributions. This increases their self-esteem and gives them the confidence to push a little further, taking on new challenges and expanding their comfort zones. Now, not only are they soaring but they are creating a powerful updraft, the strength of which multiplies the performance of each and every person in the organization.

MAINTAINING FOCUS

While a mission exists to inspire, it also contributes to updraft by providing guidance, which it does on a strategic level as well as on an operational one. Take a look at an organization called Jeremiah Program. Based in Minneapolis, Minnesota, Jeremiah Program helps single-mother families break the cycle of poverty. The program provides safe, affordable housing, childcare, coaching, access to education and employment. Their mission is "to transform families from poverty to prosperity."[137] Let's say their work in Minnesota is extremely successful and there are very few single-mother families left in need of their help. Could they extend their work to include single-father families? How about two-parent, low-income families? What about starting a fund to establish playgrounds in low-income areas?

As Gertrude Stein said, "It is important to know what is and it is important to know what is not your business."[138] Using their mission as a guide, Jeremiah Program could certainly expand to single-father or two-parent families while still carrying out their chosen mission to transform families. Some people suggest the mission should always include your target audience and even product offerings, but you can see here how that can limit growth by narrowing the focus too much. For Jeremiah Program, establishing playgrounds, while a wonderful endeavor, is outside of the scope of their mission. From a strategic standpoint, the mission allows for growth but keeps us focused on the area we want to impact and protects us from unintentional changes in direction.

The mission also serves as a powerful decision-making tool for day-to-day activities, supporting engagement and liberating you from all those operational issues. Every decision rests on the question, "Does this help us to fulfill our mission?" If the answer is no, we need to strongly question why we would do it. It isn't enough for people to memorize the mission; they need to be able to apply it to the real-life situations they encounter on a daily basis. For instance, maybe Jeremiah Program's Education and Employment Program Manager needs to decide among several new programs. The possibilities include a course in household budgeting, interviewing skills, career choice and healthy cooking. Assuming the manager has limited funds and can introduce only two new classes right now, the mission would guide her toward the budgeting, interviewing or career classes. If money were no object, the cooking class might well be included, but if a choice needs to be made, revisiting the mission will remind her of what the priority should be.

What about a course teaching kids about financial responsibility? I could argue that reaching out to these children today could help ensure the next generation prospers and never needs the assistance of the organization. They could also be more helpful to their mothers if they understood the situation better. And this, in turn, could lead to stronger, healthier families. On the other hand, I could argue that the mission is to transform families currently in need of help and that they should be the priority. The mission's scope opens

> **It isn't enough for people to memorize the mission; they need to be able to apply it to the real-life situations they encounter on a daily basis.**

it up to interpretation; sometimes it will be obvious whether and to what degree a course of action supports the work of the mission and other times it will require discussion and debate.

But updraft aside, maybe you're thinking that making decisions based on such lofty ideals isn't practical in today's environment. While it's fine for nonprofits, it's a luxury you just don't have. Not so. Consider CVS Caremark's announcement that as of October 1, 2014, they will no longer sell tobacco products at their 7,600 stores, costing the company an estimated $2 billion annually.[139] Why? Because "the sale of tobacco products is inconsistent with our purpose—helping people on their path to better health."[140]

YOUR MISSION: GET IT HEADED IN THE RIGHT DIRECTION

For example, Branta Automotive Services:

1. What do you physically do?

    We do oil changes, tune-ups, tire balancing and rotation, brake service, exhaust systems, transmissions, etc.

2. Why do you do that?

    To repair and maintain cars.

3. How does what you do affect your client's life or impact the world?

    - It allows people to rely on their cars.

    - It means that people don't have to worry about breaking down.

    - It helps people get to where they need to go.

    - It extends the lives of people's cars.

- It helps people save money by doing preventative maintenance and avoiding costly repairs.

4. So, how do you help? What is your role?

- To keep people moving.

- To keep life moving.

- To keep people mobile.

- To provide peace of mind.

- To help people fulfill their commitments.

Once you've stopped talking about products and services and have transitioned to concepts and ideas, your mission is headed in the right direction.

The simplicity and elegance of the earlier examples is deceiving, and it may take some time before you hit on the perfect wording. But that's okay; it's the idea and its ability to inspire that is important. If you don't have one, developing a mission statement is a fascinating process and one that typically won't (and shouldn't) fit into a one-hour meeting. After all, this statement has tremendous implications for your organization, and like your discussion of values, you don't want to approach it casually. If you aren't fully committed, then this exercise will come across as the "management fad of the month" and will result in an uninspiring, convoluted statement that is purely for show, beautifully framed and forgotten on the conference room wall. Needless to say, such an approach has negative consequences for integrity and trust as well as for updraft.

If you want to see forward motion like you've never seen it before, get started with an open and honest discussion with your leadership team focusing on the following:

- What aspect of our business are we passionate about?

- What approach or perspective do we bring to our industry or field that is different from others?

- Why does a client call *us*?

- What do we do from the client's point of view? How do we affect their lives from a big-picture perspective?

- What are we most proud of?

- Who do we do our best work for?

- What do we bring to the table no one else does?

Developing a mission requires an in-depth exploration of these (and many more) questions. While every business owner is concerned about how their team will react and what they will have to say, we've never been disappointed. Revealing the different and often competing perceptions of the leadership team can be an eye-opening experience and often marks a turning point for the team as well as the organization. Even business owners who were convinced they were in a business that couldn't be inspiring were pleasantly surprised.

Ultimately, everyone in a leadership and management role must be wholly committed and inspired by the mission so it engages them in a powerful way and is always top of mind. Remember Merck and the river blindness decision? Dr. Vagelos knew only too well the risks of ignoring the mission and "pointed out that failure to go forward with the product could have demoralized Merck scientists—scientists working for a company that explicitly viewed itself as 'in the business of preserving and improving human life.'"[141] Dr. Vagelos understood not only the power of the mission but the devastating effect ignoring it would have on the morale, culture and performance of the organization.

You too will have to prove every day that fulfilling your mission is the driving force behind your organization. Only then will it provide the guidance and inspiration that will propel the organization forward.

STRETCHING YOUR WINGS...

1. Look again at my favorite quote from Peter Drucker: "Profit for a company is like oxygen for a person. If you don't have enough of it, you're out of the game. But if you think your life is about breathing, you're really missing something." Do you agree or disagree?

2. How do you think your executive team would react to the quote? Who and how many would agree? Why? Who and how many would disagree? Why? How does the leadership team's view relate to your current engagement level?

3. During a self-reflection session, think back to why you started or became involved in this organization. Did you have a larger purpose? Can you see a larger purpose for your organization's existence? Devote a page to these thoughts and keep adding to the list. Eventually, a pattern will emerge which will help point you in the direction of your larger purpose.

4. Do you currently have a mission? If not, why not? If yes, does it correspond to the definition used here?

5. Is your mission's existence within the organization palpable? Is it a part of everyday decisions and discussions? If I walked through your organization, would everybody I meet be able to tell me what it is and explain it to me? Try this exercise yourself.

6. To get your mission going in the right direction, take your leadership team through the series of questions used in the Branta Automotive Services example. For a more in-depth look at the anatomy of a healthy mission statement, download *Mission Rx* from www.DeltaVstrategies.com/Resources.

CHAPTER 10

... But we're making great time

Now you have a compelling, inspiring mission to rally the troops around. But once you have that powerful mission, it begs the question, "How are you going to make progress toward it?" Your everyday activities support your mission, but don't necessarily result in significant headway. The answer, it turns out, is to develop an organizational vision. Like your mission, your vision is designed to stimulate forward motion. But in contrast to the mission, which we paint with very broad strokes, the vision is a specific, detailed imagining of where we, as a group, are headed. Your mission points you in a general direction, like a flock of geese migrating north as spring arrives. While "north" does provide some guidance and gives the flock a general sense of where they're headed, it doesn't come close to providing enough information. The idea is not to set out on a northerly route and settle down wherever they want, but to navigate to a particular destination—a very particular destination, in fact, as Canada geese return to the same area where they were born for mating and nesting.

**We always migrate to the same place:
Why do you need to buy souvenirs every year?**

If we could talk to the geese, they could describe their destination for us, in detail, specifying it is at 40.57 degrees north latitude and 75.06 degrees west longitude. They would tell us they were heading for a medium-sized pond that has a small island with one tree on it and that the pond is bordered mostly by trees on the east and west. Toward the northeast is a grassy area with a few shade trees and then a road. To the southeast is a crop field. And they expect to be there in about three weeks. Can you picture it? Well, a vision is just that—a picture. Just like the account of the pond, your vision is a clear, concise verbal description of what you want to achieve by a designated time in the future—and the more detailed, the better. It is specific, yet vision-ary, and it serves as a major stepping stone toward the achievement of your mission. As such, its scope and significance often come across as almost arrogant, especially to those outside the organization. It is a bold, challenging organizational goal that is both measurable and specific.

Visions often reference revenues, profit, market share, client base, customer service rating, fulfillment rates and the like. Some of the more inspiring, however, call for the development of a new product or capability, a radical change in distribution network or the solution to a specific problem. Some paint a picture like Bill Gates and Microsoft cofounder Paul Allen's 1975 vision of putting a computer on every desk and in every home.[142] Having just said that, please don't make the mistake of declaring that your vision is to increase sales by 125 percent over the next four years. It is the vision's connection to the organization's mission that makes it compelling, exciting and engaging, so it is important that it has significance over and above revenues and profits.

Your vision is unique. It is closely aligned with your mission and is formulated with your organization's strengths and abilities in mind. It is risky and requires total commitment, like Boeing did in the 1950s, betting almost one-quarter of their corporate net worth, as well as the future of the company, on the development of the 707.[143] Fundamentally, a vision is a goal; it's just a really big one along the lines of James Collins and Jerry Porras' BHAG—Big, Hairy Audacious Goal.[144] "All companies have goals," said Collins and Porras. "But there is a difference between merely having a goal and becoming committed to a huge, daunting challenge."[145]

> **It is the vision's connection to the organization's mission that makes it compelling, exciting and engaging, so it is important that it has significance over and above revenues and profits.**

A vision is essentially a goal on steroids, and as such, it must include all the components of a well-constructed goal, often referred to as a

SMART goal. A SMART goal is **S**pecific, **M**easurable, **A**ttainable, **R**elevant and **T**imely. Without these characteristics, what you've got is more a flight of fancy than a goal.

Specific: Exactly what are we looking to achieve? I often hear phrases like "increase sales" or "decrease production costs" or "ship faster," but these are too general to be of use. The more specific a goal is, the easier it is to begin formulating approaches and solutions. Consider the difference between "increase sales" and "increase sales by 25 percent to each of our 10 largest customers." You can see how those specifics immediately begin to goose your creative juices and focus your efforts. An ambitious, specific, challenging goal, the vision is action oriented, and as such, it can't help but stimulate progress and move the company forward. It is this forward motion that is so critical to updraft, supporting lift by providing the required airflow over our wings.

Measurable: How do we know if we've achieved it? In the example above, $1 over current sales would be increasing sales, but I doubt you'd consider that a success. Making your vision measurable allows you to track progress, something that may be even more important than you realize. We've talked about how frustrating and exhausting it is for people to hover. And it turns out, according to the research of Teresa M. Amabile and Steven J. Kramer,

> We now know what the top motivator of performance is—and, amazingly, it's the factor [managers] ranked dead last. It's progress. On days when workers have the sense they're making headway in their jobs, or when they receive support that helps them overcome obstacles, their emotions are most positive and their drive to succeed is at its peak. On days when they feel they are spinning their wheels or encountering roadblocks to meaningful accomplishment, their moods and motivation are lowest.[146]

Because the vision defines such a specific, measurable end point, it stimulates progress by initiating action. And when everyone's actions are aligned with the vision, we see consistent movement toward that goal—quite an organizational accomplishment. Add to that the ability to track our progress against a measurable target, and you have energized, motivated, action-oriented people who are getting fulfillment from the work they do every day. Make sure your vision includes detailed, objective criteria that progress can be measured against, and make sure that you keep this information front and center. Easy-to-read visuals are always helpful. That's why you often see the thermometer measuring donations outside the local firehouse. If your vision is a picture (i.e., putting a computer on every desk and in every home), be absolutely sure the picture is so vivid that everyone knows what success looks like. But also try finding ways to introduce some cold, hard numbers for tracking purposes (i.e., percentage of homes and offices with computers).

Attainable: Can it be done? In the words of Peter Ustinov, "If the world should blow itself up, the last audible voice would be that of an expert saying it can't be done."[147] History is full of inventions, achievements and concepts predicted to fail.

- In 1833, Mr. Lord Kevin, the former president of the Royal Society of Edinburgh, said "X-rays will prove to be a hoax."[148]

- In 1926, inventor Lee De Forest declared, quite categorically, "To place a man in a multi-stage rocket and project him into the controlling gravitational field of the moon where the passengers can make scientific observations, perhaps land alive, and then return to earth—all that constitutes a wild dream worthy of Jules Verne. I am bold enough to say that such a man-made voyage will never occur regardless of all future advances." [149]

- A Boeing engineer once remarked, "There will never be a bigger plane built,"[150] right after his first flight in a 247, a double-engine plane that accommodated ten passengers.

- In 1977, Ken Olson, Digital Equipment Corporation (DEC) president, chairman and founder stated, "There is no reason anyone would want a computer in their home."[151] Incidentally, he made this comment two years after Gates and Allen articulated their vision of a contradictory future.

- In 1966, in an essay called "The Futurists," *Time* magazine predicated "remote shopping, while possible, would never become popular because 'women like to get out of the house, like to handle the merchandise, like to be able to change their minds.'"[152]

As you can see, it is not as easy as it seems to determine whether something is attainable, so you will need to consider this issue carefully. A vision that is too easy won't generate the passion, excitement or creativity you want. At the same time, something deemed to be truly impossible will not be energizing either.

Relevant: Is it linked to our mission? Is it important to us? If you don't yet have a mission, don't start work on your vision. Without a connection to the mission, the vision loses its ability to inspire; it becomes just another organizational goal. But when aligned with your mission (i.e., relevant and meaningful), your vision inspires by providing a gutsy, bold, yet specific and tangible stepping stone that brings you closer to achieving your mission—and in a big way. So if you don't yet have a mission, you can't start working on your vision.

We've talked about how people are motivated by the opportunity to achieve something greater than themselves; it is your vision that really shifts this into gear. Here's how it works. Let's say you are committed to nature and the environment and are excited to get a position with the World Wildlife Fund (WWF). You are passionate about their mission to "preserve the abundance and diversity of life on Earth." But what are you and the organization really doing about that? What tangible progress have you made or are you making toward the preservation of life on earth? Their vision provides a specific, significant action that answers the question: right now, we're working to conserve 15 of the world's most ecologically important regions (by 2020). As an employee there, you can be proud you are making a difference in the world in a way that truly promotes your mission. That pride manifests itself in engagement and the creation of updraft.

Time-dimensioned: What is our deadline? As Napoleon Hill said, "A goal is a dream with a deadline."[153] So, a vision without a deadline is just a really big dream. When you remove the time dimension, your goal or ambition becomes more like a fantasy or delusion. A deadline, even one 10 years out, imposes pressure. It forces us to think ahead and plan in an effort to keep ourselves on track.

Essentially, a vision is a long-term goal. For smaller organizations, a one- to five-year window would be appropriate, while three to eight years might work better for a medium-sized organization. For large organizations, the time frame generally falls within 5 to 15 years. However, these intervals are intended strictly for guidance. For instance, a small organization striving for aggressive growth might establish a 10-year target for its vision. The vision's specific time frame as well as its scope needs to be dependent on the size of the organization as well as its ambitions. While the time dimension is often overlooked, like on Microsoft's vision, it is essential for stimulating progress. And in case you're wondering, researchers have validated everything we've just discussed about the power of goals in numerous studies of goal-setting theory and motivation.

- When a person commits to a goal, he or she focuses on goal-related activities and actively turns away from activities deemed to be irrelevant.[154]

- Setting specific, measurable goals increases productivity.[155]

- "The highest or most difficult goals produced the highest levels of effort and performance."[156]

- "Goals energize people."[157]

- Goal setting affects performance at the individual, group and organizational level.[158]

- Goals encourage people to use what they know and to acquire the knowledge or skills they need.[159]

- Goals have been shown to affect performance in intervals as short as a minute or as long as 25 years.[160]

- Concrete deadlines increase the pace of work as well as the effectiveness of the goal.[161]

- Feedback on performance is crucial to maintaining effort.[162]

Since 1968, when Edwin Locke published his landmark article "Toward a Theory of Task Motivation and Incentives," over 1,000 studies have confirmed and expanded on these findings. There is no doubt; a well-written vision is a powerful leadership tool and is extremely effective at encouraging the forward motion we need for high-altitude flying.

FORWARD MOTION

Remember Jeremiah Program? They are the Minneapolis, Minnesota, organization helping single-mother families break the cycle of poverty. In the last chapter, we talked at length about their mission "to transform families from poverty to prosperity." Their vision is to have a presence in 12 cities by 2020.[163] We just looked at the World Wildlife Fund, whose mission is to "preserve the abundance and diversity of life on Earth." Their vision is to conserve 15 of the world's most ecologically important regions by 2020.[164] While both organizations refer to these as goals, in each case the scope, time frame, ability to inspire, and alignment with their mission definitely qualifies it as a vision. What about a country with a vision? Costa Rica has committed to doubling its marine protected areas by 2015.[165]

What about corporate visions? It would be hard to discuss this subject without mentioning Walt Disney, often referred to as a visionary and for good reason. In 1934, he publicized plans for his vision of the first, full-length animated movie estimated to cost $250,000. By the time *Snow White and the Seven Dwarfs*[166] debuted on December 21, 1937, it had been dubbed "Disney's Folly." Its costs had reached almost $1.5 million, and there was much skepticism that moviegoers would sit through an animated feature about a fairy tale. Today, it is considered one of Disney's best movies, and it spawned an entire industry. Later, while watching his daughters play in a less than pristine amusement park, Disney had "a vision of a place where children and parents could have fun together."[167] As you probably realize, this was the genesis for his vision of Disneyland, which became a reality on July 17, 1955.

Today, Nokia Siemens Networks has announced its vision of having "5 billion people connected and 'always on' by 2015."[168] And Amazon has a vision "[to make] every book ever written, in any language, in print or out of print, all available within 60 seconds."[169] (Yes, Amazon's vision needs a time frame.) In general, corporate vision statements are hard to find for three main reasons. First, the vast majority of those labeled "vision statements" are not really visions at all thanks to the massive confusion surrounding the topic. Second, organizations that do have vision statements often hesitate to publicize them externally because they don't want the outside world to know what they are working on. And third, not enough organizations realize how important visions are to forward motion and the creation of updraft, and so they simply don't have them.

Oftentimes, statements purported to be visions look something like these:

> To become the *distributor* of choice for world-class products through our commitment to value, quality and teamwork.

> To be the safest and most customer-centric *fitness centers* in the world.

> To be one of the best and most respected *transportation services companies* in our industry, as determined by our employees and our customers.

> To be known as the industry leader in *construction services* by focusing on long-term relationships and exceptional service and quality.

> To be the leading *IT firm* providing quality services to our clients.

> To be the world's premier *accounting firm*.

Go back and reread these statements. Notice anything? In their current state, they are hardly unique. You can replace the italicized section with any industry or company. They are so homogenous that they don't provide any kind of strategic/competitive advantage. In addition, these statements don't really say anything. They are full of trite, vague, undefined phrases which provide neither guidance nor focus, and as a result, they don't stimulate progress. They are not the tools of leadership. Their ambiguity makes them useless (neither specific nor measurable) for strategic planning, and in fact, you can't even tell when you've achieved your goal. What does "industry leader" refer to? Sales? Profits?

New product introductions? Market share? Cutting-edge technology? Brand recognition?

For me, they seem to be stating the obvious, and my reaction is always, "No kidding? Do you know anybody who is aspiring to be the worst in their industry by ignoring customers and producing a shoddy product?" And lastly, there's no connection to the organization's strengths, strategy or mission (if they have one). As a result, these statements do nothing for inspiration or engagement. If your vision looks like one of those above, revisit it and try to remember what it was you truly wanted to accomplish. When you said "leading" or "premiere" or "customer-centric," exactly what did you mean? Start thinking about how you can make your vision specific, measurable and meaningful.

YOUR VISION: GET IT HEADED IN THE RIGHT DIRECTION

Developing a powerful vision requires an in-depth understanding of your organization: its strengths and weaknesses, its mission, its history, its values, its financial position—a whole host of topics. Many of these subjects will be explored during your strategic planning process which we will discuss in the next chapter. In the meantime, to get a feel for what you are creating, let's revisit Branta Automotive Services from the previous chapter. We'll need to make a few assumptions but will stipulate the following:

- They are a "small shop" with annual revenues of $650,000.[170]

- They have a slightly higher than average operating income of 5 percent.

- They employ 4.5 people (one owner/technician, three technicians and one flextime receptionist/ scheduler/cashier.

- They have a mission: *To keep people mobile.*

Highlights of their strategic planning discussions revealed the following:

- More and more customers have hybrids, and only one technician is certified for those repairs.

- Saturdays have become extremely busy because people can't do without a car during the week.

- Consolidation in the insurance industry has left them approved by only one insurance company.

In keeping with their mission, Branta Automotive Services decides that their vision will be to address the increasing number of hybrid vehicles coming to the shop. This will allow them to keep those people who choose to own hybrids, mobile.

Their vision is "In 18 months, to be fully servicing hybrid vehicles." If you are from a large company, this may seem small in scope to you, but it means about $15,000 in training and $2,000 in equipment.[171] It requires the efforts of the entire organization, as they will all need to pick up the slack when people are out for training and certification testing. They will also need to increase the overall workload in order to generate the extra revenues to cover the costs of this endeavor.

Note that while the insurance situation was a concern, it is essentially an administrative issue and doesn't require the efforts of the entire organization, so it was deemed unsuitable for the vision. However, the owner is considering asking the part-timer to devote some additional hours to the insurance paperwork. Your organization may well have other goals that, while relevant to your mission and your business, are not directly related to your vision. That is going to happen. You just need to be sure these other goals don't eclipse the vision; everybody must be well aware that work related to the vision takes priority.

A vision is all about seeing what is possible, from a big-picture, long-term perspective. It is leadership's way of saying to the organization, "We've thought about our future, we have a plan for our success, and here's what it looks like." We talked at length about how essential it is for you to be actively leading your organization. If the perception is that the leader doesn't know where we are going or what we are trying to achieve, how can we have confidence he or she isn't leading us off a cliff? The idea "we're lost: but we're making good time"[172] (who else, but Yogi Berra?) causes people to question leadership and undermines the confidence we've talked about. Just riding along on the thermals doesn't demonstrate leadership, but the courage to embark on a vision shows not only leadership but commitment, passion, ability to make decisions, confidence in yourself as a leader and confidence in your organization. It contributes to your status as a visionary and mobilizes the people behind you. Having a vision and the plan to realize it (more on that in Chapter 11) actively engages people and gives them confidence in their leadership and their organization.

> **A vision is all about seeing what is possible, from a big-picture, long-term perspective.**

A strong vision extends the power of each individual's updraft by providing a common goal. It establishes priorities and guides decision making on both a strategic and a tactical level, guiding resource allo-cations as well as the disposition of talent. While this is similar to the effect the mission has, it is even more powerful because the effort is so focused. This enables you to comfortably push decision making further into the organization and, once again, frees you to lead. As everyone begins moving in the same direction, morale skyrockets. This atmosphere of cooperation and teamwork helps the organiza-tion deal with the challenges that arise along the way. Rather than competing for resources and pursuing functional agendas, efforts are concentrated on vision-related activities. A spirit of camaraderie develops, creating a support structure where people are ready, willing and able to pitch in, compensating for any gaps that may result from the redeployment of resources and eliminating much of the squab-bling that occurs when we are overfocused on functional areas.

BEFORE THIS DECADE IS OUT

Probably one of the best examples of a great vision comes not from business but from government. On May 25, 1961, before a joint session of Congress, John F. Kennedy declared "This nation should commit itself to achieve the goal, before this decade is out, of landing a man on the moon and returning him safely to the earth."[173] I think this is something that is missing in America today and could be instru-mental in helping us to address some of our most challenging issues. What would this great country achieve if someone threw down another challenge? The possibilities are almost endless. How about something like, "America will, by the end of this decade, eliminate its need for fossil fuels," or, "We will, within the next eight years, wipe out hunger"? Just imagine how this would unite the country, spur progress and energize innovation.

Kennedy's challenge is a perfect example of a vision. It hits all the high points of a well-constructed goal:

Specific: Putting a man on the moon and returning him safely to earth.

Measurable: A man will walk on the moon and return home. (Notice that Kennedy painted a picture.)

Attainable: As is typical of a great vision, many doubted whether it could be done. If the common wisdom is that "it can't be done," you are almost definitely on the right track.

Relevant: Suffice it to say it was relevant to the Cold War, the "space race" and the political climate of the time.

Time-dimensioned: By the end of this decade.

Not only is this a great example of a vision but Kennedy's entire address to Congress could easily serve as the outline for the kickoff announcement of a new corporate vision. I often refer executives to Kennedy's speech when we're working on their communications; this helps them to identify talking points and understand what they are trying to get across to their organization. As we're going to see, Kennedy's words are very much an inspirational call to arms.

In that vein, imagine for a moment the United States was a business organization, John F. Kennedy was its president and landing a man on the moon was about to become the new corporate vision. The process Kennedy followed closely mirrors the steps any good leader would take. He started with a memo to Vice President Lyndon B. Johnson, asking Johnson, who was also Chairman of the National Space Council, to "be in charge of making an overall survey of where we stand in space."[174] Johnson consulted with a wide variety of scientists and experts from NASA, the military, the government and some highly-regarded citizens.[175] Then, he reported back to Kennedy with status, observations, recommendations and estimated budget requirements. (Your own budgeting process might suddenly seem less onerous when you consider that NASA provided estimates for the Vice President in less than eight days without any high-powered computers or fancy forecasting and budgeting software.) A lot of energy, time, research and discussion (i.e., strategic planning) preceded Kennedy's public announcement before Congress, ensuring not only a carefully considered decision but also the participation, input and support from much of Kennedy's staff (i.e., his "executive team").

And while we're on the subject, this is where you are going to start—not just your quest for a vision but your journey toward updraft. As Niccolo Machiavelli said, "And it ought to be remembered that there is nothing more difficult to take in hand, more perilous to conduct, or more uncertain in its success, than to take the lead in the introduction of a new order of things."[176] And that is exactly what you are doing—introducing a new order. Once you are ready to begin, be prepared to commit a significant amount of time in ongoing meetings with your leadership team or key staff members. Change is difficult, and without a cohesive leadership team, it will be impossible. Keep in mind that while you don't benefit from updraft, the birds that flank you help to diffuse the downdraft off your wings, reducing the drag that you experience.[177] However, this only occurs if the birds closest to you are supporting you in your position. Look closely at your leadership team; they are key to your success.

In Chapter 11, we're going to talk about the kinds of issues that might be discussed in these early meetings, but it is important to recognize the enormity of this endeavor and the impact just one rotten egg will have. Be prepared to make tough choices. In one organization, early in the discussions, a high-ranking executive made it clear he was not in favor of the direction the CEO was taking and would not support it. The CEO was certain he was doing what was best for his organization and recognized that how he dealt with this situation was, for him, a moment of truth that would reveal the extent of his commitment. While an extremely difficult decision, in the end he crossed the Rubicon and parted ways with that executive, who had also been a long-standing friend.

> **Change is difficult, and without a cohesive leadership team, it will be impossible.**

Once your leadership team is flying alongside you, it is time to involve the rest of the organization. Following a similar process, Kennedy's next step was to announce this vision to the entire country (i.e., his organization). As a leader, Kennedy knew he would have to touch the hearts and minds of the people of his organization in order to gain their approval and their resolve. In this case, it would mean getting the full commitment of Congress as well as the American people. After setting the stage by explaining the current situation—which I have omitted in order to save space (oh sorry, that's bad!)—he says,

> First, I believe that this nation should commit itself to achieving the goal, before this decade is out, of landing a man on the moon and returning him safely to the earth. No single space project in this period will be more impressive to mankind, or more important for the long-range exploration of space; and none will be so difficult or expensive to accomplish. . . . But in a very real sense, it will not be one man going to the moon—if we make this judgment affirmatively, it will be an entire nation. For all of us must work to put him there.[178]

Let's look a little more closely at what he did here. First, he described the current situation so everyone in the organization, even those who might not have been as informed, understood where we were and why we needed to take action. Then, with passion and decisiveness, he presented his solution. He painted an inspirational, larger-than-life picture, and then he asserted that every single person in the organization would play a critical role. He went on to outline several strategic areas that would be essential to the success of this vision, including the development of a lunar space craft, alternate liquid and solid fuel boosters, the Rover nuclear rocket, and satellite systems for worldwide communications and weather observation. He also provided estimates of the financial costs that would be required.

Your organization needs to get the same information. We spoke earlier about the importance of communication and how most people are not able to see where they are headed or how they are doing. The more they understand about the process you're using, the direction you're taking, the destination you are heading to, and the issues you may encounter on your journey, the better able they will be to embrace change and contribute to the organization's success. Opening the lines of communication with the ideas we discussed in Chapter 7 can happen as soon as you finish reading the chapter, but exactly when and how you begin communicating about your vision needs to be discussed as a part of your process (and addressed in Chapter 11). The key concept, here, is to understand that like Kennedy, you need to share not only what you want to do but why and how you came to this plan of action.

Kennedy went on to say,

> Let it be clear—and this is a judgment which the Members of the Congress must finally make—let it be clear that I am asking the Congress and the country to accept a firm commitment to a new course of action, a course which will last for many years and carry very heavy costs: 531 million dollars in fiscal '62—an estimated 7 to 9 billion dollars additional over the next 5 years. If we are to go only halfway, or reduce our sights in the face of difficulty, in my judgment it would be better not to go at all. . . .
>
> It is a most important decision that we make as a nation. But all of you have lived through the last four years and have seen the significance of space and the adventures in space, and no one can predict with certainty what the ultimate meaning will be of mastery of space.

I believe we should go to the moon. But I think every citizen of this country as well as the Members of the Congress should consider the matter carefully in making their judgment, to which we have given attention over many weeks and months, because it is a heavy burden, and there is no sense in agreeing or desiring that the United States take an affirmative position in outer space, unless we are prepared to do the work and bear the burdens to make it successful. If we are not, we should decide today and this year.[179]

Kennedy let the organization know that the issue had been carefully considered and that he and his team were well aware of the enormity of the proposal. He emphasized the difficulty and the significance of what was being considered, and he continually *asked* Congress and the American people to think it through. This is a request for support and commitment, not an order. He's saying if we, as an organization, are not prepared to see it through, we need to decide that now, together. I cannot stress the importance of this concept enough. It is a conversation I have with each and every executive and leadership team considering any kind of organizational change. Running a company that already has updraft is extremely challenging, but working to change a negative culture is nothing less than excruciating, requiring the highest levels of dedication and commitment. And there is no doubt, it is better not to start at all than to start and not see it through.

Kennedy continued, turning to the issue of resources.

> This decision demands a major national commitment of scien-
> tific and technical manpower, material and facilities, and the pos-
> sibility of their diversion from other important activities where
> they are already thinly spread. It means a degree of dedication,
> organization and discipline which have not always characterized
> our research and development efforts. It means we cannot afford
> undue work stoppages, inflated costs of material or talent, wasteful
> interagency rivalries, or a high turnover of key personnel.
>
> New objectives and new money cannot solve these problems.
> They could in fact, aggravate them further—unless every sci-
> entist, every engineer, every serviceman, every technician, con-
> tractor, and civil servant gives his personal pledge that this nation
> will move forward, with the full speed of freedom, in the exciting
> adventure of space.[180]

Kennedy set expectations around the sacrifices that would have to
be made and the priorities that would need to shift. He reinforced
the fact that this undertaking would not be an easy one and that we
cannot, for one moment, lose sight of our focus. However, he never

let us forget that he sincerely believed in our ability to be successful and that each and every one of us would share in the victory.

And inspired we were. People all over the world were captivated during those 14 days in July 1969. They tuned in and made it the most-watched television event of the time. An astounding 93.9 percent of U.S. households watched over 15 hours of Apollo 11 coverage, and some 125 million viewers watched the actual moon walk.[181]

The vision puts everything we've talked about into motion. Its ability to inspire, guide, unite and mobilize makes it cardinal to creating updraft. And achieving your vision is a huge feather in your organization's cap. But a vision goes even further, helping you not only to create updraft but also to maintain it because the achievement of your vision fundamentally changes your strategic position and sets you up for the next great challenge (i.e., the next leg of your journey). Interestingly, many organizations fail here. They pursue, achieve and celebrate the realization of their vision, but then leadership fails to set a new course. The organization becomes complacent and their momentum tapers off until there isn't enough forward motion to sustain flight. In the early 1900s, for instance, Ford rose to the top position in their industry by pursuing Henry Ford's 1907 vision to "democratize the automobile." By 1924, half the cars *in the world* were Ford Model Ts. Unfortunately, leadership didn't follow through with a new vision, and by 1927, Chevrolet's annual sales passed those of Ford's.[182]

Achieving a goal of this magnitude is exciting, motivating, confidence building and addictive. Great leaders recognize that an organization that can accomplish one visionary goal can accomplish another one. And another one. And another one. The learning and development that occurs during the pursuit of Vision 1, positions us for Vision 2—and so on. Organizations that can perpetuate this process will find that they are well on their way to internalizing the concept of updraft and that they have the Holy Grail of organizational success—a sustainable, strategic advantage.

STRETCHING YOUR WINGS. . .

1. Do you see the difference between mission and vision and how important they are to updraft? Do you have a mission? If not, go back to the previous chapter—don't attempt to develop a vision without first having a mission.

2. What goals are you currently working on? Do you have any organization-wide goals (aside from sales targets)? Get a list of your organization's current goals.

3. With your mission in mind, start brainstorming about products, services, capabilities—any ideas that would make an impact on your mission. Bring these ideas, and your list from #2 above, to your leadership team to spark discussion. (Remember that the final version of your vision must be SMART. How will it be measured? How will you keep everyone up-to-date on progress?)

4. Sharing the vision with your organization should be an exciting and inspiring event. As you begin the process, start making notes about details and information you'll want to share about the destination (your vision, of course), why you've chosen this destination, the process you've used, highlights of the current situation, the challenges you'll need to overcome, and anything else you think should be communicated. Revisit Kennedy's speech to see how he did it.

CHAPTER 11:

Filing your flight plan

A rmed with a destination (i.e., a vision), most of the leaders I meet with are eager and impatient to get moving. But setting off into the wild blue yonder without examining all aspects of the journey is short-sighted and sets you up as a sitting duck—completely unprepared and easily blindsided. We discussed the fact that your vision is designed to be a quantum leap from your current position, so you cannot get there by doing what you are doing today. Understand that you are embarking on a journey over unfamiliar terrain in unknown conditions, and whether you are expecting to cruise at 4,000 feet or 40,000 feet, you are flying without a net—and it's a long way down. Even a pilot, no matter how experienced, doesn't just jump into a plane and take off. There are charts to consult, routes to map, weather to assess, equipment to inspect, calcu-lations to solve—a lot to do before they take to the skies. And just like a pilot, you've got a lot to do to ensure that your organization arrives safely at your chosen destination.

Our avian friends, in comparison, barely stop to pack a suitcase. When conditions demand it, the geese get into formation and fly, sometimes thousands of miles, to more temperate areas where there is sufficient vegetation and open water. Then, in the spring, a strong homing instinct guides them back to their nesting grounds, right to the very place where they fledged.[183] Never having found a goose in possession of a compass or GPS device, scientists are still researching how geese and other migratory birds navigate these distances so accurately. European Starlings have been shown to orient to the position of the sun, actually compensating for the sun's movement across the sky.[184] European robins respond to magnetic fields, mallard ducks find north by using the night skies, and homing pigeons utilize their sense of smell (I had no idea birds even had a sense of smell) to return home.[185] And just like we use the bank on the corner at the third traffic light, geese use landmarks like open water, cities and mountain ranges.[186]

Canadian geese begin their long migration south.

For the birds, *how* they are going to get to their destination isn't up for discussion. Their ability to fly, in combination with whatever navigational gifts Mother Nature has bestowed upon them, is their answer. For our journey, things aren't quite so straightforward. For better or worse, we have far more options. As a result, we need to take an in-depth look at everything and anything affecting our trip—both internal and external factors.

Like a pilot, we need to understand every leg of the journey we are about to embark upon so we can prepare ourselves, our crew and our equipment. While you may not have thought of it this way, this is the exercise more commonly known as strategic planning. Let's take a look at strategic planning, focusing our discussion on what the process needs to accomplish and why, and on how it contributes to the creation of updraft.

STRATEGIC PLANNING: SEEING THE BIGGER PICTURE

Several years ago, my husband and I got the ill-conceived notion that it would be fun to rent some bikes and take a ride up into the Sierra Madre while we were on vacation in beautiful Puerto Vallarta, Mexico. While we were predominantly road bikers, we made our reservation confident that our extensive riding would allow us to adapt. Navigating the buses and cobblestone streets, we made our way to the bike shop to find that one of the guides was ill and that we would be on our own. Armed with a map sketched on a scrap of paper (no, I'm not kidding) and the two bikes, we set out. We made our way over the cobblestone streets (bumpy doesn't even begin to cover it) to the outskirts of Puerto Vallarta, where we found the dirt road that would take us up into the mountains. It was quite an adventure that included streams, horses, a burro, dogs, an angry cow and her calf, several small villages and steeper and steeper switchbacks. Just literal moments before giving up, we found our destination—Rancho Las

Pilas, where we ate and rested before heading back. It was the most refreshing beer I've ever had (and I'm not a beer drinker!).

Anyway, as we headed back down the mountain, I quickly became frustrated. Gaining speed was unavoidable, and I was not feeling in control of the bike. No matter how hard I tried, I kept hitting the many rocks in the road, sliding in the dirt and down the incline. Not a pretty picture. Finally, we stopped for a water break, and I took the opportunity to think about what I could do differently. The harder I focused on avoiding the rocks, the more I headed straight for them. But when I stepped back and contemplated the path ahead of me, suddenly my perspective changed. Looking over the handlebars at the path speeding by just four feet from the ground, all I could see were the rocks, but once I stopped and saw the bigger picture, I realized what was happening. As someone who typically rides on a paved road, I could deal with rocks and other obstacles by just swerving around them; but on a dirt road I had to change my approach because there were far too many rocks and swerving didn't work out so well on the dirt. Instead, I had to take a broader view, identifying the path that took me where I wanted to go while taking into account my level of expertise, my equipment, and all the obstacles I was aware of. It took a few minutes to retrain my brain to focus on where I wanted to go rather than on what I was trying to avoid, but the remainder of the downhill was considerably more enjoyable.

This is the general idea behind strategic planning. It is making the time to escape from our operational, day-to-day view—which speeds by like the blur I saw over the handlebars—in order to step back and look at organizational issues, realities, strengths and opportunities from new and different perspectives. It is gaining an understanding of what we have, what we need, what we know and what we don't know about our chosen journey, and then using that information to select a route that stacks the deck in our favor. Just like the pilot, we need to do our homework so we can create a detailed flight plan that maps our course, complete with vectors, landmarks, airways, airports, navigational beacons, fuel and personnel requirements, alternate routes and contingency plans.

For many people, strategic planning means a day or two off-site for a group of executives—sometimes quarterly, sometimes monthly and often intermittently—despite the fact that strategic planning, like creativity, is not an event-based effort. While these sessions should be challenging, inspiring, exhausting, and just short of life-altering from an organizational perspective, they usually miss the mark. One CEO from the health-care industry was very proud to tell me about the session he and his executive team had just returned from. They started with the perfunctory continental breakfast and went through two days of exercises and discussions. The CEO felt it had been a successful outing. With his permission, I asked a few questions:

- What did you learn that you didn't know before the session began?

- When you and your team walked into the office the next day, what was different?

- Did the session contribute to strengthening and uniting the team?

- On what issue was the team most divided?

- What did the session contribute to the organization's forward motion (i.e., progress)? What are the team's next steps?

The look on his face (he looked so deflated) and our ensuing discussion told me I had made my point. He didn't have a good answer for any of my questions. His team had spent two days reviewing and discussing financials, hearing status reports from each executive, listening to a presentation about a new IT platform, and examining a handful of specific customer and personnel issues (most of which were tabled because they didn't have enough information to resolve them). The leadership team had not gotten together in over two months, so from the CEO's perspective this was a pretty productive leadership team meeting—and I wouldn't necessarily disagree. It may have been a good meeting, but it wasn't a good strategic planning meeting. Their focus was on the day-to-day; they weren't addressing issues at the strategic level (i.e., those topics that create updraft and generate progress). Most of the CEOs and leaders I meet with believe they are engaged in strategic planning—until we dive a little deeper and find that their efforts are intermittent, incomplete or inconsistent.

© MARK ANDERSON, WWW.ANDERTOONS.COM

"Not to be a wet blanket, but I'm not sure
our strategic plan should include any idea that's
'just crazy enough to work.'"

I've probably observed as many strategy sessions as I've conducted. I've seen carefully orchestrated meetings and haphazard, meandering discussions. I've seen walls covered in flipcharts and never-ending slide shows. I've watched painful silences and angry yelling matches. What I can tell you is while there is no one way to run a strategic planning session, there are a plethora of ways not to. The most common tactical error results when leaders attempt to direct and manage these meetings but are working from an incomplete understanding of the facilitation role and, as a result, have dramatically underestimated its difficulty. In addition to guiding the meeting and keeping it focused on the objectives, a facilitator plans the meeting, prepares for the meeting, readies the participants, deals with logistics, establishes the atmosphere, gets things moving, encourages participation, monitors group interaction and body language, intervenes when necessary, and is ready to introduce tools or processes if the situation arises. A good facilitator is almost unnoticed and makes it look easy. It is considerably more complicated than it appears.

While running any kind of meeting well takes planning, an outstanding strategic planning session (and, of course, the entire process) requires extensive preparation; just checking items off an agenda won't get you where you want to go. In addition, these discussions can become very emotional, exposing concerns, beliefs and issues that had previously been hidden and are best handled by an experienced facilitator. More often than not, however, CEOs and presidents compromise the power of these sessions by their insistence on running the meeting themselves. I've coached many leaders who have worked to become very good facilitators, but part of being a great facilitator is recognizing when you aren't the best choice.

Ideally, a facilitator should be impartial and objective; it is her role to observe and guide the discussion, but not to offer opinions or pass judgment. Do you want to participate in the discussions? Or do you want to be responsible for the structure and process of the meeting—guiding discussion, monitoring group dynamics and delivering content? It is a rare bird who can switch back and forth from a facilitation role to a participation role, and it is almost impossible to do when you have a vested interest and are emotionally connected to the issues. On top of that, unless the CEO or president is extremely careful, he may inadvertently intimidate people and inhibit the open, honest discussion so critical to making these sessions successful. This is not to say the top executive never facilitates sessions within the strategic planning process; they do, but they must choose those sessions carefully.

If facilitation is the top tactical mistake, then the most likely strategic error relates to the lack of a process, often due to misconceptions around what goes into strategic planning and what you should get out of it. While there is no doubt we want to stimulate and encourage deep, insightful and even potentially difficult discussions, that is not enough. A strategy session should not be an academic exercise; if all you leave with is a warm feeling that it was a productive meeting, then you've missed the mark.

At some point in your career, I'm sure you've heard a motivational speaker. As advertised, you leave the event pumped up—you're excited and ready to go. While the inspiration that the speech gave birth to may linger, many of these speeches (not all, but many) focus on attitude, outlook and self-confidence. They don't usually go so far as to prescribe specific behaviors or actions; they don't focus on the "how." You return to work recharged and energized, but you aren't really doing anything differently. Such an outcome is fine for a motivational session but not for a strategy session. Yes, your organization needs inspiration, and while inspiration may provide some much needed thrust, it alone does not ensure long-term engagement or the creation of updraft. The strategic planning you do needs to provide the guidance your organization is seeking in the form of objectives, goals and action items that lead to the attainment of your vision. It answers questions related to heading, destination, routes, navigational cues, timelines and resources—all the information required to fill out your flight plan. And the best way to ensure you get everything you need from the session is to use a process (your own or someone else's).

HOLD THE PROCESS TOGETHER WITH T.A.P.E.™

Successful strategic planning is contingent on the ability to make good decisions, which, in turn, depend on thoroughly examining all those issues that are relevant to your understanding of where you are, where you are going and how you'd like to get there. In other words, the strategic planning process is the leadership team's flight plan for creating the organization's flight plan. I think the phrase "strategic planning" encourages people to put too much emphasis on planning and not enough on strategic. Having a process helps you resist the temptation to circumnavigate the strategic components and head straight to the planning phase.

A strategic planning process needs to contain four stages:

Strategic Planning Process

Thinking → Alignment → Planning → Execution

Strategic thinking leads to *strategic alignment,* putting us all on the same page for the actual *strategic planning,* which we then accomplish through *strategic execution.*

Step 1: *Strategic Thinking*

Strategic thinking is the most underrated part of the process, and yet it is foundational for everything that follows. Remember back in Chapter 1 when you were going to paint the living room? No matter how carefully you work or how expensive your tools, you will not be able to conceal cracks, holes, nail pops or badly taped drywall seams by painting over them. The preparation phase takes the longest but has a tremendous impact on the final product. And try as you might, going back to address those issues after the fact doesn't really work. It creates still more work and won't result in the smooth, quality finish you want. The time you take up front in the preparation stage pays off handsomely when you stand back to admire your work. Without a genuine commitment to strategic thinking, the rest of the process will not be smooth, and the results will not benefit the organization.

Creating and developing strategic thinking sessions can be quite challenging (another reason not to do it yourself unless you have expertise, or at least guidance, in this area). Although the specific components of your organization's strategic thinking sessions should be targeted to the issues within your organization, discussions often include the following:

• Vision	• Sales breakdown and analysis
• Mission	• Departmental updates
• Values	• Current situation analysis
• Executive team history	• Stages of Growth X-Ray™
• Business model	• Company history
• Competitors	• SWOT analysis
• Assumptions and beliefs	• Employee input and interviews
• Core competencies analysis	• Personnel
• Customer input and interviews	• Culture
• Vendor and partner input and interviews	• Communication issues

Stages of Growth X-Ray™ is a licensed program of FlashPoint! LLC. And: The 7 Stages of Growth is based on research conducted by James Fischer.

I mentioned earlier that part of a facilitator's job is to set the agenda, choosing the appropriate tools and processes for the situation. For instance, when I hear indications that a leadership team may not be focusing on the same priorities, I consider several options, often recommending something called a Stages of Growth X-Ray™, which helps a company understand where it is today, why it is experiencing certain issues, and how it can manage and even predict its growing pains. I rely on this particular tool for its assistance in opening the lines of communication, spurring discussion, providing a common language and ultimately helping the group understand what they, as an organization, are experiencing. Choosing the appropriate tool, however, can be harder than it seems. One client has contacted me on three different occasions for a DISC-based team session. Each time, he had a specific reason for requesting that particular session, but further discussion revealed underlying issues that would not have been addressed by that program.

While I personally enjoy the entire strategic planning process, the strategic thinking component tends to be my favorite. As the barriers begin to come down, the discussions reach levels of honesty and openness that were previously unattainable. Finally willing and able to talk turkey, the group explores issues like never before. As insights, perceptions and truths are shared, people begin to see and appreciate each other's strengths, inspiring trust and respect. Right before my eyes, the group begins to coalesce and takes the first steps toward functioning like a team. This development alone is worth the price of admission. For groups that have not historically played well together, and even for those who have, this step can be a turning point, getting issues and emotions out in the open—often for the very first time.

This spirit of collaboration, cooperation and support isn't just a welcome by-product of strategic thinking. A strong, healthy, productive executive team is a prerequisite for a strong, healthy, productive organization. While the quality of leadership at your organization may start with you, it certainly doesn't end there, and everything we've discussed about how you impact updraft (Part I) goes for your leadership team as well. Your team is either creating updraft for each other and lifting each other up—along with the rest of the organization—or they are dragging each other down—along with the rest of the organization (remember what happens to the birds flying behind them). Of course, a complete transformation is not going to happen overnight (far from it). But like a phoenix rising from the ashes, you will see glimpses of your team's true potential. Shifting their focus to the bigger picture begins uniting the team and encouraging the cooperation and collaboration that creates updraft. Organizations that resist investing in this process have not experienced its true power.

Not surprisingly, even leaders who recognize and appreciate the importance of this step tend to underestimate the time required for it, especially if this is the first time they are going through a bona fide strategic planning process. Needless to say, the strategic thinking phase cannot be rushed and is often the longest part of the process; in order to get a generous return, you'll have to invest time, money and patience into this endeavor.

> **A strong, healthy, productive executive team is a prerequisite for a strong, healthy, productive organization.**

Step 2: Strategic Alignment

Something else happens as a result of all the discussion, analysis and debate that characterizes strategic thinking. You've probably heard the parable about the blind men who were intrigued by the descriptions of an elephant and wanted to experience one for themselves. The details vary (anywhere from three to seven blind men), but the basic story is the same.[187] When the men finally encountered an elephant, one man touched the elephant's trunk and declared it was like a snake, another touched the elephant's leg and thought the animal like a tree, and still another touched its tusk and likened it to a spear. As they shared their individual observations, argument ensued as they became more and more adamant that their experience was the right one.

Blind Men and the Elephant

Like the blind men, each person on your executive team experiences the organization differently because they touch different parts of it, in different ways and from different perspectives. While the blind men could turn to a sighted person for assistance reconciling their seemingly incongruous impressions, there is no one person who can give your team the "right" answer about your organization. Each person's perceptions and observations are valid. It's not a matter of right and wrong; it's a question of how the pieces fit together so all of you are working with as accurate a picture as possible. It's like each person has a piece of the puzzle but you need to work together to figure out what the final image looks like. And, of course, unlike the very tangible elephant, the very thing *you* are trying to envision (your organization) is about as nebulous as it gets.

Little by little, the team absorbs and assimilates all this incoming information. This is not to say we have 100 percent agreement on every issue; that is not necessary. What does develop is a shared understanding of the organization, its people, strengths, issues, opportunities and so on. As a group, we recognize where we are, where we've been and where we're heading. So, in addition to strengthening the team and providing us with a more honest, objective view of the organization, strategic thinking has led us to the next step in the process—strategic alignment. Remember, in order to create updraft, we need to fly in formation. And to fly in formation, we need, quite literally, to get all our ducks in a row. This part of the process contributes greatly to the aerodynamics of your organization by getting your executive team into formation. Once there, they are positioned to create a powerful updraft for themselves and each other, as well as for all the geese that follow.

"Face it, we're never going to reach a consensus."

I mentioned that strategic planning is not a one-time event but an ongoing process. During the first iteration, a big part of the process often includes the development of the vision, but once that is established, many leaders figure all the significant issues have been thoroughly discussed and don't need to be reexamined. While it might be nice if the world would slow down for even a moment, it isn't likely. Although subsequent sessions will not be a duplication of the first, it is important to touch on both the things that change as well as those that don't. We have to monitor progress while still challenging our assumptions and incorporating new information so we can adjust our flight plan accordingly. A flight plan is not a static document. It can't be. There are too many changeable variables. Certainly anything related to atmospheric conditions can't be reliably predicted—weather, visibility and air density—but there are also things like TFRs (Temporary Flight Restrictions), which can change at a moment's notice. As a result, pilots are encouraged to check and recheck just about everything before takeoff and while en route. If, for example, Air Force One decides to make an unscheduled stop, the fact the TFR wasn't in effect when you created the flight plan will be of little consolation when you are being escorted by a couple of F-16s. What was true the last time we met might not be true today, regardless of whether that was a day, a week or a month ago.

Step 3: Strategic Planning

Now, finally, you move to the actual strategic planning phase that you've been so anxious to begin. But even this part of the process may not be what you are anticipating. Ironically, I find once the emphasis shifts to the planning stage, many of these sessions end far too soon, despite the leader's eagerness to get to this step. Strategic planning isn't just deciding where you are heading or even what your destination is. Think back to our automotive services company, and for just a moment, let's increase their size to 30 people and mandate that not everyone was at the strategic planning sessions (which would be the case at the vast majority of organizations). Now imagine you work there and you just left a meeting where the owner unveiled the new vision "to fully service hybrid vehicles within 18 months," and then sent everybody back to work. What do you do differently now that you have that knowledge? How does that pronouncement affect your day? The answer is, it doesn't. Going back to your organization with a big-picture, bird's-eye view won't produce the flurry of activity you want. It is far too abstract and theoretical.

So now, it is time to begin the actual planning. You've figured out where you are going; it's time to figure out how you are going to get there. In order to affect engagement and create the lift required for updraft, the strategic plan needs to be actionable. It needs to be broken down until divisions and departments and individuals understand not only our heading and destination, but how we will get there and what part they will play. But you need to do that without micromanaging. You need to focus their collective efforts but do it without crushing initiative and engagement. As General George Patton said, "Never tell people how to do things. Tell them what to do, and they will surprise you with their ingenuity."[188] And that's exactly what we want to do. At the highest levels, the planning phase of strategic planning is about clarifying the strategic objectives (and possibly the strategic goals— more on this in just a moment) and then bringing in the rest of the organization. Note that the leadership team will not necessarily do all of the actual planning. It is at this point we get others involved, if we haven't already.

Strategic objectives act as a bridge between your vision and your strategic goals. They outline what needs to be done. Essentially, they are the major undertakings that will be necessary for the achievement of the vision. They identify, very broadly, what needs to be accomplished, and they are an important intermediate step, helping us convert the big picture into actionable items. Notice, however, they do not dictate "how" to achieve the objectives, just what they are. We want to direct action but leave a high degree of flexibility in order to encourage initiative, creativity and updraft.

> **The strategic plan should direct action but leave a high degree of flexibility in order to encourage initiative, creativity and updraft.**

Strategic objectives, however, are still too expansive to drive daily actions, so they need to be broken down even further into strategic goals. (Notice we've moved back to the word "goal," indicating that they need to be SMART in order to be of use.) Strategic goals are the component parts of the strategic objective and bring with them all the benefits that goals provide. They are smaller in scope but are not necessarily small. Then, the next step, operational goals, brings us into the project management arena, where these operational goals will be broken down into goals and possibly several layers of subgoals. At this point, we've got discrete, individual action items that can be incorporated into a person's daily plan.

So, what does this process look like? What it looks like can vary dramatically from organization to organization depending on several variables including its size, Stage of Growth™, current levels of updraft, history, experience with such an endeavor, and communication up until now. Earlier, I mentioned that the leadership team doesn't do all the work in the planning phase. Generally, they are responsible for the vision, and once that has been established, others can be brought in at any time. Some executive teams want additional input while they are working on the vision and some go so far as to create the strategic objectives themselves and then present everything to the organization. (Note that some level of communication with the broader organization should be occurring all the while.) Sometimes, we'll have a kickoff once the vision has been established in order to generate excitement. We'll ask the organization to start thinking about what will need to be done, making sure the lines of communication are wide open, and we'll incorporate those thoughts into the creation of the strategic objectives. However, once we start talking about strategic goals and operational goals, the entire organization must be involved. At this point, we want those who are doing the work to be involved in the planning.

STRATEGIC OBJECTIVES, STRATEGIC GOALS AND OPERATIONAL GOALS Branta Automotive Services			
MISSION	To keep people mobile		
VISION	In 18 months, to be fully servicing hybrid vehicles		
STRATEGIC OBJECTIVE #1		**STRATEGIC OBJECTIVE #2**	**STRATEGIC OBJECTIVE #3**
Acquire and set up equipment for repairing and maintaining hybrid vehicles. ↓		Get mechanics certified. ↓	Publicize new capabilities. ↓
STRATEGIC GOAL #1.1	**STRATEGIC GOAL #1.2**	**STRATEGIC GOAL #2.1**	**STRATEGIC GOAL #3.1**
Acquire the equipment (7 months) ↓	Set up the equipment (12 months) ↓	Arrange for training (15 months) ↓	Launch marketing program (15 months) ↓
OPERATIONAL GOALS			
1. Research vendors and equipment (3 months) 2. Analyze financing options and financial impact (3 months) 3. Purchase equipment (7 months) – MILESTONE	1. Design new floor plan (5 months) 2. Consult with electrician (7 months) 3. Rearrange equipment (9 months) 4. Take delivery (10 months) 5. Equipment is ready for use (12 months) - MILESTONE	1. Research training options (2 months) 2. Work out employee/ employer training agreement (3 months) 3. Register for courses and schedule absences (4 months) 4. Take courses (15 months) 5. Each certification MILESTONE	1. Meet with marketing consultant (9 months) 2. Approve program (10 months) 3. Launch marketing program (15 months)

ADDITIONAL CONSIDERATIONS

There are a few additional issues that tend to be overlooked but should be a part of the planning phase.

- **Communication:** Canada geese use the same wintering grounds, breeding grounds and stopover sites year after year after year. They are quite unusual, however, in that mom, dad and the kids stay together for up to a year and continue to migrate in family groups. As a result, researchers have hypothesized that the young learn the navigational routes from their parents and/or grandparents.

In similar fashion, you and your team must decide how you will communicate the details of the journey to the entire flock, ensuring the information reaches everyone in your organization. We talked earlier about how essential communication is to creating an environment that supports engagement and updraft. Part of the strategic planning process must include the development of a communication plan designed to get the information into every corner of the organization. Every person needs to understand the "big picture" but also the "whys" and "hows" of the plan. This is important not just for updraft but for the success of the journey. It's no coincidence that communication increases to a frenzy just before a gaggle of geese takes to the sky.

And while geese are known for their orderly v-formations, on the other end of the spectrum are starlings, famous for their murmurations. A beautiful and awe-inspiring sight, a starling murmuration can consist of several dozen to over a million birds that appear to swoop, veer and turn simultaneously, prompting thoughts of avian ESP. While often unnoticed, a falcon or other bird of prey is typically nearby,[189] serving as the murmuration's dance partner. As Grainger Hunt explains, the movements and gyrations of the flock result as each starling "strives to place others between itself and the falcon.... The whole display is a grand interaction of predator and prey."[190] These birds of a feather flock together because for them, there truly is safety in numbers.

While a mesmerizing spectacle, it is the level of coordination and synchronicity of movement that has both amazed and puzzled scientists. I'm sure you remember the game Operator or Telephone where one person whispers a word or phrase to another and it continues down the line until the last person delivers the final, usually funny message, out loud to the group. What started as "my old Corvette has brand-new wheels," turns into "my hovercraft is full of eels."[191] What researchers have discovered is that starlings are masters of this game, able to disseminate information to every member of the flock, almost instantaneously, without compromising the integrity of the message.[192] The flock's survival depends on its ability not only to detect predators but also to alert the flock so it can react immediately.

Similarly, every member of your flock needs to be in the crow's nest, on the lookout for obstacles, issues, opportunities, and predators (competitors). However, they can only do this effectively if they are aware of the situation as well as the plan and, like the starlings, are equipped with a mechanism for quickly and easily transmitting that information back through the flock. In the same way your ability to develop a great strategic plan depends on timely, accurate and objective information, so too does your ability to execute that plan. Conditions change and your people are often in a position to see and hear things before you do. You must have a plan that not only gets information out but also ensures that it is getting back to you.

- **Milestones:** We mentioned earlier that geese find their way using a combination of tools, often using landmarks as navigational cues. Waterfowl have been observed making sharp, sudden turns as they approach rivers, cities and bodies of water.[193] Incorporating milestones into our route is essential because they aid in the translation from strategic to operational, but maybe more importantly, they lend a degree of "tangibility." Milestones make it easier for people to track and see progress (something we already know to be related to engagement), and they typically mark the achievement of a major stepping stone, fueling excitement and giving people a reason to cheer.

  If you look back at the list of strategic objectives, strategic goals and operational goals for Branta Automotive Services on page 240, you'll notice several milestones are identified: the purchase of the equipment at 7 months, the installation of the equipment at 12 months, and the ongoing certifications. These milestones encourage the creation of updraft by keeping people inspired and energized and by providing reasons to celebrate while we're still en route.

- **Resources:** During especially cold winters you may see geese resting at creeks and streams even though they prefer open water like ponds and lakes. Responsible for providing the resources needed by the flock, the lead bird has had to adjust his plan in order to make sure the flock has what it needs to make the trip successfully. Ensuring the organization has what it needs is a critical part of leadership's job, so you and your team must address issues proactively and continue to monitor this issue once the journey has begun. A bird with insufficient resources won't be able to keep up with the flock, won't have the energy to make the trip, and won't have the strength to create updraft.

- **Contingencies:** Migration distances vary drastically from the record-setting 44,000-mile trip taken by the arctic tern[194] to the Canada geese's more typical 2,000- to 3,000-mile flight. To prepare for such a trip, migrating birds enter hyperphagia, a period of excessive eating where they increase their body weight by 20 to 50 percent, storing fat to be used as the energy for their journey. While the bar-tailed godwit wins the prize for longest *nonstop* flight, logging an amazing 7,100 miles in 9 days,[195] most birds stop en route to rest and eat. But what if a cold snap has frozen the water at their usual stopover site or a field of crops has been converted into an urgently needed mini-mall? Hyperphagia provides the extra resources that allow the birds to adapt when weather, terrain or other conditions force them to change course.

  While you may have planned your course as the crow flies, you too need to be prepared for obstacles that force you to alter your plans. Of course, you won't be able to prepare for every situation, but taking the time to consider these issues allows you, as an organization, to react quickly and intelligently when conditions threaten to take you off course. (This is yet another place where your organization may astound you with their forethought and analysis.)

- **Reality checks:** In some areas, people have begun to wonder why they are seeing Canada geese year-round, and the answer, it turns out, is quite simple. Geese migrate because as temperatures drop, food sources become scarce and water freezes. As this occurs, geese families take to the skies and head south to their chosen destination in search of food and water. However, changing weather patterns have sometimes resulted in warmer than normal temperatures, leaving water and food available throughout the winter season. The geese recognize this and determine that they don't need to leave. You and your team can't be so enamored with your plan that you ignore updates and incoming information. Putting blinders on now is just as dangerous as wearing them during the strategic thinking phase.

by HAGEN

So I said to myself: Fred, you have Pay-TV, CDs, DVDs, a VCR, Computer Games, no need to go South this winter...

Remember Henry Ford and the Model T? We talked about the fact that while Ford achieved its vision to "democratize the automobile," a new vision was not established. Henry Ford, it turns out, was so attached to the Model T that he refused to make any changes despite input the industry was changing. Customers were becoming more sophisticated, looking for styling and other options, something his staff recognized even if he wasn't willing to. In fact, "once, while [Ford]...was away on vacation, employees built an updated Model T and surprised him with it on his return. Ford responded by kicking in the windshield and stomping on the roof."[196] You must be constantly reevaluating and reassessing the situation (remember our discussion about the dangers of the ivory tower) to ensure that your route is still the right one for the organization. The goal isn't to follow the flight plan no matter what, but to arrive safely at the chosen destination.

Step 4: Strategic Execution

I know by this point, the team is eager to fly the coop, but before you can *move* into the next phase of your strategic planning, you need to *discuss* the next phase—execution—to ensure the strategic execution phase doesn't turn into a wild goose chase. So often, strategic planning efforts become discrete, isolated events. But as we said, strategic planning is not a one-time session, nor should it be an academic exercise. Part of the planning phase must include a discussion of the execution phase, addressing, at the very least, issues like what the next steps are, how often the leadership team will meet, how information is to be shared and other logistical issues. You know how easily day-to-day and operational issues insinuate themselves, quickly eroding focus and threatening momentum. Making this a part of your process is a commitment to making something happen—like the difference between "yeah, I'll call you" and "let's put something on the calendar right now." Taking off on a wing and a prayer leaves too many issues to chance, making your strategic plan as vulnerable as a clay pigeon just waiting to be shot out of the sky.

Finally, congratulations are in order. You and your team have accomplished a lot, and it is important to acknowledge and celebrate that. But before you start strutting around like the cat that swallowed the canary, remember—all this work just gets you to the starting gate. There's a whole lot to be done. Unfortunately, having a brilliant, well-thought-out strategy guarantees you absolutely nothing if you can't deliver on it. The reality is that most strategic initiatives lay an egg. Strategic plans fail more often than they succeed with a failure rate estimated to be in the 70 to 90 percent range. While we've already touched on a whole host of reasons for that (i.e., no process, unsuitable facilitator, insufficient resources, lack of honesty and/or objectivity, etc.), there are two reasons I see most often. First is an unrealistic expectation of how quickly progress should be made—especially in organizations lacking updraft. Just announcing our destination doesn't make it happen without all the other factors we've discussed. And second is a lack of commitment and accountability from the very people who developed the plan—leadership. It is at this point everything we've talked about comes together and leadership either earns its wings or falls out of the sky.

STRETCHING YOUR WINGS...

1. What do you see as the purpose of strategic planning? Have your past efforts been fruitful?

2. How long ago was your last strategic session? And the one before that? Were these truly strategic planning sessions, or were they executive meetings focusing on status and updates?

3. Think about your most recent off-site sessions. What did they emphasize? What process did you use? What did you get out of them? What did they contribute to the organization's journey? Lead a discussion with your leadership team to find out what they thought about these sessions.

4. What phase of the process have your sessions typically focused on—Thinking, Alignment, Planning or Execution? Think about those aspects that your process doesn't address. Start researching strategic planning processes and/or consultants, find one you connect with and get the process moving.

5. Don't wait. Change the focus of your leadership team meetings from the day-to-day to more strategic topics. Work on your facilitation skills, encouraging and guiding the conversation but not monopolizing it.

CHAPTER 12:

Sustaining the wind beneath their wings

Execution at the leadership level is complex and challenging—but then, you already knew that. It requires constant, unwavering attention to all the ideas we've discussed. It is where integrity, strategy, vision, mission, people and culture all come together. What you do on a daily basis matters far more than you realize; and yet, we know from the research that leaders are not focusing on those issues and behaviors most critical to updraft and engagement.[197] Earlier, we defined leadership as the ability to supercharge the organization's most important asset—its people. And to do that, we said leadership needs to address resources, culture and direction. While just three words, these terms encompass a broad array of issues we now know to be essential for updraft. At this point, however, it might be more accurate to say that your job, leadership's job, is to supercharge the organization's most important asset by focusing on those factors affecting the creation of updraft at both the individual and the organizational level. By doing so, you inject the positive leadership energy that supercharges your entire organization, stimulating the creation of updraft in every corner.

Back in Chapter 1, we discussed the aerodynamics of the v-formation. We talked about how the lead bird has the hardest job because he is flying into undisturbed air and taking the brunt of the headwind. But in all the time I've worked with leaders, I've never had one complain about having to work hard. Frustrated with results? Yes. Disappointed with performance? Yes. Annoyed with the lack of progress? Most definitely. Earlier, we talked about how most leaders are spending too much time in the wrong places and on the wrong issues, acting more like my rear-wheel drive Nissan 200SX than the front-wheel drive Acura Integra. But when you put your energy in the right places, shifting your focus to the creation of updraft, you will see progress like you've never seen before. This change will not make your job easier, but then I never said creating updraft through great leadership was easy. (You can go back and check. I'll wait.) I said it was extremely fulfilling and worth the effort—but definitely not easy. Allow me to illustrate.

IF YOU CAN'T STAND THE HEAT...

Have you ever watched a chef oversee the preparation and serving of a meal? I have, and it is one of the most organized and chaotic events you'll ever witness. Several years ago, I had the opportunity to observe the kitchen while Chef Michael Salmon[198] of The Hartstone Inn, Camden, Maine, prepared dinner at the James Beard House in New York City for 80 guests. The James Beard Foundation is a nonprofit whose "mission is to celebrate, nurture, and honor America's diverse culinary heritage through programs that educate and inspire."[199] Their events are designed to "educate people about American cuisine and to support and promote the chefs and other industry professionals." (If you get the opportunity to attend an event, go!) An invitation to cook at the James Beard House is quite an honor, so Chef Salmon was accompanied by nine top-flight assistants, a menu designed to encourage Maine tourism, and the meat from 240 lobsters.

The main section of the kitchen at the James Beard House[200] is about ten feet by seventeen feet, smaller than the average one-car garage. Along the left side are cabinets with all kinds of dishes, and on the right, pots, pans, additional countertop space and a sink. In the middle of the room is a large u-shaped counter with the horizontal base of the "u" running parallel to the left wall and centered about 2 feet from the wall. The far vertical section of the "u" is counter space, and there is a stovetop on the other vertical section. Additional freezers, ovens, ranges and refrigerators are in nearby areas.

Chef Salmon began by bringing everyone together around the counter, reviewing the menu and addressing any questions. Then, he handed out assignments, and the group turned into a blur of white coats, retrieving equipment and ingredients. One person began working on the cucumber and dill panini while another started on the Riesling poached Maine lobster tails it would be served with. Another mixed up the spicy lemon aioli that would be needed for one of the four passed hors d'oeuvres. And yet another started on the Maine lobster and scallop timbale that would be part of the first of five dinner courses. (Hungry yet?) As they weaved back and forth around the kitchen, it looked like a choreographed dance with the cooks using trays, hot pans and stacks of dishes as partners.

Chef Salmon never stopped moving. One moment he was scanning the room to see what everyone was doing, the next creating his special sauce at the stove, the next reminding someone that the Parmigiano-Reggiano crisps should come out of the oven in 10 minutes, and the next tasting and discussing the Smoked Tomato Confit with the cook making it. He continually moved around the kitchen, not only checking on what was being done but also on how it was done. He used some of the most amazing project management skills to plan, delegate and

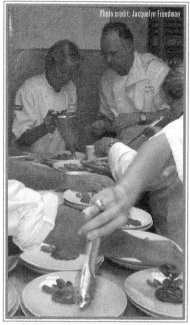

Chef Michael Salmon at the James Beard House

monitor progress, ensuring everything was prepared perfectly and ready at the proper time. And while all of this was going on, he was providing guidance and creating teaching moments as the opportunity arose. At every moment, Chef Salmon knew the status of every single component of the meal, what still needed to be done, and how much time was left. Then, when it came time to plate the dish, the chef was right there demonstrating how it should be done, helping out, and ensuring that every single dish leaving the kitchen conformed to his vision and quality standards. And he wasn't finished until he got feedback from the diners, made sure that everything was put away and that the kitchen was clean and ready for the next event.

Think about that within the context of execution. Before Chef Salmon stepped into the kitchen, he chose the menu (direction), procured the appropriate ingredients, and recruited some of the most talented people he knew (resources). Once the evening began, he was involved in overseeing the production of the product and its delivery, reinforcing and upholding his standards and values (culture) and using the experience to further develop the staff. On top of that, his evening wasn't over until he had been in touch with his "clients," either directly ("How was everything tonight?") or through his staff, to understand how the meal was received. This is Execution with a capital "E," and it only just begins to illustrate how complex and challenging execution is. Just like Chef Salmon, you need to focus on those areas responsible for achieving milestones along the strategic path while simultaneously ensuring that updraft is occurring in all departments, in all areas and for all people.

So, how can you possibly do all that? Well, notice where the chef is: he's right smack in the middle of the action, not in his office. In Japanese, the term *gemba* means "the real place"[201] and refers to the place where things are happening. You need to see things first-hand, and to do that, you need to "go where the action is." In business, *gemba* typically refers to where the work is done or where the value stream is created. The continuous improvement and quality control field has embraced the concept of *gemba* and uses expressions like "walking *gemba*" or "going to *gemba*." Stories abound regarding Taiichi Ohno, Toyota's Vice President of Manufacturing and the man behind the Toyota Production System, who taught his engineers how to observe by making them stand in a chalk circle on the manufacturing floor (*gemba*) and take notes about what they saw.[202] What an amazing and powerful lesson for both leadership and management: the only reliable way to know what is going on inside your organization is to see it and experience it firsthand. Can we say with any confidence that a restaurateur who doesn't spend time in the kitchen really knows what is going on in his restaurant? What about an hotelier who doesn't visit the front desk or hasn't walked into a guest room? Ten minutes in *gemba* beats ten years in the office any day.

L-GEMBA

Your reasons for going to *gemba*, however, are a bit different from those of the engineers or even your managers, as their responsibilities are more focused on their functional areas or on specific processes or problems. Everything you do in leadership *gemba* (let's call this *L-gemba* just to differentiate it from the definition used in manufacturing and continuous improvement) should be related to seeing, with your own eyes, anything and everything that is relevant to updraft.

- Is updraft being created? What is getting in the way of its creation?

- Are we living our values?

- Is progress being made on our vision and goals?

- Are the "right" messages reaching every single person?

- Do people have what they need?

- Are people excited about their work and their contribution?

- Are managers and executives doing the things that matter most?

Like the engineers, you are in *L-gemba* to study your organization. But unlike them, you are not restricted to a chalk circle. In fact, if your presence is somewhat unusual, just showing up and standing around watching will probably make people rather uncomfortable until they understand what you are trying to accomplish. Instead, using your time in *L-gemba* to its fullest advantage has you walking around and covering as much territory as possible. Once inside *L-gemba*, you must remember that your job is leadership. Execution comes not from your direct participation in the work being done, but from the updraft created by your presence. While a manager's job is to get operationally involved, your job in *L-gemba* is to observe and get feedback (although that is not to say a manager won't or shouldn't do these things as well). During your visits you are touching base and checking in with individuals at all levels of the organization, encouraging them to chat with you and listening to what they have to say. You are checking on progress and providing support and encouragement. You are welcoming a new employee and thanking someone for his or her recent suggestion. And you are using your keen powers of observation to make sure you are aware of the realities of your organization.

When you are in *L-gemba*, the challenge is striking the right balance. I accompanied one leader as he walked through his building, nodding and saying hello to people, but he was not really seeing what was in front of him. He was oblivious to the three or four people trying to get his attention, didn't notice the person "fighting" with the printer, missed the abject look of frustration on another's face, and passed by two people who immediately averted their eyes and hid behind their computers. While the intention was sincere, the execution was incomplete; there was a lot there to learn, and our discussion revealed he

> **Execution comes not from your direct participation in the work being done, but from the updraft created by your presence.**

had missed pretty much all of it. On the other end of the spectrum, another leader made it a point to stop at almost every desk in our path, asking specific questions about what the person was working on. Rather than exuding support and inviting interaction, he was being perceived as an unwelcome interruption. His approach was more akin to micromanaging and was obviously making people tense and uncomfortable.

The good news is that observing, like listening, can be practiced and learned. In fact, the most important condition for being a skillful observer is the same one you need for being a good listener: being fully present. In other words, you need to slow down and give the effort your complete attention. If you allow your mind to wander while you are observing, you won't see what is right in front of you in much the same way that extraneous thoughts can lead you to "tune out" when someone is speaking with you. In addition, it isn't possible to see the little things—how someone's demeanor has changed or the way two people are interacting—if you race through *L-gemba*.

While something may hit you right between the eyes, keep in mind that vision or sight actually occurs in your brain, which processes and sorts an astounding amount of information. Physically, "neurons devoted to visual processing...take up about 30 percent of the cortex, as compared with 8 percent for touch and just 3 percent for hearing. Each of the two optic nerves, which carry signals from the retina to the brain, consists of a million fibers; each auditory nerve carries a mere 30,000."[203] To process all that information, the brain automatically filters out anything it deems irrelevant or unnecessary. However, careful observation is all about retraining your brain to pay attention to those details it might have previously disregarded. When you begin "listening with your eyes," pay special attention to body language, group dynamics, and the general feeling or mood of the place—these tell you volumes, making them a great place to start.

- Do people look happy and relaxed?

- Are they comfortable in the space?

- Is anything or anybody out of place?

- What kind of energy fills the building?

- Do you see evidence of teamwork and collaboration?

Be sure to let go of your own perceptions of how things are and focus on seeing what is in front of you. Use this general information to guide your inquiries. Someone seems frustrated and unhappy? *Approach them, or talk with their immediate manager to find out more about the person's history and whether the manager is aware of anything that has changed either personally or professionally. Have the manager talk with the person to see what has been going on and how "we" can help.* Notice an executive whose conversations quickly escalate to anger? *Make a note to pull them aside, check on how things are going, and remind them of the organization's values and of how people are to be treated.* Watching a production manager and a few of his people who seem to be struggling to get a machine online? *Speak with them to find out what is going on, and make sure they have what they need.* The more time you spend observing, the more you will learn about your organization and what is interfering with the creation of updraft.

In addition, because you spend time in *L-gemba*, you will know months (years?) before the scheduled launch that R&D is having issues with the development of "brilliant widget #1," a new product which is key to attaining your vision. Or that customer service is struggling to reach their customer satisfaction metrics due to technology issues which are out of their control. Or that morale in a department seems to have slipped since the hiring of a new department head. Execution, from the leadership perspective, is ensuring that the organization's strategy is being appropriately translated into daily activities. It is constantly assessing the organization's abilities and its alignment to its vision, mission, goals and values; and then, it is stepping in to provide guidance or resources, when necessary. And on top of all that, it is making sure updraft is being created throughout the organization.

Understanding where *L-gemba* is today supercharges your effectiveness, clarifying your priorities and indicating where your valuable time needs to be spent. Determining *L-gemba* requires that you have an operational mindset guided by your strategic vision. Operationally, you need to consider those areas related to the organization's core processes. But you also need to consider those places where the bulk of the organization's current strategic efforts are taking place. For Chef Salmon, the choice is relatively straightforward—the vast majority of the time, *L-gemba* will be the kitchen. Similarly, for the owner of Branta Automotive Services, *L-gemba* will usually be the garage floor where he can 1) provide guidance, support and instruction, 2) check on how the design for the new floor plan is coming and keep tabs on other activities related to the vision, 3) attend to his own work, and 4) monitor the factors that create updraft.

Unfortunately, the more functional areas and responsibilities your job includes, the more challenging it will be to identify *L-gemba*, especially if you don't have the benefit of a well-crafted vision and mission to focus your efforts. For instance, let's say you are the Director of Research and Development back at Catbird Industries, our designer and manufacturer of cat-related products. As such, *L-gemba* is most likely in the product development area, where you would look in on the design, fabrication and prototyping of potential new products, paying particular attention to any product or development efforts that support the current vision. Your excellent work results in a promotion to Director of Manufacturing, which encompasses both product development and production, forcing you to reevaluate *L-gemba*. Since product development is operating well and you know it so thoroughly, you might initially designate the manufacturing floor as *L-gemba*, being sure to investigate the status of any strategic objectives, strategic goals and operational goals that are linked to manufacturing. Then, once you have a more complete understanding of manufacturing, you might expand *L-gemba* to encompass the design lab and the manufacturing floor.

Your hard work pays off, once again, and you find yourself moving into the Vice President of Operations' office. Now you are accountable not only for product development and manufacturing but for shipping, receiving, procurement and customer service. While your responsibilities have increased, the length of a day has not, which is why it is so important to reassess *L-gemba* every time your role changes. Before you do so, however, you will need to gather information regarding the following:

- The current and historical performance of the area.

- Any problems or issues as well as achievements.

- The strength of the managers and supervisors.

- The degree to which updraft is being generated.

- The people in those areas.

- The status of any strategic objectives, strategic goals and operational goals.

Only once you have a thorough understanding of what kind and how much attention each area needs can you determine where *L-gemba* should be.

But don't make the mistake of trying to pigeonhole *L-gemba*. A problem in shipping or a new department manager may require you to extend *L-gemba* to include that area temporarily. As things change, *L-gemba* will shift, expand and contract. Time constraints and other commitments require you to make deliberate and conscious choices about where you spend your time. By prioritizing and focusing efforts on vision-related activities and those areas in need of attention, you will have the greatest impact on your company's progress and success.

But what about the rest of the organization? The reality is while the entire organization needs constant, daily attention, the leader must be able to rely on his leadership team to be monitoring, guiding and supporting those areas which are currently not in *L-gemba*. Having said that, great leaders will create opportunities to check in on these other areas—in person. For instance, rather than request information or answer a question by email or phone, she may take a walk, enabling her to keep tabs on areas that are not top priority at the moment. "Walking around is how I learn what's really happening in my company, what's working and what's not. It can take a long time for an issue to work its way up a company, but if I'm saying hi and asking people how they're doing, they volunteer the information I need to know,"[204] explains Steve Grubbs, CEO of Victory Enterprises. Great leaders create opportunities that allow them to "be present" throughout the organization. People like to know they matter, and nothing says "you are important" more than a personal visit from leadership. (By the way, having people come to you, even with a heartfelt and welcoming open-door policy, doesn't send the same message.)

> **People like to know they matter, and nothing says "you are important" more than a personal visit from leadership.**

THE EXTERNAL SHIFT

It would be great if our discussion of execution could end here, as you already have plenty to juggle, but so far we've focused on the leader's internal responsibilities. More than anyone else, however, leaders must be aware of what's going on outside their organization as well as what's going on inside. Their responsibilities extend to keeping abreast of industry, market and competitive trends, dealing with board members, clients, bankers and other stakeholders, and representing the company and all it stands for. It is a delicate and difficult balancing act, requiring leaders to move seamlessly from one environment to the other. I refer to this as the Cetacean cycle (after all, leadership is a whale of a job—sorry, couldn't resist), requiring that *we* move from one environment to another, temporarily diving out of the sky, like the northern gannet, into a marine environment.

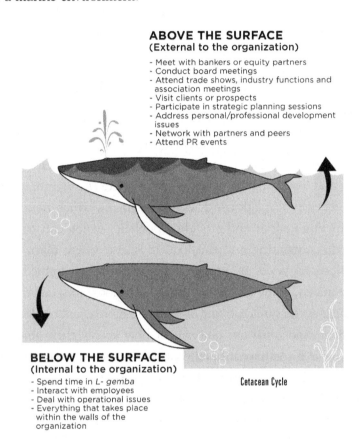

ABOVE THE SURFACE
(External to the organization)

- Meet with bankers or equity partners
- Conduct board meetings
- Attend trade shows, industry functions and association meetings
- Visit clients or prospects
- Participate in strategic planning sessions
- Address personal/professional development issues
- Network with partners and peers
- Attend PR events

BELOW THE SURFACE
(Internal to the organization)

- Spend time in *L- gemba*
- Interact with employees
- Deal with operational issues
- Everything that takes place within the walls of the organization

Cetacean Cycle

As you probably know, the order Cetacea includes the aquatic mammals (whales, porpoises and dolphins) who breathe oxygen just like we do. Over time, their "noses" (more correctly known as blowholes) evolved to a position toward the top of their heads, allowing them to breathe without fully surfacing. Unlike most mammals, however, cetaceans are conscious breathers.[205] This means they decide when to rise to the surface and take a breath. Leaders need to behave in similar fashion. Although much of their time is spent below the surface working inside their organizations, they must decide when, how often and for how long to surface. During that time, they deal with the issues that impact the organization but are external to it. They may meet with bankers or equity partners, conduct board meetings, attend industry functions, interact with consultants, see clients, network with partners and peers, and then dive back into their organizations to complete the cycle.

World-class execution, leadership and strategy require this additional external component. It ensures the organization and its mission and vision remain relevant within the context of industry, economy and world change. It is the place where the organization, as a whole, receives accolades and acknowledgment, which nourish the culture, fueling updraft and providing publicity which can positively impact sales, recruiting and the like. It is also where many of the organization's resources are procured and relationships formed.

Unfortunately, many CEOs and executives choose to spend the bulk of their time at the surface. Some of them are more comfortable in that environment, and some are unaware of how keenly their absence is felt. Of course, if you have infused your organization with a strong mission, vision, values and culture, you can be assured it will continue to thrive even in your absence. In the same way the leadership role moves seamlessly among the strongest and most experienced geese, your leadership team and others from within your organization will be eminently capable of guiding the flock. But even though you have the utmost confidence your leadership team understands the updraft concept and everything it requires of them, you must remain vigilant—painfully aware of how fragile culture is and how easily updraft dissipates. Even when you must be away, find ways of getting firsthand information—attend a few conference calls (ones you don't necessarily need to be on), call and chat with a variety of people to get a handle on what is happening, and check in with those responsible for strategic and operational goals. Remember, just as if you were walking through the building, you are looking to check in and support, not micromanage.

Managing these competing priorities is endemic to the job of leadership, and striking the appropriate balance is a tremendous challenge. The longer you are away from your organization, the further you get from firsthand information. Keep in mind that the most reliable way to gauge the organization's progress and the power of its updraft is to witness it from your chalk circle in *L-gemba*.

STRETCHING YOUR WINGS...

1. What percentage of your time is spent in the office versus outside the office? When you are in, how much time is spent behind your desk and in meetings? Get up and take a stroll through your organization. Right now. Start practicing the art of observation.

2. How many employees do you have? How many do you know by name? How many do you interact with on a weekly basis? Pick a number and make it a point to touch base with at least that many people in your organization every week.

3. Look at your current strategic objectives. Where do you need to be to monitor their progress?

4. Think about where *L-gemba* is for you right now. This can be tricky especially if you don't have a well-defined mission and vision as a guide. Devote a self-reflection session to brainstorming where *L-gemba* is for you.

5. Are you more comfortable at the surface than inside your organization? If so, think about why that is and how you can change that.

Final Thoughts

I wrote this book because I believe in the power of leadership. I wrote this book because I believe what I said way back in Chapter 1—that leadership can be learned. And even if you're not quite sure, *I* am confident you can be a great leader *and* enjoy it at the same time. You can't go wrong striving to create updraft—it is a win-win-win, benefitting you, your people and your organization as a whole.

You can do this; just set your expectations appropriately. In the same way an airplane will stall if it tries to climb too quickly, recognize that you cannot transform your organization overnight. You'll need to become comfortable with all that updraft requires and share that knowledge with your executives. Then, as a team, you can work together to bring updraft to the entire organization.

- Are you ready to soar?
- Are you ready to watch your organization make progress like you never thought possible?
- Are you ready to enjoy being a leader?

Then it's time to take to the skies. Pilots have been surprised to see Canada geese flying at 9,000 feet,[206] and bar-headed geese achieve amazing heights in excess of 19,000 feet[207] during their migration across the Himalayas. What amazing heights can your organization reach?

Endnotes

CHAPTER 1: HOW DOES LEADERSHIP CREATE UPDRAFT?

1. Gallup, Inc., *State of the Global Workplace: Employee Engagement Insights for Business Leaders Worldwide*, (Washington, D.C., 2013), 83, accessed November 22, 2013, http://www.gallup.com/services/178517/state-global-workplace.aspx.

2. "Hewitt Analysis Shows Steady Decline in Global Employee Engagement Levels," Aon, July 29, 2010, accessed July 17, 2012, http://aon.mediaroom.com/index.php?s=25825&item=585.

3. Corporate Leadership Council, *Driving Performance and Retention Through Employee Engagement*, (Washington, D.C., 2004), 6, accessed April 2, 2014, https://www.stcloudstate.edu/humanresources/_files/documents/supv-brown-bag/employee-engagement.pdf

4. AonHewitt, "Managers – a critical link in employee engagement," September 2011, Slideshow, 10, accessed January 1, 2015, http://www.slideshare.net/AonHewitt/aon-hewitt-employee-engagement-2011-presentation-9630948.

5. Richard Wellins, Paul Bernthal and Mark Phelps, DDI, *Employee Engagement: The Key to Realizing Competitive Advantage*, (Pittsburgh: 2005), 5, accessed November 17, 2013, http://www.ddiworld.com/DDIWorld/media/monographs/employeeengagement_mg_ddi.pdf?ext=.pdf.

6. Gallup, 84.

7. Steven J. Portugal, Tatjana Y. Hubel, Johannes Fritz, Stefanie Heese, Daniela Trobe, Bernhard Voelkl, Stephen Hailes, Alan M. Wilson and James R. Usherwood. "Upwash exploitation and downwash avoidance by flap phasing in ibis formation flight." *Nature* 505 (January 16, 2014): 399.

8. Thea Cunningham, ed., *Come fly with me*, YouTube video, 6:35, posted by "nature video," January 15, 2014, accessed March 23, 2014, http://www.youtube.com/watch?v=fKkzqk3RMLc.

9. Portugal, et. al., 399.

10. Portugal, et. al., 400-402.

11. Ethan Decker, "Self-Organizing Systems," University of New Mexico, accessed March 25, 2014, http://sev.lternet.edu/~bmilne/bio576/instr/html/SOS/sos.html.

12. Laurence J. Peter and Raymond Hull, *The Peter Principle: Why Things Always Go Wrong* (New York: William Morrow & Co., Inc., 1969), 25.

13. Michael McCarthy, "Phil Mickelson adds 'mental coach' to entourage," *USA Today*, August 12, 2011, accessed February 21, 2014, http://content. usatoday.com/communities/gameon/post/2011/08/phil-mickelson-adds-mental-coach-to-entourage-at-pga-championship-julie-elion-tiger-woods-butch-harmon-bones-mackay/1.

14. James MacGregor Burns, *Leadership*, (New York: Harper & Row Publishers, Inc., 1978), 2, accessed March 10, 2014, http://www.amazon.com/ Leadership-Harper-Perennial-Political-Classics/dp/006196557X.

15. Matthew Boyle, "The Wegmans Way," *CNN Money*, January 24, 2005, accessed September 6, 2014, http://archive.fortune.com/magazines/fortune/ fortune_archive/2005/01/24/8234048/index.htm.

16. "Company Overview," Wegmans, accessed April 2, 2014, http://www. wegmans.com/webapp/wcs/stores/servlet/CategoryDisplay?storeId=10052&iden tifier=CATEGORY_2441.

17. "Frequently Asked Questions: We found some abandoned Canada goose eggs; how do we incubate them and raise the goslings?" Coalition to Prevent the Destruction of Canada Geese, accessed June 18, 2014, http://www.canadageese.org/faq5.html.

18. T.R. Michels, "T.R.'s Tips: Waterfowl Hunting," Trinity Mountain Outdoor News, accessed June 18, 2014, http://www.trmichels.com/WaterfowlArticles.htm.

19. "Canada Goose," The Cornell Lab of Ornithology: All About Birds, accessed June 18, 2014, http://www.allaboutbirds.org/guide/canada_goose/ lifehistory.

CHAPTER 2: ARE YOU WORTHY OF BEING FOLLOWED?

20. "Gandhi for Children," Gandhi Memorial Center, accessed June 18, 2014, http://gandhimemorialcenter.org/activities/educational-programs/ children/.

21. Kevin Kruse, "Norman Schwarzkopf: 10 Quotes on Leadership and War," *Forbes*, December 27, 2012, accessed December 18, 2014, http://www.forbes.com/sites/kevinkruse/2012/12/27/norman-schwarzkopf-quotes/.

22. "FAQ," Blue Angels, accessed September 30, 2014, http://www. blueangels.navy.mil/show/faq.aspx.

23. Mike Hixenbaugh, "Pulling 7 Gs with the Navy's Blue Angels," *The Virginian-Pilot*, September 20, 2014, accessed September 30, 2014, http://hamptonroads.com/2014/09/videos-pulling-7-gs-navys-blue-angels.

24. Stephen Covey, *The 7 Habits of Highly Effective People* (New York: Simon & Schuster Inc., 1989), 188-203.

CHAPTER 3: ARE YOU AIRWORTHY?

25. Michelle Ortlipp, "Keeping and Using Reflective Journals in the Qualitative Research Process," *The Qualitative Report* 13:4 (December 2008): 695-705, accessed August 20, 2014, http://www.nova.edu/ssss/QR/QR13-4/ortlipp.pdf.

26. Crystal Holyn Holdefer, "Understanding Yourself and Increasing Your Professional Value through Self-Reflection," Intercom, accessed August 20, 2014, http://intercom.stc.org/2014/01/understanding-yourself-and-increasing-your-professional-value-through-self-reflection/.

Graham Gordon Ramsay and Holly Barlow Sweet, *A Creative Guide to Exploring Your Life: Self-Reflection Using Photography, Art, and Writing* (London: Jessica Kingsley Publishers, 2008) accessed August 20, 2014, http://www.amazon.com/Creative-Guide-Exploring-Your-Life/dp/1843108925/.

27. Peter F. Drucker, "Managing Oneself," *Harvard Business Review*, January 2005, accessed August 21, 2014, http://hbr.org/2005/01/managing-oneself/ar/1.

28. "New Study Shows Nice Guys Finish First," AMA, October 7, 2010, accessed August 21, 2014, http://www.amanet.org/training/articles/New-Study-Shows-Nice-Guys-Finish-First.aspx?pcode=XCRP.

29. Robert A. Caro, *Master Of The Senate: The Years of Lyndon Johnson* (United States: Vintage Books, 2002), 120, accessed December 18, 2014, http://www.amazon.com/Master-Senate-Years-Lyndon-Johnson/dp/0394720954/.

30. Victoria Gill, "Barn owl wings adapted for silent flight," BBC, January 19, 2012, accessed February 21, 2014, http://www.bbc.co.uk/nature/16593259.

31. April Holladay, "Owls: Dead-shot in the dark," *USA Today*, September 6, 2005, accessed July 28, 2014, http://usatoday30.usatoday.com/tech/columnist/aprilholladay/2005-08-31-owls-hearing_x.htm.

32. "Northern Gannet," The Cornell Lab of Ornithology: All About Birds, accessed May 21, 2014, http://www.allaboutbirds.org/guide/northern_gannet/id.

33. P.Y. Daoust, G.V. Dobbin, R.C.F. Ridlington Abbott and S.D. Dawson, "Descriptive anatomy of the subcutaneous air diverticula in the Northern Gannet Morus bassanus," Seabird 21, (2008): 64-76, accessed May 21, 2014, http://www.seabirdgroup.org.uk/journals/seabird_21/SEABIRD%2021%20(2008)%20Daoust%20et%20al.64-76.pdf.

34. Bai Vue, Louis N. Quast, Bruce A. Center, Chu-Ting Chung and Joseph M. Wohkittel, "Managerial Behavior Associated with Managerial Derailment in the U.S. and Several Asian Countries," (University of Minnesota, 2011), accessed June 28, 2014, http://www.cehd.umn.edu/olpd/research/StudentConf/2011/VueManagerDerailment.pdf.

Jean Brittain Leslie and Ellen Van Velsor, *A Look at Derailment Today: North America and Europe*, (Greensboro: Center for Creative Leadership, 1996), accessed June 28, 2014, http://wenku.baidu.com/view/91a640ea81c758f5f61f6776.html.

Louis N. Quast, Joseph M. Wohkittel, Bruce A. Center, Chu-Ting Chung and Bai Vue, "Managerial Behavior Associated with Managerial Derailment in the U.S. and Nine European Countries," (University of Minnesota, 2012), accessed June 28, 2014, http://www.ufhrd.co.uk/wordpress/wp-content/uploads/2012/11/UFHRD2012Leadership91.pdf.

35. Bill Bonnstetter, Judy Suiter and Randy Widrick, *The Universal Language DISC: A Reference Manual*, (Target Training International, Ltd., 1993).

36. Elizabeth Huff, "In matters of style, swim with the current... (Quotation)," The Jefferson Monticello, June 8, 2011, accessed March 10, 2014, http://www.monticello.org/site/jefferson/matters-style-swim-currentquotation.

37. Aristotle, *Nicomachean Ethics: Book II*, trans. W.D.Ross, The Internet Classics Archive, accessed December 18, 2014, http://classics.mit.edu/Aristotle/nicomachaen.2.ii.html.

38. Dr. Izzy Justice, *Emotional Intelligence*, YouTube video, 4:33, posted by "DrIzzyJustice," January 8, 2009, accessed October 7, 2012, http://www.youtube.com/watch?v=l03MifVvY8M&feature=relmfu.

39. Julia Layton, "How Fear Works," HowStuffWorks.com, accessed September 30, 2014, http://science.howstuffworks.com/life/inside-the-mind/emotions/fear2.htm.

Júlio Rocha do Amaral and Jorge Martins de Oliveira, "Limbic System: The Center of Emotions," The Healing Center On-line, accessed September 30, 2014, http://www.healing-arts.org/n-r-limbic.htm.

40. Robert Sapolsky, *Why Zebras Don't Get Ulcers: The Acclaimed Guide to Stress, Stress-Related Diseases, and Coping*, 3rd ed. (New York: Henry Holt and Company, 2004), 30-32.

41. Sapolsky, 4-5.

42. J.D. Mayer and P. Salovey, "What is Emotional Intelligence?" in *Emotional Development and Emotional Intelligence*, ed. P. Salovey and D.J. Sluyton (New York: Basic Books, 1997), 3-31, accessed November 4, 2010, http://www.unh.edu/emotional_intelligence/EI%20Assets/Reprints...EI%20Proper/EI1997MSWhatIsEI.pdf.

John Mayer, "Emotional Intelligence Information," accessed September 30, 2014, http://www.unh.edu/emotional_intelligence/index.html.

Peter Salovey and John Mayer, "Emotional Intelligence," *Imagination, Cognition, and Personality* 9 (1990): 185-211, accessed October 7, 2011, http://www.unh.edu/emotional_intelligence/EI%20Assets/Reprints...EI%20Proper/EI1990%20Emotional%20Intelligence.pdf.

43. Daniel Goleman, *Working with Emotional Intelligence* (New York: Bantam Books, 1998).

44. Jorn K. Bramann, "A Look at Lao Tzu and the Tao Te Ching," Frostburg State University, accessed December 18, 2014, http://faculty.frostburg.edu/phil/forum/Laotzu.htm.

CHAPTER 4: ARE YOU GOING THE WAY OF THE DODO?
45. "Dodo bird a resilient island survivor before the arrival of humans, study reveals," *Smithsonian Science*, September 26, 2011, accessed March 16, 2014, http://smithsonianscience.org/2011/09/dodo-bird-was-a-resilient-island-survivor-before-the-arrival-of-humans/.

46. BlessingWhite, *Engagement Report: 2011*, (Princeton: 2011), 3, accessed April 2, 2014, http://www.blessingwhite.com/EEE__report.asp.

47. "My Life as a Turkey: Who's Your Mama? The Science of Imprinting," PBS, November 16, 2012, accessed April 2, 2014, http://www.pbs.org/wnet/nature/my-life-as-a-turkey-whos-your-mama-the-science-of-imprinting/7367/.

48. Stephen Gandel, "How Blockbuster Failed at Failing," *Time*, October 17, 2010, accessed March 25, 2013, http://content.time.com/time/magazine/article/0,9171,2022624,00.html.

49. Austin Carr, "Blockbuster: Please, Please Change Your Habits," *Fast Company*, July 8, 2011, accessed March 25, 2013, http://www.fastcompany.com/1765646/blockbuster-please-please-change-your-habits.

50. Austin Carr, "Blockbuster CEO Jim Keyes on Competition From Apple, Netflix, Nintendo, and Redbox," *Fast Company*, June 8, 2010, accessed March 25, 2013, http://www.fastcompany.com/1656502/blockbuster-ceo-jim-keyes-competition-apple-netflix-nintendo-and-redbox.

51. Austin Carr, "Blockbuster Bankruptcy: A Decade of Decline," *Fast Company*, September 22, 2010, accessed March 25, 2013, http://www.fastcompany.com/1690654/blockbuster-bankruptcy-decade-decline.

52. Beth Jinks, "Kodak Moments Just a Memory as Company Exits Bankruptcy," Bloomberg, September 3, 2013, accessed June 19, 2014, http://www.bloomberg.com/news/articles/2013-09-03/kodak-exits-bankruptcy-as-printer-without-photographs.

Scott Dengrove, "Kodak: It's hard to believe," Dengrove Studios Blog, March 21, 2012, accessed March 25, 2013, http://www.dengrovestudios.com/blog/tag/kodak-downfall/.

53. Mary Bellis, "The Invention of VELCRO ® - George de Mestral," About.com, accessed September 7, 2014, http://inventors.about.com/library/weekly/aa091297.htm.

"Velcro Industries History And George de Mestral," Velcro Industries, accessed September 7, 2014, http://www.velcro.com/About-Us/History.aspx.

54. "HISTORY TIMELINE: Post-it® Note notes," 3M, accessed September 7, 2014, http://www.post-it.com/wps/portal/3M/en_US/PostItNA/Home/Support/About/.

55. Roger Von Oech, *A Whack on the Side of the Head: How You Can Be More Creative*, (New York: MJF Books, 1998), 6.

56. Erin Gruwell, ed., *The Gigantic Book of Teachers' Wisdom*, (United States: Skyhorse Publishing, 2007), 129, accessed December 18, 2014, http://www.amazon.com/Gigantic-Book-Teachers-Wisdom/dp/1602391777.

CHAPTER 5: WHAT KIND OF WOODPECKER ARE YOU?

57. *Abbott & Costello Who's On First*, YouTube video, 8:03, posted by "NYYGehrig," August 15, 2012, accessed September 30, 2014, https://www.youtube.com/watch?v=kTcRRaXV-fg.

58. "Acorn Woodpecker," The Cornell Lab of Ornithology: All About Birds, accessed April 2, 2014, http://www.allaboutbirds.org/guide/Acorn_Woodpecker/lifehistory.

59. "Red-headed Woodpecker," The Cornell Lab of Ornithology: All About Birds, accessed April 2, 2014, http://www.allaboutbirds.org/guide/red-headed_woodpecker/lifehistory.

60. "About Us: Who We Are," Wegmans, accessed June 11, 2011, http://www.wegmans.com/webapp/wcs/stores/servlet/CategoryDisplay?storeId=10052&identifier=CATEGORY_507.

61. "Vision, Mission and Values," Ingram Micro, accessed March 30, 2014, http://corp.ingrammicro.com/About-Us/Vision-Mission-Values.aspx.

62. "Enron's 1998 Annual Report, Our Values," Yale School of Management, accessed June 11, 2011, http://faculty.som.yale.edu/shyamsunder/FinancialFraud/Fraud2005Material/Enron%20Values.doc.

63. David Bollier, *Aiming Higher: 25 Stories of How Companies Prosper By Combining Sound Management and Social Vision* (New York: AMACOM, 1996), 280-293.

Mectizan Donation Program, accessed October 5, 2012, http://www.mectizan.org/.

Michael Useem, *The Leadership Moment: Nine True Stories of Triumph and Disaster and Their Lessons for Us All* (New York: Three Rivers Press, 1998), 10-30.

64. Useem, 23.

65. Brenda D. Colatrella, email message to Daniel Freedman, November 25, 2014.

66. *Our Values and Standards: The Basis of our Success (Code of Conduct: Edition III)*, Merck, 4, accessed January 30, 2014, http://www.merck.com/about/code_of_conduct.pdf.

CHAPTER 6: IT'S ALL ABOUT THE FLOCK

67. Jeff Scott, "V-Formation Flight of Birds," Aerospaceweb.org, July 17, 2005, accessed November 12, 2012, http://www.aerospaceweb.org/question/nature/q0237.shtml.

68. Torkel Weis-Fogh, "Energetics of Hovering Flight in Hummingbirds and Drosophila," *The Journal of Experimental Biology* (1972), accessed January 24, 2014, http://jeb.biologists.org/content/56/1/79.full.pdf.

69. Paul Ehrlich, David S. Dobkin and Darryl Wheye, *The Birder's Handbook: A Field Guide to the Natural History of North American Birds* (New York: Simon & Schuster, 1988), 327, accessed January 25, 2014, http://www.amazon.com/The-Birders-Handbook-Natural-American/dp/0671659898.

70. "The Graduate: Trivia," IMDb, accessed May 21, 2014, http://www.imdb.com/title/tt0061722/trivia?ref_=tt_trv_trv.

71. "The Dark Knight: Trivia," IMDb, accessed May 21, 2014, http://www.imdb.com/title/tt0468569/trivia?ref_=tt_trv_trv.

72. "Elizabeth Taylor: Biography," IMDb, accessed May 21, 2014, http://www.imdb.com/name/nm0000072/bio#trivia.

73. Linda Ray, "Employee Turnover Statistics in Restaurants," Chron, accessed August 15, 2014, http://smallbusiness.chron.com/employee-turnover-statistics-restaurants-16744.html.

74. "Hay Group Study Finds Employee Turnover in Retail Industry is Slowly Increasing," Bloomberg, May 8, 2012, accessed December 31, 2012, http://www.bloomberg.com/article/2012-05-08/aWdgOKjbTBXY.html.

75. Eliot Burdett, *Sales Trends from 2012 CSO Insights: Sales Rep Performance*," Peak Sales Recruiting, June 14, 2012, accessed August 15, 2014, http://www.peaksalesrecruiting.com/sales-trends-from-2012-cso-insights-sales-rep-performance/.

76. Russell Huebsch, "Standard Employee Turnover in the Call Center Industry," Chron, accessed August 15, 2014, http://smallbusiness.chron.com/standard-employee-turnover-call-center-industry-36185.html.

77. "Using Benchmarks to Reduce Turnover and Increase Profitability," TTI Success Insights, accessed August 15, 2014, http://www.ttisuccessinsights.com/casestudies/cs_entries/using-benchmarks-to-reduce-turnover-and-increase-profitability.

78. Jessi Hempel, "A CEO takes on the war for talent," *Fortune*, October 24, 2012, accessed August 15, 2014, http://fortune.com/2012/10/24/a-ceo-takes-on-the-war-for-talent/.

79. "Netsuite Announces Fourth Quarter And Fiscal 2013 Financial Results," NetSuite, January 30, 2014, accessed August 15, 2014, http://www.netsuite.com/portal/company/pressreleases/01-30-14b.shtml.

80. "Famous Quotes by Babe Ruth," Babe Ruth, accessed March 10, 2014, http://www.baberuth.com/quotes/.

CHAPTER 7: CAN YOU HEAR THE HONKING?

81. "Canada Goose: Branta Canadensis," Ducks Unlimited Canada, accessed February 28, 2014, http://www.ducks.ca/learn-about-wetlands/wildlife/canada-goose/.

82. T.R. Michels, "T.R.'s Tips: Waterfowl Biology & Behavior," Trinity Mountain Outdoor News, accessed April 15, 2013, http://www.trmichels.com/WaterfowlArticles.htm.

83. T.R. Michels, "T.R.'s Tips."

84. Larry King with Bill Gilbert. *How to Talk to Anyone, Anytime, Anywhere: The Secrets of Good Communication* (New York: Three Rivers Press, 1994), 40, accessed April 3, 2014, http://www.amazon.com/Talk-Anyone-Anytime-Anywhere-Communication-ebook/dp/B0012SMGPQ.

85. Gallup Inc., *The State of the Global Workplace: A worldwide study of employee engagement and wellbeing*," (Washington, D.C., 2010), 25, accessed June 22, 2012, http://www.gallup.com/services/176300/state-global-workplace.aspx.

86. Brian Brim and Jim Asplund, "Driving Engagement by Focusing on Strengths," Gallup, November 12, 2009, accessed September 21, 2011, http://gmj.gallup.com/content/124214/driving-engagement-focusing-strengths.aspx.

CHAPTER 8: WHAT IS THE ROOSTER'S JOB?

87. Jane J. Lee, "How a Rooster Knows to Crow at Dawn," *National Geographic*, March 18, 2013, accessed February 3, 2014, http://news.nationalgeographic.com/news/2013/03/130318-rooster-crow-circadian-clock-science/.

88. Jonathan Bailey, "Comparing the Jonah Lehrer and Jayson Blair Plagiarism Scandals," *Plagiarism Today*, January 9, 2013, accessed June 17, 2013, http://www.plagiarismtoday.com/2013/01/09/comparing-the-jonah-lehrer-and-jayson-blair-plagiarism-scandals/.

89. Gary Strauss, "How 'Opal Mehta' got shelved," *USA Today*, May 7, 2006, accessed June 17, 2013, http://usatoday30.usatoday.com/life/books/news/2006-05-07-opal-scandal_x.htm.

90. "Isley Feels Vindicated In Bolton Case," *Billboard*, accessed June 17, 2013, http://www.billboard.com/articles/news/78775/isley-feels-vindicated-in-bolton-case.

91. Garson O'Toole, "A Man May Do an Immense Deal of Good, If He Does Not Care Who Gets the Credit," Quote Investigator, December 21, 2010, accessed December 20, 2014, http://quoteinvestigator.com/2010/12/21/doing-good-selfless.

92. "'The Buck Stops Here' Desk Sign," Harry S. Truman Library and Museum, accessed March 11, 2014, http://www.trumanlibrary.org/buckstop.htm.

93. Viridiana Linares, Lauren E. Shore, Stephanie L. Rojas and Kimberly A. Barchard, "It's not my fault! Emotional Intelligence and Blaming Others," Faculty Websites: University of Nevada, Las Vegas, April 2009, accessed June 28, 2014, https://faculty.unlv.edu/img/lab/conference%20posters/Scapegoat_handout.pdf.

94. Jeanna Bryner, "Passing the buck: Blaming others is contagious," NBCnews.com, January 19, 2010, accessed June 21, 2013, http://www.nbcnews.com/id/34940422/ns/health-behavior/t/passing-buck-blaming-others-contagious/.

Nathanael J. Fast and Larissa Z. Tiedens, "Blame contagion: The automatic transmission of self-serving attributions," *Journal of Experimental Social Psychology* 46 (2010): 97–106, accessed December 17, 2014, http://www-bcf.usc.edu/~nathanaf/blame_contagion.pdf.

95. Nancy Gohring, "Motorola CEO: Open Android store leads to quality issues," *Computerworld*, June 3, 2011, accessed June 20, 2013, http://www.computerworld.com.au/article/388831/motorola_ceo_open_android_store_leads_quality_issues/.

96. Gohring, "Motorola CEO."

97. Pete Swabey, "Oracle blames its own sales force for duff quarter," *Information Age*, March 21, 2013, accessed June 20, 2013, http://www.information-age.com/industry/software/123456911/oracle-blames-its-own-sales-force-for-duff-quarter.

98. Gary A. Davis, "Barriers to Creativity and Creative Attitudes." in *Encyclopedia of Creativity*, ed. Mark A. Runco and Steven R. Pritzker, vol. 1 (San Diego: Academic Press, 1999), 165-174, accessed July 5, 2014, http://books.google.com/books?id=cjPlhZ9WBqgC&lpg=PP1&dq=isbn%3A0122270762&pg=PP1#v=onepage&q&f=falseon.

99. Adobe, *State of Create Study: Global benchmark study on attitudes and beliefs about creativity at work, school and home,* (April 2012), 13, accessed July 5, 2014, http://www.adobe.com/aboutadobe/pressroom/pdfs/Adobe_State_of_Create_Global_Benchmark_Study.pdf.

100. Kaomi Goetz, "How 3M Gave Everyone Days Off and Created an Innovation Dynamo," *Fast Company*, February 1, 2011, accessed July 2, 2014, http://www.fastcodesign.com/1663137/how-3m-gave-everyone-days-off-and-created-an-innovation-dynamo.

101. John Maynard Keynes, *The General Theory Of Employment, Interest, And Money* (New York: Harvest Book/Harcourt, Inc., 1964), viii, accessed January 1, 2015, http://www.amazon.com/General-Theory-Employment-Interest-Money/dp/0156347113.

102. "Famous Pablo Picasso Quotes," Pablo Picasso, accessed December 18, 2014, http://www.pablopicasso.org/quotes.jsp.

103. Darya L. Zabelina and Michael D. Robinson. "Child's Play: Facilitating the Originality of Creative Output by a Priming Manipulation," *Psychology of Aesthetics, Creativity, and the Arts* 4:1 (2010): 57–65, accessed July 5, 2014, http://www.psychologytoday.com/files/attachments/34246/zabelina-robinson-2010a.pdf.

Elizabeth Rosenblatt and Ellen Winner. "The Art of Children's Drawing." *Journal of Aesthetic Education* 22:1, Special Issue: Art, Mind, and Education (Spring, 1988): 3-15, accessed July 3, 2014, http://www.jstor.org/stable/3332960.

Kyung Hee Kim, "The Creativity Crisis: The Decrease in Creative Thinking Scores on the Torrance Tests of Creative Thinking," *Creativity Research Journal* 23:4 (November 9, 2011): 285-295, accessed July 3, 2014, http://dx.doi.org/10.1080/10400419.2011.627805.

Mark A. Runco, "Fourth Grade Slump," in *Encyclopedia of Creativity*, ed. Mark A. Runco and Steven R. Pritzker, vol. 1 (San Diego: Academic Press, 1999): 743-744, accessed July 5, 2014, http://books.google.com/books?id=cjPlh Z9WBqgC&lpg=PP1&dq=isbn%3A0122270762&pg=PP1#v=onepage&q&f= false.

Paul E. Torrance, "Scientific Views of Creativity and Factors Affecting Its Growth," *Daedalus* 94:3 (Summer, 1965): 663-681, accessed July 5, 2014, http://www.jstor.org/stable/20026936.

Sam McNerney, "Killing Creativity: Why Kids Draw Pictures of Monsters & Adults Don't," Big Think, April 22, 2012, accessed July 3, 2014, http://bigthink.com/insights-of-genius/killing-creativity-why-kids-draw-pictures-of-monsters-and-adults-dont.

CHAPTER 9: JUST SURVIVING ISN'T ENOUGH

104. "Altitude Sickness, WebMD, October 4, 2012, accessed February 9, 2011, http://www.webmd.com/a-to-z-guides/altitude-sickness-topic-overview.

105. "Theory of Flight," Massachusetts Institute of Technology, March 16, 1997, accessed February 9, 2014, http://web.mit.edu/16.00/www/aec/flight.html.

106. Joanna Tong and Adele Schwab, "The Flight of Birds," MIT Open Courseware, accessed February 9, 2014, http://ocw.mit.edu/courses/materials-science-and-engineering/3-a26-freshman-seminar-the-nature-of-engineering-fall-2005/projects/flght_of_brdv2ed.pdf.

107. Elizabeth Pennisi, "Geese ride aerial roller coaster across the Himalayas," *Science*, January 15, 2015, accessed February 5, 2015, http://news.sciencemag.org/biology/2015/01/geese-ride-aerial-roller-coaster-across-himalayas.

108. Nell Greenfieldboyce, "Highflying Geese Save Energy By Swooping Like A Roller Coaster," NPR, January 15, 2015, http://www.npr.org/2015/01/15/377321027/highflying-geese-save-energy-by-swooping-like-a-roller-coaster.

109. "Peter Senge's Necessary Revolution," *BloomburgBusinessWeek*, June 11, 2008, accessed March 10, 2014, http://www.businessweek.com/stories/2008-06-11/peter-senges-necessary-revolutionbusinessweek-business-news-stock-market-and-financial-advice.

110. "Museums and Awards," Dyson, accessed June 21, 2011, http://content.dyson.com/insideDyson/default.asp#MUSEUMSANDAWARDS.

111. "How we work," Dyson, accessed December 31, 2014, http://www.careers.dyson.com/about/default.aspx.

112. "Company," Google, accessed June 21, 2011, http://www.google.com/corporate/.

113. "About Us," Merck, accessed June 21, 2011, http://www.merck.com/about/our-values/home.html.

114. "Company and Founder," Mary Kay, accessed April 3, 2014, http://www.marykay.com/en-US/About-Mary-Kay.

115. "About Nike, Inc.," Nike, accessed June 21, 2011, http://nikeinc.com/pages/about-nike-inc.

116. "About," Microsoft, accessed June 21, 2011, http://www.microsoft.com/about/en/us/default.aspx.

117. "About Wawa," Wawa, accessed June 21, 2011, http://www.wawa.com/WawaWeb/About.aspx.

118. "About Us," Nokia, accessed June 4, 2013, http://www.nokia.com/global/about-nokia/about-us/about-us/.

119. "Who We Are: Facts," Girl Scouts, accessed June 21, 2011, http://www.girlscouts.org/who_we_are/facts/.

120. "Masthead," *Focus*, November/December, Vol. 32, No. 6 (Washington, D.C.: World Wildlife Fund, 2010).

121. "Who We Are," Monster, accessed September 8, 2014, http://www.about-monster.com/content/who-we-are#mission.

122. "About: Our Mission," Revolution Foods, accessed July 10, 2014, http://revolutionfoods.com/about/.

123. "Our Mission: Our Mission Statement," Trentham Construction, accessed July 7, 2014, http://trenthamconstruction.com/our-mission.

124. "Police Department: The department 411," VCU Police, accessed July 7, 2014, http://police.vcu.edu/about/index.html.

125. "Information: Mission Statement," Bloomington Photography Club, accessed July 7, 2014, http://bloomingtonphotoclub.org/mission-statement/.

126. "Information: Mission Statement," Aurora Photography, accessed July 7, 2014, http://auroraphotoblog.com/mission-statement/.

127. "Mission Statement," Cypress, LLP, accessed July 7, 2014, http://cypressllp.com/approach/mission-statement-and-statement-of-values/.

128. "About: Mission and Vision," Zach Theatre, accessed July 7, 2014, http://www.zachtheatre.org/about/mission-vision.

129. "About Us: Our Mission Statement," La Porte Insurance Agency, accessed July 7, 2014, http://www.laporteinsuranceagency.com/Our-Mission-Statement.1.htm.

130. "Wellness Center Information And Regulations," Seneca PT & Wellness Center, accessed July 8, 2014, http://www.senecapt.com/files/pdf/wellness-forms.pdf.

131. "About Us," Oasis Landscapes & Pools, accessed July 8, 2014, http://www.oasisusa.net/about_us.php.

132. "NYPL's Mission Statement," New York Public Library, accessed July 8, 2014, http://www.nypl.org/help/about-nypl/mission.

133. "Planning Commission," City of Saratoga California, accessed July 8, 2014, http://www.saratoga.ca.us/cityhall/comms/planning/default.asp.

134. "Fire Department," City of Chanhassen Minnesota, accessed July 8, 2014, http://www.ci.chanhassen.mn.us/index.aspx?nid=221.

135. "Message From Our Founder," Susan G. Komen, accessed June 21, 2011, http://ww5.komen.org/AboutUs/MessageFromOurFounder.html.

136. Mardy Grothe, *Viva La Repartee: Clever Comebacks and Witty Retorts From History's Great Wits & Wordsmiths* (New York: HarperCollins Publishers, 2005): 57, accessed December 31, 2014, http://www.amazon.com/Viva-Repartee-Comebacks-Historys-Wordsmiths/dp/0060789484.

137. "About Us," Jeremiah Program, accessed June 21, 2011, http://www.jeremiahprogram.org/about-us/.

138. "Know What Is and Isn't Your Affair, Gertrude Stein Tells Institute in Talk," *The Columbia Spectator*, November 21, 1934, accessed December 20, 2014, http://spectatorarchive.library.columbia.edu/cgi-bin/columbia?a=d&d=cs19341121-01.2.34#.

139. "CVS Caremark to Stop Selling Tobacco at all CVS/pharmacy Locations," CVS Caremark, February 5, 2014, accessed March 31, 2014, http://www.cvshealth.com/content/cvs-caremark-stop-selling-tobacco-all-cvspharmacy-locations.

140. "CVS quits for good," CVS Caremark, accessed March 21, 2014, http://info.cvscaremark.com/cvs-insights/cvs-quits.

141. James Collins and Jerry Porras, *Built to Last: Successful Habits of Visionary Companies* (New York: HarperCollins Publishers, Inc., 1994), 47.

CHAPTER 10: . . . BUT WE'RE MAKING GREAT TIME

142. "A history of Windows," Windows, accessed December 31, 2014, http://windows.microsoft.com/en-us/windows/history.

143. Collins and Porras, 91-93.

144. Collins and Porras, 91-114.

145. Collins and Porras, 94.

146. Teresa M. Amabile and Steven J. Kramer, "The HBR List: Breakthrough Ideas for 2010 – 1. What Really Motivates Workers," *Harvard Business Review*, January 2010, accessed June 21, 2011, http://hbr.org/2010/01/the-hbr-list-breakthrough-ideas-for-2010/ar/1.

147. Warren Allen Smith, *Celebrities in Hell* (New York: chelCPress, 2010), 379, accessed December 18, 2014, http://www.amazon.com/Celebrities-Hell-Warren-Allen-Smith/dp/0557837529.

148. Josef, "History: 25 Biggest False Predictions Concerning Technology," List25, May 13, 2013, accessed July 17, 2014, http://list25.com/25-biggest-false-predictions-concerning-technology/.

149. Josef, "False Predictions."

150. Josef, "False Predictions."

151. Josef, "False Predictions."

152. Erin Skarda, "Top 10 Failed Predictions: Very, Very Wrong - Online Shopping Will Flop," *Time*, October 21, 2011, accessed July 14, 2014, http://content.time.com/time/specials/packages/article/0,28804,2097462_2097456_2097474,00.html.

153. Barry J. Farber, *Diamond Power: Gems of Wisdom from America's Greatest Marketer* (United States: The Career Press, Inc., 2004), 60, accessed December 18, 2014, http://www.amazon.com/Diamond-Power-Americas-Greatest-Marketer/dp/1564146987.

154. Gary P. Latham, "The Motivational Benefits of Goal-Setting," *The Academy of Management Executive* (1993-2005) Vol. 18, No. 4, (November 2004): 126-129, accessed July 15, 2014, http://www.jstor.org/stable/4166132.

155. Edwin A. Locke, Karyll N. Shaw, Lise M. Saari and Gary P. Latham, "Goal Setting and Task Performance: 1969-1980," DTIC Online, June 1980, accessed June 15, 2014, http://www.dtic.mil/dtic/tr/fulltext/u2/a086584.pdf.

156. Edwin A. Locke and Gary P. Latham, "Building a Practically Useful Theory of Goal Setting and Task Motivation: A 35-Year Odyssey," *American Psychologist* 705, Vol. 57, No. 9 (September 2002): 705–717, accessed July 15, 2014, http://www-2.rotman.utoronto.ca/facbios/file/09%20-%20Locke%20&%20Latham%202002%20AP.pdf.

157. Gary P. Latham, "The Motivational Benefits of Goal-Setting."

158. Edwin A. Locke and Gary P. Latham, "Building a Practically Useful Theory."

159. Gary P. Latham, "The Motivational Benefits of Goal-Setting."

160. Edwin A. Locke and Gary P. Latham, "Building a Practically Useful Theory."

161. Fred C. Lunenburg, "Goal-Setting Theory of Motivation," *International Journal Of Management, Business, And Administration* Volume 15, Number 1, 2011, accessed July 15, 2014,

http://www.nationalforum.com/Electronic%20Journal%20Volumes/
Lunenburg,%20Fred%20C.%20Goal-Setting%20Theoryof%20Motivation%20
IJMBA%20V15%20N1%202011.pdf.

162. Edwin A. Locke and Gary P. Latham, "Building a Practically Useful
Theory."

163. "History," Jeremiah Program, accessed June 11, 2011,
http://www.jeremiahprogram.org/about-us/history/.

164. WWF, accessed June 11, 2011, http://www.worldwildlife.org/who/
index.html.

165. Curtis Runyan, "Forever Costa Rica," The Nature Conservancy,
Spring 2011, accessed June 11, 2011, http://www.nature.org/magazine/
magazine-forever-costa-rica.xml.

166. Sarah Pruitt, "Celebrating the 75th Anniversary of 'Snow White
and the Seven Dwarfs,'" History, December 21, 2012, accessed July 13, 2014,
http://www.history.com/news/celebrating-the-75th-anniversary-of-snow-white-
and-the-seven-dwarfs.

167. Brad Aldridge, "Disneyland's History," JustDisney.com, accessed July
12, 2014, http://www.justdisney.com/disneyland/history.html.

Brad Aldridge, "Walt Disney's Disneyland," JustDisney.com, accessed July
12, 2014, http://www.justdisney.com/walt_disney/biography/w_disneyland.
html.

168. "Nokia Siemens Networks: Preparing to Connect the World," Nokia,
February 12, 2007, accessed July 12, 2014, http://networks.nokia.com/ru/news-
events/press-room/press-releases/nokia-siemens-networks-preparing-to-connect-
the-world.

169. Alex Pham, "Amazon's Kindle opens new chapter for publishing
industry," Los Angeles Times, December 29, 2010, accessed July 12, 2014,
http://www.latimes.com/business/la-fi-amazon-kindle-qanda-20101229-story.
html.

170. "Auto Repair Shops: Industry Snapshot," Pacific County Economic
Development Council, accessed July 16, 2014, http://www.pacificedc.org/
Library%20Docs/Auto%20Repair%20Shop%20Industry%20Report.pdf.

171. "Cost to get into the HEV/EV repair business," Auto Career
Development Center, accessed July 16, 2014, http://www.fixhybrid.com/cost-
to-get-into-the-hev-ev-reapir-business/.

172. Yogi Berra, The Yogi Book: I Really Didn't Say Everything I Said!
(New York: Workman Publishing Co., Inc., 1999), 51, accessed December 18,
2014, http://books.google.com/books?id=VX3GrYIT2cEC&printsec=frontcove
r#v=onepage&q&f=false.

173. John F. Kennedy. "Special Message to the Congress on Urgent
National Needs, May 25, 1961," John F. Kennedy Presidential Library and
Museum, May 25, 1961, accessed October 7, 2012, http://www.jfklibrary.

org/Research/Research-Aids/JFK-Speeches/United-States-Congress-Special-Message_19610525.aspx.

174. John F. Kennedy, "Memorandum for Vice President, 20 April 1961," National Aeronautics and Space Administration, April 20, 1961, accessed June 11, 2011, http://history.nasa.gov/Apollomon/apollo1.pdf.

175. Lyndon B. Johnson, "Memorandum for the President, Evaluation of Space Program," National Aeronautics and Space Administration, April 28, 1961, accessed June 11, 2011, http://history.nasa.gov/Apollomon/apollo2.pdf.

176. Nicolo Machiavelli, *The Prince*, trans. W.K. Marriott, Oregon State University, accessed January 26, 2015, http://oregonstate.edu/instruct/phl302/texts/prince/prince.html.

177. Jeff Scott, "V-Formation Flight of Birds."

178. John F. Kennedy, "Special Message."

179. John F. Kennedy, "Special Message."

180. John F. Kennedy, "Special Message."

181. "Apollo 11 Footage Missing," Television Obscurities, July 20, 2009, accessed June 11, 2011, http://www.tvobscurities.com/2009/07/apollo-11-footage-missing/.

182. "The Automobile Industry, 1920–1929," Bryant University, accessed July 27, 2014, http://web.bryant.edu/~ehu/h364/materials/cars/cars%20_30.htm.

CHAPTER 11: FILING YOUR FLIGHT PLAN

183. Tina Yerkes, "How Ducks Navigate," Ducks Unlimited, accessed July 7, 2013, http://www.ducks.org/conservation/waterfowl-biology/how-ducks-navigate.

184. "Migration of Birds: Orientation and Navigation," USGS, accessed July 9, 2013, http://www.npwrc.usgs.gov/resource/birds/migration/orient.htm.

185. "Migration Basics," National Park Service, accessed July 9, 2013, http://www.nps.gov/akso/parkwise/students/referencelibrary/general/migrationbasics.htm.

186. Michael L. Wege and Dennis G. Raveling, "Factors Influencing the Timing, Distance, and Path of Migrations of Canada Geese," *The Wilson Bulletin*, Vol. 95, No. 2 (June 1983): 209-221, accessed April 3, 2014, http://www.jstor.org/stable/4161751.

187. John Godfrey Saxe, "The poems of John Godfrey Saxe/The Blind Men and the Elephant," Wikisource, accessed April 3, 2014, http://en.wikisource.org/wiki/The_poems_of_John_Godfrey_Saxe/The_Blind_Men_and_the_Elephant.

188. "General George S. Patton, Jr. Quotations," The Official Website of General George S. Patton, Jr., accessed March 10, 2014, http://www.generalpatton.com/quotes/index3.html.

189. Grainger Hunt, "A Darwinian Dance," The Cornell Lab of Ornithology: All About Birds, accessed March 12, 2014, http://www. allaboutbirds.org/Page.aspx?pid=2588.

190. Grainger Hunt, "A Darwinian Dance."

191. Graham Chapman, John Cleese, Terry Gilliam, Eric Idle, Terry Jones and Michael Palin, *The Complete Monty Python's Flying Circus: All the Words Vol. Two* (New York: Pantheon Books, 1989) 16.

192. Andrea Cavagna, Alessio Cimarelli, Irene Giardina, Giorgio Parisi, Raffaele Santagati, Fabio Stefanini and Massimiliano Vialea, "Scale-free correlations in starling flocks," PNAS, May 11, 2010, 11865-11870, accessed March 12, 2014, http://www.pnas.org/content/early/2010/06/11/1005766107. full.pdf+html.

193. Frank Bellrose, *Ducks, Geese & Swans of North America*, (Pennsylvania: Stackpole Books, 1976), 42.

194. Mark Kinver, "Bird sets record as UK's oldest Arctic tern," BBC, September 21, 2010, accessed March 31, 2014, http://www.bbc.co.uk/news/ science-environment-11375618.

195. Carl Zimmer, "7,000 Miles Nonstop, and No Pretzels," *The New York Times*, May 24, 2010, accessed February 21, 2014, http://www.nytimes. com/2010/05/25/science/25migrate.html?pagewanted=all&_r=0.

196. Daniel Gross, *Forbes Greatest Business Stories of All Time* (United States: John Wiley and Sons, Inc., 1996) 86, accessed January 1, 2015, http:// www.amazon.com/Forbes-Greatest-Business-Stories-Time/dp/0471196533.

CHAPTER 12: SUSTAINING THE WIND BENEATH THEIR WINGS

197. BlessingWhite, *Engagement Report: 2011*, 3 and 20.

198. "Meet the Chef," Hartstone Inn, accessed 1 January 2015, http://www.hartstoneinn.com/dining/meet-the-chef/.

199. "About Us," James Beard Foundation, accessed January 1, 2015, http://www.jamesbeard.org/about.

200. "Kitchen Floor Plan," James Beard Foundation, accessed January 1, 2015, http://www.jamesbeard.org/sites/default/files/downloads/kitchen_floor_ plan.pdf.

201. "Gemba," BusinessDictionary.com, accessed March 10, 2014, http://www.businessdictionary.com/definition/gemba.html.

202. Richard Steel, "Tales from the Gemba-Circle of Chalk," Kaizen Institute, accessed September 21, 2012, http://nz2013.kaizen.com/?id=4498.

203. Denise Grady, "The Vision Thing: Mainly in the Brain," *Discover*, June 1, 1993, accessed August 8, 2014, http://discovermagazine.com/1993/jun/ thevisionthingma227.

204. Steve Grubbs as told to Reshma Yaqub, "The Way I Work: Steve Grubbs, Victory Enterprises," *Inc. Magazine* (April 2012): 116.

205. Tom Harris, "How Whales Work," How Stuff Works, accessed September 21, 2012, http://science.howstuffworks.com/environmental/life/zoology/marine-life/whale1.htm.

FINAL THOUGHTS

206. "About Canada Geese," Canada Geese New Jersey, accessed April 3, 2014, http://www.canadageesenewjersey.com/Canada%20Geese%20Facts.htm.

207. L.A. Hawkes, S. Balachandran, N. Batbayar, P.J. Butler, B. Chua, D.C. Douglas, P.B. Frappell, Y. Hou, W.K. Milsom, S.H. Newman, D.J. Prosser, P. Sathiyaselvam, G.R. Scott, J.Y. Takekawa, T. Natsagdorj, M. Wikelski, M.J. Witt, B. Yan and C.M. Bishop, "The paradox of extreme high-altitude migration in bar-headed geese *Anser indicus*," *Proceedings of the Royal Society* (October 31, 2012): 4, accessed March 13, 2014, http://rspb.royalsocietypublishing.org/content/early/2012/10/25/rspb.2012.2114.full.pdf+html.

Index

Would you like to bring Updraft into your organization?

I hope you enjoyed this book and I thank you for taking the time to read it. If you found it to be thought-provoking and would like to hear more about leadership, engagement and updraft, then I invite you to connect with me.

Visit my website at www.deltavstrategies.com to find out more about how I work with leaders and their teams to bring updraft to their organizations.

While you're there, feel free to read my blog, find out where I'm speaking and check for new resources.

CPSIA information can be obtained at www.ICGtesting.com
Printed in the USA
BVOW06*0519170216

437023BV00005B/62/P